D0087149

*Stormwater
Management
in Urbanizing
Areas*

Stormwater Management in Urbanizing Areas

WILLIAM WHIPPLE

NEIL S. GRIGG

THOMAS GRIZZARD

CLIFFORD W. RANDALL

ROBERT P. SHUBINSKI

L. SCOTT TUCKER

Prentice-Hall, Inc., Englewood Cliffs, New Jersey   07632

Library of Congress Cataloging in Publication Data
Main entry under title:

Stormwater management in urbanizing areas.

Includes bibliographical references and index.
1. Urban runoff.   2. Storm sewers.   3. Flood
damage prevention.   4. Urban hydrology.   I. Whipple, William.
TD657.S76   628'.212   82-2193
ISBN 0-13-850214-5   AACR2

Editorial/production supervision and interior design by Anne Simpson
Manufacturing buyer: Joyce Levatino

© 1983 by Prentice-Hall, Inc., Englewood Cliffs, N.J. 07632

All rights reserved. No part of this book
may be reproduced in any form or
by any means without permission in writing
from the publisher.

Printed in the United States of America
10 9 8 7 6 5 4 3 2 1

ISBN   0-13-850214-5

Prentice-Hall International, Inc., *London*
Prentice-Hall of Australia Pty. Limited, *Sydney*
Prentice-Hall Canada Inc., *Toronto*
Prentice-Hall of India Private Limited, *New Delhi*
Prentice-Hall of Japan, Inc., *Tokyo*
Prentice-Hall of Southeast Asia Pte. Ltd., *Singapore*
Whitehall Books Limited, *Wellington, New Zealand*

We dedicate this book to our colleague
Robert P. Shubinski
who was killed in a plane crash, January 1982.
He was a fine engineer and a good friend.

Contents

**CHAPTER 3.   STORM HYDROLOGY AND
CHANGING LAND USE   29**

Neil S. Grigg, Bruce H. Bradford, and Robert P. Shubinski

CHAPTER 6.   EROSION AND STORMWATER   123

William Whipple

Preface

Over a period of about ten years the six principal authors of this book, although widely separated in different states, have been engaged in various studies, research, publications, conferences, and consulting activities involving flooding and polluting effects of runoff in urbanizing areas. Gradually our activities began to change from the analytical mode to the remedial and preventive. We were parts of a movement in which the engineering profession and officials of many counties and municipalities were beginning to develop the technology of stormwater management; and in several parts of the country, the objectives of stormwater management began to be extended to the control of runoff pollution in urbanizing areas. Several of the authors were active initiators of this new development. When the idea of a book on the new aspects of stormwater management was broached, it turned out that four of the six of us were already considering the idea, and the others agreed to participate as soon as asked.

The combined experience and expertise of the coauthors is extraordinary. Neil Grigg is Director of the Water Resources Research Institute of the University of North Carolina, currently on leave of absence to act as Assistant Secretary for Natural Resources in North Carolina's Department of Natural Resources and Community Development. Thomas Grizzard is Director of the Occoquan Watershed Monitoring Laboratory and Adjunct Professor of Civil Engineering with the Virginia Polytechnic Institute and State University. Clifford W. Randall is Lunsford Professor of Civil Engineering, and Director of the Occoquan

Watershed Monitoring Program of the Virginia Polytechnic Institute and State University. Robert P. Shubinski was Vice President of the consulting firm of Camp Dresser and McKee, Inc., until his recent death. L. Scott Tucker is Executive Director of the Denver's Urban Drainage and Flood Control District. My own background includes service as Brigadier General, Corps of Engineers, and Director of the Water Resources Research Institute of Rutgers University. Currently a research professor, on leave of absence, I am with the New Jersey Department of Environmental Protection as Administrator, Water Supply and Watershed Protection Administration in the Division of Water Resources.

Each chapter was written by a principal author and one or more coauthors, as indicated in the chapter headings, subject to overall review and editing of the text as a whole. In addition to the principal authors, Mr. Bruce H. Bradford is a coauthor of Chapter 3, and Larry A. Roesner of chapter 5.

The aim of the book is to be useful primarily to the many thousands of municipal and county engineers, planners, and administrators throughout the country who deal with land use control, urban drainage, water quality, and control of flooding at the local level. It is directed equally towards the thousand or so engineering firms that provide service for these operations. Secondly, it should be useful to planners and administrators at state, regional, and federal levels and to university faculty members who are concerned with these matters. It is not designed to deal with the complex problems of cities such as Chicago and San Francisco, or the problems of the major rivers, which must be solved by large scale engineering undertakings beyond the scope of this work.

The drawings in the book were made by Ms. Ginger Docktor. Photographs of floods were made available by the courtesy of the American Red Cross. The typing was done at Rutgers University by able secretaries Ursula Lubreski and Marjorie Krespach, and by other secretaries in the offices concerned.

Any branch of service, particularly a rapidly developing one, develops its own specialized nomenclature. The knowledge achieved by research and analysis is stated in these terms. Accordingly, with all due respect to the English language, a number of technical terms are used in this book. They are defined when first used in the text, but are collected and more completely defined in the glossary.

The authors hereby apologize to all of the fine students and analysts, including some of our good friends, whose writings and research achievements are not adequately covered, and regret that many interesting related aspects were omitted. In order to accomplish the main objectives of the book and to cover the basic essentials in a short space, we had to concentrate on basics. We hope that our work will be useful.

William Whipple
Princeton, N. J.

List of Figures

*Same as Fig. 8-9

*Same as Fig. 6-4

*Stormwater
Management
in Urbanizing
Areas*

1

Introduction

This book describes how rapidly developing urbanization increases flooding and stream erosion and creates pollution of storm runoff, and how programs called *stormwater management* can prevent such environmental damage. Stormwater management is a new approach, which consists of the control of storm runoff, onsite or in small streams, by means of programs which may include land use control, detention/retention of runoff, erosion control, and drainage. Stormwater management in the headwaters is a necessary supplement to programs of flood control and floodplain management, which have been applied to problems of larger streams and rivers. The authors have combined recent research results with experience from various parts of the country to explain how important the management of new developments and of small streams is to national environmental and economic approaches.

MICROCOSM

Harry's Brook is a small stream, about a mile long, in an attractive setting of prosperous homes, with one branch draining the business district of Princeton, New Jersey. Mr. and Mrs. A. have a home in this watershed, which was flooded three times during 1979, although there was no unusual rainstorm. The A's blame the restrictive culvert, which takes the flow of the little tributary under the road just downstream from them. In fact, all of the culverts in the Harry's Brook watershed are too small to carry floodwaters. Last year when the county rebuilt one, it was widened from 6 to 20 feet, with the same height as before. Some of the citizens of the town wonder why the municipal and county engineers, in a town which has generally been well managed, were so stupid in earlier days as to put in such inadequate culverts. Mr. and Mrs. A. bought their house only recently. They were told that the property sometimes flooded from the brook, but they didn't realize that it would rise high enough to come into the house. Their discomfort over this situation is somewhat alleviated by the fact that the federal government, through flood insurance, compensates them for the damages suffered.

Mr. and Mrs. B., also in the Harry's Brook watershed, have an exasperating problem. The stream has eroded a long strip of their garden, undermining trees and shrubs. They blame this on a small dam, which they thought was owned by the municipality. Actually, the dam was built by the earlier owners of their property and that of neighbor C. across the stream. The water pouring over the dam has dug a deep hole and threatens the house of the neighbor, Mr. C. He, in turn, put rocks in the channel, which diverts the main flow across to the neighbor's property, causing erosion.

The B's and C's and their neighbors enjoy their little stream's generally clear water. What they do not realize, however, is that whenever it rains, the turbid waters take in considerable lead and petroleum hydrocarbons, and also are highly unsanitary, on account of sewer overflows which frequently dump raw sewage into the stream.

Mr. and Mrs. E., who live on Harry's Brook, are an elderly couple who enjoy photograph albums showing the early growth of their children. These early photographs, compared to conditions seen today, clearly show that not only is the stream channel much larger today, but its bed is about a foot and a half deeper. Other neighbors, who built masonry walls to protect their properties from erosion, have found these masonry walls mysteriously undermined and toppled over towards the stream. One man, in exasperation, hired heavy trucks to bring in huge boulders weighing over a thousand pounds each. *His* property, at least, will no longer be eroded by this exasperating little stream.

Mr. F., on another part of the watershed, also has an annoying problem. His house is built high enough above the brook that floodwaters do not reach it. However, the culvert upstream backs up the water, which flows out on the road and pours onto Mr. F.'s property from the rear, down his driveway, and into his garage and garden.

Several years ago, the township, concerned about flooding problems in this stream, engaged an engineering firm to make a floodplain study. This study computed the area that would be flooded by an estimated 100-year flood. The study showed that most of the houses along the brook and its tributaries had been prudently built high enough to be safe from the predicted floodwaters. However, there were some areas, one in particular, where homes seemed to be located on a completely different basis, right in the natural floodplain. Local residents praised the accuracy of the flood line, but they reported that the 100-year flood line had been reached 4 times during the past 25 years.

What was wrong in the management of Harry's Brook? Such conditions are not a horrible example of exceptionally poor planning; they are pretty much characteristic of rapidly urbanizing areas.

The explanation of how such conditions arise, and what can be done about them, is what this book is about.

URBANIZATION AND INCREASED FLOODING

Rapidly developing or urbanizing regions are exposed to growing environmental pressures as the effects of land development increase floods, accentuate channel erosion, and degrade the quality of streams with runoff pollution. Over a period of years, as an area changes from grassland and forests to suburban development, the peak flood flows produced by rain storms of a given magnitude may double or triple,[1] and the total quantity of runoff also increases, although to a lesser extent. These increased flood flows almost always cause flood damages, because the early settlers built homes based upon their perceptions of the original flood situation; and even if they evaluated it correctly, the unanticipated increase in flood heights causes damage. For example, a federal flood study of Four Mile Run, near Alexandria, Virginia, some 30 years ago, made an estimate of a 100-year frequency flood that is now completely outdated. The original terrain had an absorbent covering of turf and tree mulch, which absorbed the rainfall. The virtually complete urbanization of the watershed has brought paved streets, parking lots, and roofs, from all of which water rushes in torrents. The original "100-year" flood now occurs every 4 or 5 years. For most small streams there is no accurate estimate of the statistical probability of floods in the original condition of the watershed, and development occurs much more slowly than in the Four Mile Run watershed, so that such striking increases are not usually noted. However, as explained in Chap. 3, intensive development of land characteristically intensifies stormwater runoff in a predictable manner.

Along with the increased flooding comes a greater tendency for erosion of the bed and banks of a stream. This tendency was not recognized until recent years, and it has now been explained in more detail as a result of recent research. (See Chap. 6.)

The water quality of streams is also degraded as a result of development. In part, this is due to erosion of the soil, with its nutrients and mineral constituents, during construction; but more largely, runoff pollution results from other human activities. Industrial and commercial facilities, although largely controlled by water pollution control agencies, generate pollutants from various leakages, illegal dumping of wastes, spills, runoff from the vicinity of operations, and dust and fumes in the air which precipitate out along with rainfall. Agricultural contributions to water pollution come from cattle feed lots and dairies, nutrients from fertilizers, and pesticides. Even the runoff from residential areas includes pollutants originating from garbage, pets, automobiles, eroding metals, and lawns and gardens. Water quality analysts refer to this dispersed pollution as *nonpoint source* to distinguish it from *point source* pollution, which is the wastes and effluents from sewage treatment plants and the larger industries. Although the Environmental Protection Agency has spent billions of dollars annually to build treatment plants for point sources, Congress has not authorized the expenditure of federal funds to build works to treat nonpoint sources.[2] The extensive sewerage systems that collect human and point source wastes for treatment usually leak, and sewage-contaminated overflow in wet weather adds materially to the pollution of many streams.

Various proposals have been suggested to reduce illegal discharges and solid waste disposal from industrial plants; but dealing with the more dispersed pollutants which cannot be eliminated at source will probably have to be handled largely through stormwater management, as outlined in Chap. 7. This approach is a development of recent research, which was first applied on a substantial scale during 1980.

CHARACTER OF URBANIZING AREA DEVELOPMENT

Traditional patterns of land use in the United States were characterized by a generally rural countryside on which villages, towns, and cities were interspersed in a fairly orderly hierarchy, each one a growing center of habitation and business activity. Increasingly, different patterns are emerging. Many of the large central cities are growing slowly or not at all. Substantial amounts of new housing are built as large developments, which are laid out like carpet across the countryside, in increments that range in size up to several thousand housing units. Large shopping centers in between the older towns are attracting more and more of the trade and generating more of the pollution. (See Fig. 1-1.)

Figure 1-1 Suburban Development

The forces creating these new patterns include the increasing mobility of homeowners due to automobile transportation, and the fleeing of prosperous elements of society from the crowded, dirty, expensive, and sometimes dangerous environments of the big central cities. The general availability of truck transportation has relaxed the bonds which previously attracted industries to the railroads; and the availability of trained labor in suburbia has motivated many industries and corporate headquarters to move to more dispersed locations. These conditions now generally characterize the eastern megalopolis and are developing

Figure 1-2 Shopping Center

elsewhere, although in other parts of the country some of the towns and cities are still growing along traditional lines.

To describe these conditions of urban sprawl is not to recommend them. Although the actions of the developers and planning boards are generally legal and in accordance with our traditional concepts of freedom of personal choice, there are some undesirable by-products in the accompanying social and economic distress of the big cities. These include the increasing vulnerability of the economic structure to any restriction of the supply of petroleum, and the disruption of the environment by inconsiderate and poorly controlled development. Planners and analysts are struggling to redirect and control the dynamics of urbanization more adequately. From the viewpoint of stormwater management, it is necessary to recognize the new conditions, to devise approaches and methodology adapted to limiting certain undesirable effects, and to take advantage of the new opportunities offered.

TYPE AND SCALE OF FLOODS

Stormwater management consists of the array of approaches available for addressing urban drainage and flood problems on the smaller streams. Stormwater management is to be differentiated from larger flood control projects used to address flooding problems on large river systems.

The federal government became concerned with flooding on a national level following the disastrous Mississippi inundations of 1927, the Ohio River flood of 1937, and similar events on other large rivers. Floods on small streams were also recognized, but were largely considered in an agricultural context. Accordingly, the Corps of Engineers initiated the most prominent part of a national flood control program, which was mainly devoted to large rivers, with some smaller local projects in urban areas; and the Soil Conservation Service started its program oriented to control agricultural runoff by land treatment measures and systems of "small" dams. These SCS dams are small compared to Corps of Engineers' structures, but generally many times larger than detention dams being built by developers today. These and other federal systems[3] comprised a national flood control program, which was limited in its size and scope only by the time and money available, and by its lack of attention to the smaller streams in urbanizing and urban areas.

Figure 1-3 Flood Damage

During the 1950s, Dr. Gilbert White initiated studies which led to major changes in national flood control policy. He found that despite the expenditure of many billions of dollars, the national total of flood damage was not being reduced at all, but was actually increasing, even in "real" terms.[4] This paradox he and other analysts attributed to the continued tendency to occupy floodplains ever more densely, and particularly to the movement into the portions of floodplains that had been partially protected by federal projects. As a consequence, a national program of floodplain management was adopted, financed by federal flood insurance, and directly enforced by nonfederal laws and ordinances. However, this approach was based upon the assumption that the cycle of floods of the past would be repeated in the future, with no essential change in frequency and severity. Thus, this program was not designed to deal with the increasing floods in urbanizing areas, which were just beginning to be understood at that time.

In putting these various federal programs into perspective, as is done in the next chapter, it is important to recall that the floods on the large rivers are not increasing in frequency and severity due to urbanization, as are those of the small streams. In fact, the Mississippi had its greatest flood of record in 1843, and both the Columbia and Missouri Rivers had their maximum known floods in the 1880s, all three cases occurring at times when development was extremely sparse. The relative stability of the larger rivers is understandable because the watersheds of our large rivers still are largely undeveloped, and also because the flood control reservoirs have a restraining effect. Moreover, the great accentuation of flood peaks on small streams in developed areas has practically no effect on a large river; it is only the much smaller proportionate increase in total runoff that adds to the magnitude of floods on major rivers.

Figure 1-4   Flood Wave   (Photo courtesy of *Providence Journal-Bulletin.*)

On all rivers, large and small, the damaging floods are mainly the very large ones. Most of the flood damage and loss of life from flooding each year occurs in a few very large floods, such as those which hit Jackson, Mississippi, and Rapid City, South Dakota, within recent years. Generally these floods are greater than the statistically calculated 100-year flood. The 100-year flood, as every flood analyst knows, has a probability of 0.01 of being equalled or exceeded in any one year, that is, it is the flood which would be equalled or exceeded once for every hundred years of a very long record, if no changes in basic conditions occurred. Usually, unless facilities are grossly mislocated, there is little damage from floods having a statistical frequency of once every 5 or 10 years. With adequate floodplain zoning, the damages from floods up to 100-year frequency can be prevented from increasing, and in some cases reduced. However, if the peak flood discharges for a given rainfall continue to be increased by changing land use throughout the watershed, there will continue to be damage from the occasional great floods.

If the contiguous United States is visualized as comprising about 25,000 watersheds, each of 100 square miles, it could be expected that, each year, on the average, 250 of these watersheds would have floods equal to or greater than 100-year frequency. If we consider the two or three largest floods occurring in a given year on watersheds of this size in the United States, if follows that such floods have a statistical probability of occurring around once in 10,000 years. However, when very damaging floods occur in heavily urbanized areas,

Figure 1-5 Flood Damage

such as the Green Brook flood in New Jersey in 1973, they may represent
rainfall of much more frequent occurrence, rendered damaging by the high
proportion of impervious surfaces and the intensive development of the valley.
Conventional floodplain zoning cannot cope with such floods (although it does
reduce the damage), and by the time the urbanized condition develops, it has
usually become infeasible to obtain land for conventional flood control structures. It is for these reasons that stormwater management in urbanizing areas
is a necessity.

RESEARCH AND TECHNOLOGY DEVELOPMENT

It is a fact of life, although a regrettable one, that in the fields of flood damage
mitigation and of environmental protection generally, there is little support
for research unless there is either a commercial interest involved or a federal
agency with a direct responsibility for the function. The federal EPA, Soil
Conservation Service, and Corps of Engineers each has large annual appropriations for research into functions directly related to its mandated responsibilities. Capital-heavy programs using a lot of machinery, such as waste
treatment plant construction, benefit from industrially sponsored research and
product development. However, there is no federal agency charged with stormwater management or with urban drainage, nor is there any large industry with
an interest sufficient to stimulate major research. Responsibilities rest largely
at the municipal level, and outside of a few large cities, such as New York,
San Francisco, and Chicago, local government staffs are relatively small. Cities
and states do not usually invest in research. Each federal agency supports and
advocates its own program, which is useful as far as it goes; but the comprehensive viewpoint is not taken by any one agency. As a result, single purpose
projects and programs are extended to solve problems involving other important aspects, and the potentialities of multiple purpose programs are not realized. Whether or not there should be a federal program of general stormwater
management might be debated; but the authors of this book will not advocate
such a step. We believe that the states and substate agencies are best equipped
to handle such matters. However, some federal agency, such as the National
Science Foundation, should provide funds for applied research in this field, in
order to make sure that adequate technology is developed for the aspects of
stormwater management that remain a nonfederal responsibility.

Even without special support, recent research into stormwater management has been very productive; many new concepts and potentialities have
become available within the last few years. However, some quite primitive
approaches of the past remain in general use, partly because some'of the new
ideas require methods too complex for general application, and partly because
of professional inertia.

FLOOD HAZARD MITIGATION POLICY

Several opposing views on this subject are current and are dealt with in detail in the chapters that follow. The earlier extreme conservationist view that floods could be generally eliminated by reforestation and natural growth is less often advocated, after reflection on the huge floods of the historic past, which occurred in largely forested areas. A strong voice of opinion, in Washington and elsewhere, maintains that comprehensive floodplain management, including flood warnings, flood proofing, and removal of buildings in particularly vulnerable areas, will solve the national flood problems. However, these advocates do not go so far as to recommend the abandonment of New Orleans and other cities in flood plains.

In many localities, engineers are still maintaining as a policy the solving of local flood problems by getting rid of the water as fast as possible, by means of larger culverts and drains, channel enlargement and straightening, and channel lining. This parochial approach is not advocated nationally, but on a local level, since for many upstream communities it is undoubtedly the least expensive way of handling the problem. In effect, the problem is not solved; it is passed downstream to other communities.

The National Association of Soil Conservation Districts seems to feel that stormwater management can be handled through the various districts, acting in concert with the local governing bodies concerned. In midwestern states particularly, such opinions seem to have considerable appeal. However, Soil Conservation Service spokesmen are correct and circumspect in their official positions.

The EPA for a time showed a disposition for adopting a federal approach to stormwater management through federally funded water quality planning agencies, organized under Section 208 of the Water Pollution Control Act. However, there seems to have been insufficient support for such local machinery. There remains a possibility that if specific programs of stormwater management were adopted as "best management practices," they might be incorporated in the EPA's program, for implementation by the states. The legal authority granted by Congress for pollution control purposes might be held to be adequate for such purposes, although this appears unlikely.

Meanwhile, however, initiative in stormwater management has been taken by many municipalities and other substate agencies. It has been realized that if flooding and other environmental degradation are caused by development, it is both legal and equitable to require developers to incorporate stormwater management measures into their development plans, to prevent such degradation, or at least to minimize it. Once stated in that way, the principle is usually acceptable to all. However, a host of problems remain. The measures designed to control floods are not effective in solving other problems unless modified. Some structural dual purpose or multiple purpose programs can solve two or more problems at little more than the cost of one; but how are such potentialities to be compared to nonstructural single purpose programs? The complicated planning methodology outlined by the federal Water Resources Council[5] is probably too complex an approach, but what approach should be used? Some of the proposals to eliminate runoff pollution, such as street sweeping, must be compared to the alternative of developing detention storage, with the settling of particulate forms of pollution in detention basins and their subsequent removal. Detention basins can also be useful for recreation, or for groundwater recharge in appropriate cases. The creation of a multitude of small detention basins, one to each developed tract, is manifestly more costly and difficult to maintain than a well-planned system of larger basins; but how are the larger master ("regional") basins to be planned, constructed, and maintained? What about the assurance of future maintenance of any privately owned basins; can property owners' associations be organized for such purposes? What levels of government or other agency should control stormwater management? It is clear that many problems remain to be resolved.

CHARACTER OF STORMWATER MANAGEMENT

Stormwater management developed at the "grass roots" level without either a sponsoring federal agency or a nationally known intellectual to establish the doctrine and popularize it. Despite its diverse origins, its various manifestations have many points in common. Stormwater management is a program related to very localized problems, many of which are met by small structures built by developers. It is mainly important on small streams and headwaters, in areas undergoing the process of urbanization. It is of little interest to sparsely developed areas; and on land devoted to agriculture, it takes the form of the soil and water conservation programs of the Soil Conservation Service. From a practical viewpoint, a great strength is that it can be funded in a preventive mode by requiring provision to be made at the time of new development, at the cost of developers. However, in established urban and suburban areas, remedial programs, funded by government, are necessary and are much more difficult to implement.

SCOPE OF THIS BOOK

This book is intended to provide methodology to support the planning, design, and administration of stormwater management systems, including both structural and nonstructural measures. It is designed primarily to serve the thousands of municipal engineers, county governments, environmental commissions, planning boards, municipal councils, and administrators who deal with such problems, and also to serve the many consulting firms who provide engineering advice to them. For more details on the various technical aspects, references are given, since all of the complex relationships involved could never be covered in a single volume.

NOTES—CHAPTER 1

1. The effect on large floods is proportionately less than that on small floods, as explained in Chap. 3.
2. Except for agricultural nonpoint sources, under certain conditions.
3. Both the Tennessee Valley Authority and the Bureau of Reclamation also build reservoirs in aid of flood control.
4. In terms of dollars corrected for currency inflation and price increases.
5. U.S. Water Resources Council, "Principles and Standards for Planning Water and Related Land Resources," 38 *Federal Register*, No. 174, Pt. 3, 10 Sept. 1973.

2

Governmental Aspects of Stormwater Management

WILLIAM WHIPPLE

L. SCOTT TUCKER

Responsibility for stormwater management rests primarily with local governments such as municipalities, townships, cities, and counties. There are state and federal programs, however, that can support or influence local government efforts. While federal involvement with various aspects of flood hazard mitigation is manifold, this involvement generally is oriented toward flood control and floodplain management. Only the Soil Conservation Service has long-standing programs of stormwater management. The purpose of this chapter is to present and discuss various federal, state, and substate programs and policies related to stormwater management. Government programs and policies change, however, and it will be up to the reader to pursue the specifics of any area of special interest.

FEDERAL PROGRAMS

There are many federal agencies involved in flood hazard mitigation. Such federal involvement is direct and largely controlling for flood control, and very important in floodplain management. Although there is no one federal agency with a direct mandate to plan and implement general programs of stormwater management, there are several agencies with more limited concerns, which are engaged in, or could engage in, related activities. A listing of federal agencies officially stated to be concerned in such matters is given in Table 2 — 1.[1]

The following discussion summarizes some of the more important federal programs and authorizations.

Soil Conservation Service (SCS)

The SCS is authorized, first, to plan and carry out a national soil and water conservation program and second, to provide technical and financial assistance in planning and carrying out works of improvement to protect, develop and utilize the land and water resources in small watersheds and to assist states and other federal agencies preparing comprehensive plans for the development of water and related land resources.[2] This work is done partly through field offices, and partly through Soil Conservation Districts, organized in each county of most of the United States. Other Department of Agriculture agencies and the Agricultural Extension Service of state universities also contribute assistance. In practice, Soil Conservation Service programs related to stormwater management take two main forms: (1) structural programs of small dams and channel improvement undertaken for flood control and related purposes and (2) land treatment, especially in agricultural areas, designed to retain soil and water on the land. In addition, by state legislation, Soil Conservation Districts in some states have been given certain powers over all new construction in order to prevent soil erosion prior to the establishment of permanent cover. It has been suggested that such authorities could be extended to establish criteria of storm-

TABLE 2-1   Federal Agencies Concerned
with Flood Hazard Mitigation

Department of Agriculture
  Agricultural and Rural Economic Research
  Agriculture Stabilization and Conservation
    Service
  Farmers Home Administration
  Forest Service
  Soil Conservation Service
Department of the Army
  Corps of Engineers
Department of Commerce
  National Oceanic and Atmospheric
    Administration
  Economic Development Administration
Department of Energy
  Federal Energy Regulatory Commission
Department of Health, Education, and Welfare
  Public Health Service
Department of Housing and Urban Development
  Community Planning and Development
  Federal Housing Administration
Department of the Interior
  Bureau of Land Management
  Heritage Conservation and Recreation Service

  Geological Survey
  Fish and Wildlife Service
  Water and Power Resources Service
  Office of Water Research and Technology
Department of Transportation
  Coast Guard
  Federal Highway Administration
Federal Emergency Management Agency
  Federal Disaster Assistance Administration
  Federal Insurance Administration
  Civil Defense Preparedness Agency
Small Business Administration
Tennessee Valley Authority
Water Resources Council
National Science Foundation

water management for all new construction in states having such legislation.

The basic authorizations of the Soil Conservation Service would undoubtedly allow providing assistance to local agencies in planning stormwater management systems, if appropriations for that purpose were provided. However, there is no federal authorization for the Soil Conservation Service to set stormwater management standards and to enforce such standards, except through the programs noted above.

Environmental Protection Agency (EPA)

The main business of the Environmental Protection Agency is the control of water, land, and air pollution. Although the EPA is not officially listed among the agencies concerned in flood hazard mitigation,[3] it has some important activities and legal powers related to stormwater management. Under Section 208, P. L. 92-500, the EPA launched a series of areawide planning activities, starting in 1975. These "208 plans" could have included programs of stormwater management in the joint interest of flood control and water quality; it did in fact include at least a few tentative proposals of this nature. However, these planning activities are now being directed toward narrower goals.

In 1978, the EPA and the U.S. Geological Survey initiated a major new activity, the Nationwide Urban Runoff Program. In this program at approximately 30 locations in various parts of the United States, field studies are being carried out on the origin of pollutants in urban runoff and on the efficacy of detention basins in removing them. However, this program of research, analysis, and demonstration does not appear to have any clear and direct relationship to Section 208 planning.

The third activity of the EPA that is related to stormwater management, and which may be significant for the future, stems from a little-noticed definition in the basic federal water pollution control legislation, P. L. 92-500, and successor legislation. This proviso defines "point sources" of pollution to include any polluting material which enters a steam through a pipe, ditch, or channel. This definition, in conjunction with other language setting up the National Pollutant Discharge Elimination System (NPDES), apparently has the effect of authorizing the EPA, acting either directly or through the states, to set maximum limits of pollutant discharge for storm sewers and open ditches anywhere in the United States. If this were done, municipalities concerned would presumably be legally required to comply. Of course it would still remain to be determined in each case whether or not stormwater management would constitute the means by which such requirements would be met. So far, these powers have only been invoked sporadically, and it is not clear that this sort of authorization could be used to establish such a sweeping control over local governments as would be entailed by a nationwide system of stormwater management. It seems unlikely that Congress had any such intent when it passed the legislation. Most probably, new legislative powers would be sought before starting such a program.

Corps of Engineers

Originally it was believed that the structural programs of the Corps of Engineers and Soil Conservation Service would be sufficient to eliminate serious flooding in the United States. However, by the mid-'60s, despite over $11 billion spent for such purposes, it became apparent that flood damages were still increasing due to continued encroachment upon floodplains. Accordingly, a new federal policy arose, with emphasis on nonstructural approaches, particularly floodplain management. Although some enthusiasts thought that nonstructural means would substitute for structural programs almost entirely, it is now apparent that this is just as illusory as the earlier confidence in structural measures alone. In most cases, both structural and nonstructural programs are needed for a permanently satisfactory and cost-effective solution to flood problems.

The long-established statutory authority of the Corps of Engineers for planning and building flood control works has been supplemented by authorizations to consider nonstructural alternatives as well. If authorized by Congress, they can be funded federally. This has been done in a few cases.

There is nothing in the law itself to indicate how small a flood control project can still be eligible for construction by the Corps of Engineers; in fact, even the smallest of detention basins could be said to be a project in the interest of flood control. In practice, however, the Corps is limited to the larger projects. The office of Management and Budget has set a guideline of 800 cubic feet per second (cfs) as the minimum flood flow for the 10-year frequency, below which a project ordinarily should not be authorized for Corps participation. However, an even more effective line of demarcation is set by the long and complex planning procedure with which the Corps of Engineers must comply, and by the necessity for congressional authorization of each project individually. It is very difficult for any but large projects to be authorized and built under such a system.

There is nothing to prevent the Corps of Engineers, in the course of planning structural flood control for large basins, from considering complementary systems of floodplain management, and from requiring adoption of such a system as a condition for federal financing of the structural program. In fact, the Flood Hazard Mitigation Report[4] recommended such a linkage. A similar relationship could be considered for stormwater management. However, the effect of even very complete systems of stormwater management upon the flood crests of large rivers would be so slight that it hardly seems it would be useful for the Corps of Enginners to recommend such a condition being extended as part of a flood control plan. Stormwater management is much more relevant to the flood heights on the smaller rivers and streams, and therefore to floodplain management systems, than it is to construction of major flood control reservoirs.

The Corps of Engineers, and several other agencies, make technical studies of the incidence of flooding valley lands, which can be useful to local communities.

Federal Emergency Management Agency (FEMA)

This agency has two principal programs and a coordinating role. The Federal Assistance Administration "provides assistance to states, local governments, and individuals in alleviating suffering and hardship resulting from emergencies or major disasters declared by the president."[5] The Federal Insurance Administration (FIA) has the objective of promoting wise floodplain management practices in the nation's flood prone areas, and it administers the federal flood insurance program.

FEMA's most important objective, that of promoting wise floodplain management practices, is implemented largely through the federal flood insurance program. In its original concept, the flood insurance program was supposed to contribute to the deferral of unwise building in floodplains by the costs of the (mandatory) flood insurance, which was to be reinforced by denial of emergency relief to those communities not participating. However, very few communities have a fully implemented regular insurance program in which all new buildings must pay the actuarial costs of new insurance; and in practice the planned denials of relief funds have not usually been carried out. Under the so-called emergency program, the insurance is heavily subsidized. In this situation, the subsidized federal insurance functions primarily as financial relief to flood victims, and secondarily as the incentive to communities to adopt floodplain zoning ordinances, as required by FLA as a prerequisite to granting the federal insurance. Incidentally (and undesirably), the subsidized insurance provides a financial incentive to maintain facilities in the floodplain which might otherwise be relocated.

It is noteworthy that by using the subsidized insurance program as the "carrot" to obtain floodplain zoning ordinances, any possible constitutional objection to the program was avoided. The federal government does not have the legal right to issue floodplain ordinances directly; but it does have the power to require their issuance by means of financial incentives.

Many federal agencies have played a part in floodplain management, and even more in disaster relief and rehabilitation. Some lack of coordination and planning deficiencies have been noted. Accordingly, in July 1980, the Office of Management and Budget issued a directive creating an interagency task force under the leadership of FEMA. Its mission is to promote the use of nonstructural measures for flood loss reduction and to encourage preparation of both pre-disaster and post-disaster plans for reducing flood losses and encouraging wise use of floodplains. The directive also provided for FEMA leadership in team efforts towards this end. This policy has now been implemented by interagency agreement.

Tennessee Valley Authority (TVA)

The Tennessee Valley Authority has the functions of providing structural flood control and of making studies of the incidence of flooding within its area. Its flood information studies have been particularly successful.

Forest Service and Bureau of Land Management

These agencies have responsibility for planned land use and management practices in large areas of publicly owned land, with resultant impacts on stream flows, and in some instances on the dedication of land for floodways.

Bureau of Reclamation

In some instances, it provides for structural flood control through multiple purpose projects.

National Oceanic and Atmospheric Administration (NOAA)

The NOAA assists coastal states to develop management programs for land and water resources of its coastal zone, and assists in the administering of coastal zone management programs approved by the Secretary of Commerce. Such programs may include both floodplain management and stormwater management elements, as appropriate. It also provides flood warnings in all states, through the National Weather Service.

Other Agencies

Department of Housing and Urban Development. The Office of Community Planning and Development has the objective of strengthening planning and decision-making capabilities of chief executives of states, and of local governments and areawide planning organizations, and also of encouraging development of well-planned new communities. Potentially, this type of federal program could provide major assistance to the planning of stormwater management and floodplain management, if appropriations were budgeted for such purposes.

Geological Survey (USGS). Its mission includes the provision of water information for best use of water resources and the carrying on of research in hydrology. The USGS is participating in the important National Urban Runoff Studies, jointly with the EPA.

Fish and Wildlife Service. The acquisition and management of wildlife areas frequently involve lowland/wetland areas, which may form significant parts of a floodplain management plan.

Federal Highway Administration. The most important relationship to flood matters comes at the time of the important decisions as to either rebuilding or relocating demaged bridges and highways after disastrous floods.

Such decisions must be made promptly after the flood, and are often of critical importance to the plan of rebuilding and rehabilitation of a community.

Small Business Administration, Public Health Service, Federal Housing Administration, Farmers' Home Administration, and Agriculture Stabilization and Conservation Service. These agencies, as well as several of the agencies mentioned above, participate in disaster relief after floods. The American Red Cross also still carries out its traditional role in disaster relief, including flood situations.

Discussion of Federal Approaches

There is a wide variety of methods by which the federal government exerts its influence on flood matters. In some, such as the major structural flood control program of the Corps of Engineers, the federal agency consults with local agencies, but carries out the function with its own field offices and staff, through the states of planning, construction, operation, and maintenance. As another alternative approach, the Soil Conservation Service has created a nationwide network of conservation districts. These districts carry out many important functions on their own responsibility, while other functions are carried out by the federal staff. In the case of floodplain management, the federal agency (FEMA) is establishing a fairly complete federal control, although the actions affecting individuals are legally mandated by state laws and local ordinances. In this case, the financial incentives of the flood insurance program provide a prime motivating force for obtaining the state legislation and local ordinances required.

In the field of stormwater management, no federal agency has attempted to assume general responsibility and control. Action taken to date has been very largely under local initiatives. There is some substate regional action, and a few states are becoming interested in the possibility of statewide policies and programs. As noted above, there are several federal agencies that have authorities which might be extended into this field.

STATE PROGRAMS

Flood Control

In the field of flood control, states play only a small part, having most importantly an informal veto power to prevent authorization and appropriation in any particular case. Sometimes state governments become influential advocates of a given project, or influence its scope and design. Always the state and the local governmental entities are consulted. However, the federal government plays the predominant role. There is no legal obstacle to a state or substate entity or a river basin commission undertaking flood control improvements on its own. However, the availability of federal funding for any program makes it very difficult to obtain funding at other levels of government for such a purpose. Consequently, states and interstate organizations generally do not implement flood control programs, except in cases of particular interest. For example, the Delaware River Commission is formally charged with planning and implementing comprehensive plans including flood control; but in practice the building of flood control reservoirs, in that basin as elsewhere, is dependent upon obtaining Congressional authorization and funding through the Corps of Engineers.

Floodplain Management

Many states have adopted laws permitting or mandating floodplain management at the local level. This activity has been stimulated by the federal flood insurance program, and the state and local efforts are in compliance with federal standards. This is rapidly becoming a general institutional pattern. Although progress in obtaining the necessary mapping is slow, the federal control of policy and criteria is substantial.

However, the form in which the state legislation is enacted varies considerably, being either permissive or mandatory. For example, Massachusetts has permissive legislation, which authorizes zoning of land ". . . subject to seasonal or periodic flooding . . ." so that it cannot be used ". . . to endanger the health or safety of the occupants."[7] The municipality may or may not decide that it needs such legislation, or that it needs the flood insurance for which such provisions are a requirement. On the other hand, New Jersey requires local governments to enact floodplain zoning, once the state has delineated the floodplain.

About half of the states have some form of floodplain enabling legislation. Some states have active programs in which state staff members provide technical and program assistance and generally promote sound floodplain management and flood hazard mitigation. In other states, floodplain management exists mainly "on paper" and municipalities deal directly with federal officials.[8] A strong state role is almost essential to effective floodplain management, since it is impracticable for the federal government to keep track of all the details involved in thousands of local governments.

Stormwater Management

Stormwater management programs other than in rural areas have originated and still exist largely at the substate level. Generally, stormwater management is enforced by local ordinances, which are very different in character even in immediately adjacent areas.

It seems important that states determine their own policies of stormwater management, in order to apply reasonable, uniform criteria. Otherwise, a hodgepodge of local ordinances may allow developers to play off one local entity against another by concentrating developments in those jurisdictions where ordinances or their enforcement are most lenient. Because of local governments' desire to increase their tax revenue, considerable pressure can be exerted by developers. Some states are considering instituting stormwater management programs. If most states choose not to initiate action of their own, interested groups and federal agencies may obtain authorization of a federal stormwater management program. In view of the great diversity of conditions from one state to another, it would be difficult to formulate a federal policy and criteria satisfactory to all. Even within a single state there may be major differences.

Examples of State Programs

Pennsylvania. One of the few state stormwater management programs is that of Pennsylvania. The Pennsylvania program was authorized in the Stormwater Management Act, passed in 1978 by the Commonwealth General Assembly. The policies and purposes of the Stormwater Management Act are to:

"1. Encourage planning and management of stormwater runoff in each watershed which is consistent with sound water and land use practice.

2. Authorize a comprehensive program of stormwater management designated to preserve and restore the flood-carrying capacity of Commonwealth streams: to preserve to the maximum extent practicable natural stormwater runoff regimes and natural course, current, and cross-section of water of the Commonwealth; and to protect and conserve ground waters and ground-water recharge areas.

3. Encourage local administration and management of stormwater consistent with the Commonwealth's duty as trustee of natural resources and the people's constitutional right to the preservation of natural, economic, scenic, aesthetic, recreational, and historic values of the environment."

The heart of the program is the preparation and adoption by each county of a watershed stormwater management plan. A watershed plan must be prepared for every watershed, designated by the state, which is located in the county. The watershed plans are to be adopted by the counties within two years following promulgation of guidelines by the State Department of Environmental Resources. The watershed plans are to include the identification of problems, assessment of land development patterns, analysis of development in floodplains, review of stormwater collection systems, identification of existing and proposed flood control projects, identification of solutions, standards for control of runoff from existing and new development, a 10-year implementation plan, designation of priorities, and provisions for periodic review and updating of the plan.

The state reviews and approves county watershed plans. The state can enforce the act through mandamus actions to compel counties to adopt and submit plans, through issuance of notice of violation to noncomplying municipalities, and through withholding of state funds payable to a noncomplying municipality.

The Pennsylvania Stormwater Management Program is a companion effort to an active floodplain management program which requires all local governments to adopt floodplain management regulations. The state's floodplain management program,[9] coordinated by the state's Department of Community Affairs, provides technical assistance for ordinance adoption, administration, and enforcement, and provides a continuing training program for local officials. Program innovations include a pilot project to study the feasibility of adopting flood insurance study maps for flood warning and evacuation purposes. Also, the state has used flood disaster bond money to acquire flood damaged properties for open-space use.

While several states have relatively active floodplain management programs and most states have developed some floodplain management program materials, few states have gotten actively involved in stormwater management. The Pennsylvania program is unusual in this regard.

Florida.   Another unusual state program is Florida's program to mitigate the degradation of the quality of receiving waters from stormwater discharges. Florida requires licenses (permits) for urban stormwater discharges that are determined to be significant by the state. Existing discharges are also subject to permitting authority if determined to have significant impact. There is provision for delegation of this authority to local regional governments where they demonstrate the capability to administer the program.

SUBSTATE PROGRAMS

Flood Control

Important substate entities may assume more of a role in flood control than does the state, because of particular local pressures and the inability to obtain federal funding corresponding to local plans and proposals. Sometimes state funding is available in aid of such programs. Most large cities are concerned with storm drainage problems of a character involving flooding and control of floods. Probably the largest and most noteworthy of such undertakings is the "Tunnel and Reservoir Plan" (TARP) of the Metropolitan Sanitary District of Chicago. This huge project, which combines elements of flood control and water quality improvement, will require funds from federal, state, and local levels before it is completed. Other active programs on a substate level include those of the Urban Drainage and Flood Control District of the Denver metropolitan area, the California flood control districts, and the Fairfax County, Virginia, and Florida water management districts.

Floodplain Management

Floodplain management is largely implemented at the local government level. As previously discussed, however, there is considerable federal influence in terms of minimum requirements and criteria, and in some states there is active state involvement. Local governments are the ones that regulate floodplains, establish building codes, and review development of plans, since local government is the level of government in general control of the process of land development.

Stormwater Management

As previously indicated, stormwater management programs exist largely at the substate level. Generally stormwater management programs are funded and implemented by local government and enforced by local ordinances. Local programs generally vary considerably from community to community even within the same metro regions.

There are a few stormwater management systems covering areas larger than a single municipality. The Metropolitan Sanitary District of Chicago administers controls throughout its multijurisdictional area. The Delaware and Raritan Canal Commission of New Jersey enforces stormwater management to protect an old historic canal, which is both a state park and an important aqueduct. It covers 35 municipalities in 5 counties and controls runoff in such a manner as to reduce particulate pollution as well as to reduce flooding. Water Management Districts in Florida, particularly the South Florida and Southwest Florida Districts, are multicounty organizations involved in stormwater management.

Examples of Substate Regional Organizations

All local governments to some extent address flood control, floodplain management, and stormwater management problems. The large cities have large and trained staffs, but small towns and counties in many cases have minimal capabilities to address these problems. In multijurisdictional metropolitan areas, difficulties arise in developing consistent and compatible programs from community to community. This difficulty has been addressed in some metropolitan areas by the establishment of special purpose multijurisdictional organizations.

Examples are multicounty regional drainage and flood control authorities such as the Albuquerque Metropolitan Arroyo Flood Control Authority and the Denver Area Urban Drainage and Flood Control District. The Urban Drainage and Flood Control District (UDFCD), for example, includes 29 municipalities in the six-county Denver metropolitan region. The UDFCD has developed a regional drainage criteria manual,[10] adopted floodplain regulation criteria, delineated flood hazard areas, developed a program of annually sending flood hazard brochures to floodplain occupants, designed and constructed regional drainage and flood control facilities, developed early flood warning systems, held seminars and conferences, and maintained drainage and flood control facilities. The UDFCD is governed by a 15-member Board of Directors made up of 13 locally elected officials appointed by various appointing authorities and 2 professional engineers appointed by the other 13 board members. Funding is provided by a 0.1-mill levy for engineering and operations, 0.4-mill levy for capital construction, and 0.4-mill levy for maintenance and preservation of floodways and floodplains. The assessed valuation of the UDFCD exceeded $6.5 billion in 1980. The UDFCD has police power authority to control development in floodplains, has powers of condemnation, and can charge drainage fees. The UDFCD was established by special state statute and is the only organization of its kind in Colorado. In New Mexico, there is a similar organization covering the Albuquerque metropolitan area called the Albuquerque Metropolitan Arroyo Flood Control Authority (AMAFCA). The AMAFCA is also unique to New Mexico.

Florida statutes have created five multicounty water management districts.[11] These districts were created to provide for management of water and related land resources; to promote the conservation, development, and proper utilization of surface and groundwater; to provide water storage for beneficial purposes; to prevent damage from floods, soil erosion, and excessive drainage; to preserve natural resources, fish, and wildlife; and to promote recreational development. The South Florida Water Management District (SFWMD), for example, consists of about 17,000 square miles in 16 counties and includes almost 50% of Florida's 8-million population.[12] An important aspect and basic activity of the SFWMD is a surface water management permitting program. Most new construction projects within the District must be permitted with the exception of those adequately addressed by other agencies. Four primary areas of concern in terms of quantity are: (1) discharges within receiving water capability; (2) ability to meet local regulations; (3) determination of 100-year flood elevations; and (4) maintenamce of reasonable groundwater elevation. Even with such a state level commitment through the Water Management Districts, local government will most likely continue to be the unit of government to address stormwater management problems. Most stormwater management solutions are closely related to local land use decisions, and it is difficult for other levels of government to deal with them. From every perspective it appears that local government will continue to be the most logical level of government for addressing stormwater management situations.

Countywide flood control districts are fairly common in the southwest and west, such as the Harris County Flood Control District of the Houston area, the Maricopa County Flood Control District of the Phoenix area, the Los Angeles County Flood Control District, and the Orange County Flood Control District, the latter two located in southern California. In some cases these districts are a part of county government and in other instances they operate autonomously from other county government functions. County flood control districts generally exist in metropolitan areas that involve several municipalities, although this is not necessarily the case.

Nongovernmental Activity

The fact that federal agencies have generally not supported stormwater management, except for the agriculturally oriented programs of the SCS, has left the roles of research and technology development largely to nongovernmental organizations. The American Society of Civil Engineers, especially its Urban Water Resources Research Council, and the American Public Works Association are among those which contributed materially. Also, a good deal of university research occurred, encouraged by support from the Office of Water Research and Technology, Department of the Interior. Since there is no large industry closely involved in stormwater management, these lightly funded activities provided the main sources of technical guidance to the organizations described in this chapter.

NOTES—CHAPTER 2

1. "Flood Hazard Mitigation Study," National Science Foundation, 1980.
2. "Catalog of Federal Domestic Assistance," Office of Management and Budget, Executive Office of the President, 1978, with update.
3. Catalog of Federal Domestic Assistance, 1978.
4. Flood Hazard Mitigation Study, 1980.
5. Catalog of Federal Domestic Assistance, 1978.
6. Flood Hazard Mitigation Study, 1980.
7. Flood Hazard Mitigation Study, 1980.
8. Flood Hazard Mitigation Study, 1980.
9. Patricia A. Bloomgren, "Strengthening State Flood Plain Management," draft, by the Association of State Flood Plain Managers, for the U.S. Water Resources Council, 1980.
10. Wright-McLoughlin Engineers, *Urban Drainage Criteria Manual, Vols. I and II*, Urban Drainage and Flood Control District, Denver, Colo., 1969.
11. "Management and Storage of Surface Waters," *Permit Information Manual, Vol. IV*, South Florida Water Management District, (no date).
12. "Urban Stormwater Management," *Proceedings of a Southeast Regional Conference* held April 10–11, 1979, Water Resources Research Institute of the Univ. of North Carolina.

3

Storm Hydrology and Changing Land Use

NEIL S. GRIGG

BRUCE H. BRADFORD

ROBERT SHUBINSKI

INTRODUCTION

Storm hydrology applies hydrological science to the calculations necessary for predicting storm runoff, with emphasis on the hydrological effects of urbanization and land development. Storm management is concerned with several aspects of hydrology. This chapter deals with peak flood flows, which are related to flood damages and to the design of structures, and also with temporal characteristics of flood flows, which affect the routing of floods through channels and detention structures. The chapter sets forth procedures necessary for estimating the effects of urbanization upon runoff, and summarizes effects of this nature which occur due to changing land use. The discussion includes the background of storm hydrology and procedures for implementation. Then procedures for estimating storm rainfall are presented, including estimation of ordinary and extreme design storms, with a discussion of the merits of design storms versus simulation. Several procedures for calculating runoff in small and large basins are presented. These subjects can fill several volumes, so they have necessarily been distilled to essential applied methods. The methods presented are practical, and research topics have been avoided.

Hydrology has as its objective the analysis and prediction of movements of water in and under the ground; but it is inescapably linked to meteorology, because the data on precipitation are much more extensive and more susceptible to statistical analysis than the data on water movement. Therefore, the frequency of given rainfall occurrences is used in varying contexts of soil, land use, and ground cover characteristics, to predict the corresponding occurrences of surface and underground water. Like other earth sciences, hydrology has evolved over the years and is in a continuous stage of evolution. Procedures are improving and more data become available daily.

From the beginning, hydrology has taken on an engineering character, due to the urgent need for answers to practical problems. In the 19th century, procedures of hydrology were mostly empirical. Many rules-of-thumb were in use, and large errors in the use of hydrological approaches were inevitable. Procedures improved in the 20th century, but only after World War II did urban hydrology develop. During the late 1950s and in the 1960s, research increased greatly. The results have been sumarized in the volumes and papers issued by the ASCE Urban Water Resources Research Program.

STORM RAINFALL ANALYSIS

Stormwater management requires a careful analysis of expected rainfall duration, intensity, and distribution in time and space. It is necessary either to study the effects of a large number of storms which actually happened or to use statistics compiled from studies of many storms in an area of concern. Modern statistical hydrology tends toward the use of actual storm data when computers and models are used. Other approaches often use a design storm derived from the statistical data.

To fully understand the analysis of rainfall, examine the isohyetal lines from the historical storm shown in Fig 3-1. The actual rainfall mass curves shown in Fig. 3-2 might well result from this storm. Each of the rainfall mass curves represents an entirely different distribution of rainfall, even though they occurred within the same basic rainfall event within a few miles of each other.

With such great variations of rainfall in time and space, it has become necessary to average rainfall quantities for use in analysis. Rainfall is averaged both in time and in space. For example, a basic record of 60-minute rainfall values provides values falling within 1-hour time blocks; these time blocks may hide very intense 5, 10, and 30-minute rainfalls, averaging them over the full 60 minutes. Rainfall maps are produced by averaging rainfall values over areas. Point rainfall values are recognized to have higher maxima than areawide values. The well-known relationship shown in Fig. 3-3 demonstrates this phenomenon.

The U. S. Weather Bureau, now the National Weather Service (NWS),

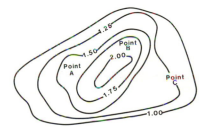

Figure 3-1 Isohyetal Lines Over Area

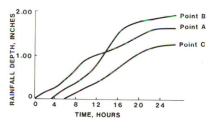

Figure 3-2 Rainfall Mass Curves for Individual Storm

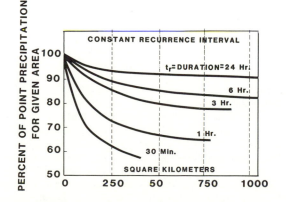

Figure 3-3 Area-Depth Curves for Use with Duration-Frequency Values (after National Weather Service)

part of the NOAA, has produced a wealth of rainfall depth-duration-frequency maps which can be used in stormwater studies if averaged data are to be used. If actual data are preferred, they can be obtained from the NWS at the National Climatic Center, Asheville, North Carolina. Jens[1] has summarized data available from the NWS as shown in Table 3-1.

**TABLE 3-1 A Summary of National Weather Service[a]
Precipitation Data**

A. *Durations to 1 day and return periods to 100 years:*
    NOAA Technical Memorandum NWS HYDRO-35, "5 to 60-Minute Precipitation Frequency for Eastern and Central United States," 1977.
    Technical Paper 40. 48 contiguous states (1961).
    (Use for 37 contiguous states east of the 105th meridian for durations of 2 to 24 hours. Use NOAA NWS HYDRO-35 for durations of 1 hour or less.)
    Technical Paper 42. Puerto Rico and Virgin Islands (1961).
    Technical Paper 42. Hawaii (1962).
    Technical Paper 47. Alaska (1963).
    NOAA Atlas 2. Precipitation Atlas of the Western United States (1973).

Vol. I, Montana	Vol. II, Wyoming	Vol. III, Colorado
Vol. IV, New Mexico	Vol. V, Idaho	Vol. VI, Utah
Vol. VII, Nevada	Vol. VIII, Arizona	Vol. IX, Washington
Vol. X, Oregon	Vol. XI, California	

B. *Durations from 2 to 10 days and return periods to 100 years:*
    Technical Paper 49. 48 contiguous states (1964).
    (Use SCS West Technical Service Center Technical Note—Hydrology—PO-6 Rev. 1973, for states covered by NOAA Atlas 2.)
    Technical Paper 51. Hawaii (1965).
    Technical Paper 52. Alaska (1965).
    Technical Paper 53. Puerto Rico and Virgin Islands (1965).

C. *Probable maximum precipitation:*
    Hydrometeorological Report 33. States east of the 105th meridian (1956).
    (Use Fig. 4-12, NWS map for 6-hour PMP (1975). This map replaces ES-1020 and PMP maps in TP-40[b] which are based on HM Report 33 and TP-38.)
    Hydrometeorological Report 36. California (1961).
    Hydrometeorological Report 39. Hawaii (1963).
    (PMP maps in TP-43[b] are based on HM Report 39.)
    Hydrometeorological Report 43. Northwest States (1966).
    Technical Paper 38. States west of the 105th meridian (1960).
    Technical Paper 42[b] Puerto Rico and Virgin Islands (1961).
    Technical Paper 47[b] Alaska (1963).
    Unpublished Reports:
    Thunderstorms, Southwest States (1972).[c]
    Upper Rio Grande Basin, New Mexico, Colorado (1967).

---

[a]National Weather Service (NWS), National Oceanic and Atmospheric Administration (NOAA), U.S. Department of Commerce (formerly U.S. Weather Bureau).
[b]Technical Papers listed in both A. and C. have been replaced by Hydrometeorological Report No. 51, "Probable Maximum Precipitation East of the 105th Meridian for Areas from 10 to 20,000 Square Miles and Durations from 6 to 72 Hours," available as of 1977.
[c]Being replaced by Hydrometeorological Report No. 49, "Probable Maximum Precipitation, Colorado and Great Basin Drainages."

As as example, the 100-year, 60-minute map for part of the United States is produced as Fig. 3-4. Other maps are similar and can be obtained from the NWS publications. The most current rainfall map for the area of interest should always be used.

The reader must understand thoroughly the concept of "frequency" as used herein. The term means the average recurrence interval of events expected over very long periods of time. For example, a 100-year frequency refers to an event expected once every 100 years, on the average. The 100-year event has a 1% probability of occurrence each year, but is not expected to occur even at approximately 100-year intervals.

Design storms of all kinds can be prepared from these rainfall maps and publications. As an example, if the rainfall intensity is needed for a 100-year, 1-hour storm, the value is simply taken from the map. If values not on the map are desired, it is necessary to prepare curves and interpolate. If a hyetograph is needed, it can be prepared from depth-duration curves. Examples of each will be given after an explanation of how basic rainfall data are collected and analyzed.

The NWS collects basic data from its network of stations. From the data at any point, appropriate statistics can be calculated. An appropriate sta-

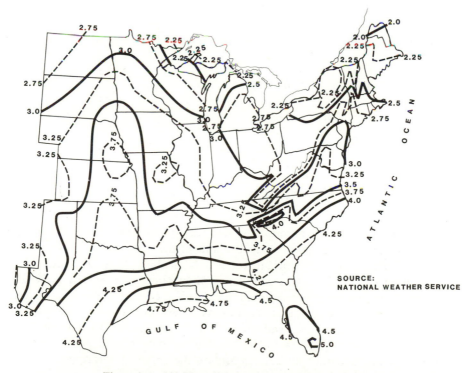

Figure 3-4   100-Year 60-Minute Precipitation (inches)

tistical distribution is used. The NWS has been using the Fisher-Tippett Type I distribution with a fitting procedure developed by Gumbel. It is beyond the scope of this discussion to go into the details of the statistics; the reader should understand that the statistical study will yield probability data for any given duration of rainfall, corresponding to the period of record analyzed. The probabilities can then be converted to frequencies by using the return period.

Once rainfall maps are available, the depth-duration-frequency curve is a useful format for employing the data. An example is given in Fig. 3-5.

From this information, design storm hyetographs can be prepared. This is illustrated in Table 3-2. The 6-hour duration storm shown in Fig. 3-6 resulted from the 25-year return period curves shown in Fig. 3-5. The rainfall pulses are normally arranged with the maximum intensity near the center of the storm and with the lowest intensities at the beginning and end of the storm.

TABLE 3-2   Atlanta 25-Year Rainfall Depths

Duration (h)	Depth (in.)	Δ Depth (in.)	Time (h)	Δ Depth (in.)
0	0		0	
		2.58		0.24
0.75	2.58		0.75	
		0.54		0.28
1.50	3.12		1.50	
		0.30		0.30
2.25	3.42		2.25	
		0.28		2.58
3.00	3.70		3.00	
		0.28		0.54
3.75	3.98		3.75	
		0.26		0.28
4.50	4.24		4.50	
		0.24		0.26
5.25	4.48		5.25	
		0.22		0.22
6.00	4.70		6.00	

For simplicity, a 45-minute time step was shown here. The actual choice of the time step depends on the response time of the watershed and is normally around 5 to 15 minutes for urban watersheds of about 1 square mile.

Extreme rainfall must be considered when safety and security are examined. Probable maximum precipitation (PMP) is a concept developed for estimating maximum meterological conditions which might occur for practical design purposes. Values are available for certain portions of the United States and references were given in Table 3-1. Unfortunately, it is not possible to define with any accuracy either an absolute maximum of precipitation, or a value against which it is safe to design. As regards design criteria for protec-

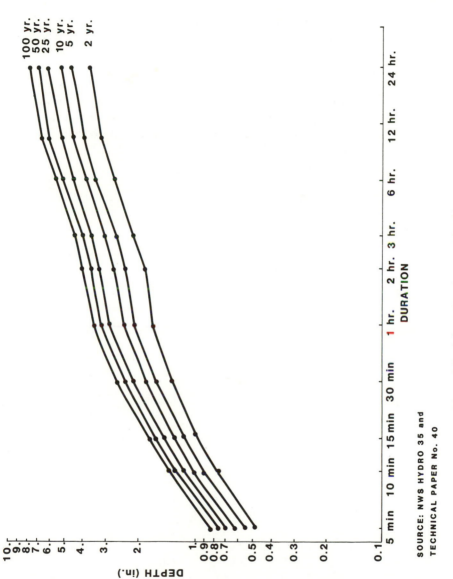

Figure 3-5   Atlanta Depth versus Duration

tion, it is usual to consider storms no larger than 100-year probability in storm-water management and floodplain management, with safety against 500-year floods sometimes required in locations of key facilities. However, in the planning of large flood control reservoirs and in the preparation of flood warning plans for particularly vulnerable areas, much larger storms may be taken into consideration. In the design of spillways, very large and unusual floods must always be taken into consideration.

A common misconception is that a particular storm will have an associated single value return period. However, not only is an actual storm spatially varied (see Fig. 3-1), but its temporal variation is also quite variable. For example, the temporal pattern of a storm measured at the Atlanta Airport on April 12–13, 1979 is given below.

Date	Time	Depth Increment (in.)	Date	Time	Depth Increment (in.)
4/12	5 p.m.		4/13	5 a.m.	
		0.00			0.88
	6 p.m.			6 a.m.	
		0.00			0.30
	7 p.m.			7 a.m.	
		0.48			0.22
	8 p.m.			8 a.m.	
		0.08			0.00
	9 p.m.			9 a.m.	
		0.46			0.02
	10 p.m.			10 a.m.	
		0.11			1.13
	11 p.m.			11 a.m.	
		0.01			0.26
	12 midnight			12 noon	
		0.16			0.09
4/13	1 a.m.			1 p.m.	
		0.60			0.10
	2 a.m.			2 p.m.	
		0.18			0.10
	3 a.m.			3 p.m.	
		0.01			0.23
	4 a.m.			4 p.m.	
		0.14			0.02
	5 a.m.			5 p.m.	

In order to compare this with the precipitation frequency curve for Atlanta, one must determine the maximum depth of precipitation for various durations. This is shown for the above storm as follows:

Duration (h)	Total Depth (in.)	Intensity (in./h)	Period
1	1.13	1.13	4/13 10 a.m.–11 a.m.
2	1.39	0.70	4/13 10 a.m.–12 noon
3	1.48	0.49	4/13 10 a.m.–1 p.m.
6	2.55	0.43	4/13 5 a.m.–11 a.m.
12	3.90	0.33	4/13 12 midnight–12 noon
18	5.04	0.28	4/12 7 p.m.–4/13 1 p.m.
24	5.58	0.23	4/12 7 p.m.–4/13 7 p.m.

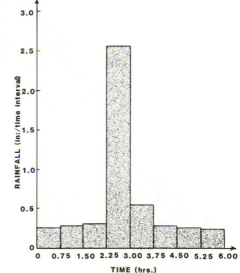

Figure 3-6 Rearranged Atlanta 25-year
Storm Distribution

In Fig. 3-7, this intensity-duration curve is superimposed on the Atlanta curves based upon past records. It is seen that it constitutes about a 10-year frequency storm for durations of 18 and 24 hours, about a 5-year storm for 12 hours and less than a 2-year storm for shorter durations. The values listed represent maximum "clock hour" values. Intensities recorded would undoubtedly have been greater if a continuous record were available, particularly for the shorter durations.

A basic equation can be developed to relate rainfall intensity to duration and frequency.

$$I = \frac{KT^x}{t^b} \tag{3-1}$$

where I = rainfall intensity in inches per hour; T = return period in years, t = rainfall duration in minutes; b and x = regional constants.[2] This equation, valid only within certain ranges, is often useful in modeling studies.

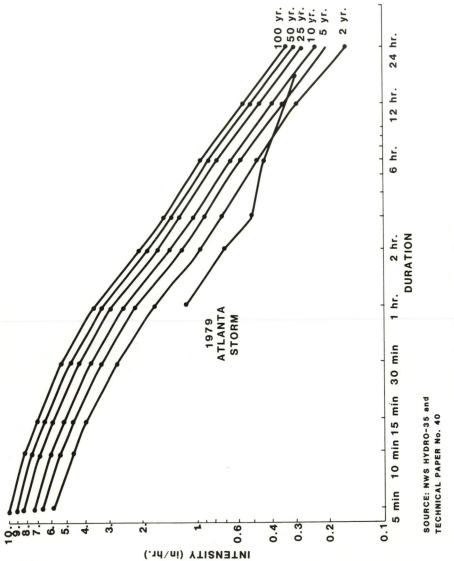

INTENSITY (in/hr.)

SOURCE: NWS HYDRO-35 and
TECHNICAL PAPER No. 40

Figure 3-7   Atlanta Intensity-Duration-Frequency

Examples of Preparing Design Storms

With the basic data available from NWS publications, it is possible to compile all of the approximate data that might be needed for stormwater planning. Jens has presented a good detailed description of the procedures;[3] they are summarized here.

1. Preparation of depth-duration-drequency curves.
    a. Using the appropriate reference for the eastern or western U.S. (see Table 3-1), compile the available rainfall-depth data for the location of interest.
    b. Array the data in a table listing depths by duration and by return period.
    c. Plot the data on an appropriate graph paper such as log-log (see Fig. 3-5).
2. Preparation of design hyetographs.
    a. From the depth-duration-frequency curves, determine the incremental rainfall for each unit interval of time such as 10 minutes, 30 minutes, or whatever is appropriate (see Table 3-1).
    b. Plot the pulses of rainfall on a graph to study the time variation of the rainfall intensities.
    c. Rearrange the rainfall pulses to approximate worst case or other rainfall conditions for the watershed (see Fig. 3-6).
3. Preparation of intensity-duration-frequency curves.
    a. When the rational method is to be used, it is convenient to convert the depth-duration-frequency data to intensity-duration-frequency data by dividing each depth by the appropriate duration.
    b. Plot the resulting intensities on log-log paper (see Fig. 3-7).

RUNOFF CALCULATION PROCEDURES

The calculation of runoff involves passing the estimated rainfall through a transformation to arrive at estimated runoff. There are numerous approaches that can be used, ranging from simple empirical approaches to very elaborate methods. Modeling methods are explained in Chap. 5.

In this section methods for small and large basins will be described. Much of the development of these methods is empirical. To fully understand the evolution of watershed hydrology and the limitations of our present tools, it is necessary to see that current methods are really extensions of earlier concepts. Since we now have much more data to calibrate our methods, as well as much better computational machinery, we can take advantage of improved techniques. On the other hand, it makes little sense to reject methods which may be old but are still useful.

Methods for Small Basins

Hydrological estimation techniques begin with small basins, smaller than about 200 acres. The smaller the basin, the more accurate the runoff estimate can be, provided the rainfall input and the characteristics of the basin are known accurately. Runoff estimation techniques for large basins are based on summations of small basins acting together; thus, the foundation for all runoff calculations is small basin estimation theory.

The ideal case for small basin estimates is a uniform rain falling on a smooth rectangular flat plate. The literature contains several examples of theoretical analyses of runoff from flat plates. Actually, a watershed can be simulated as a collection of flat plates connected together.

The essence of all small watershed theory is that rainfall impacts an area with certain hydrologic characteristics. A certain amount runs off, different in rate and timing from the rainfall. This "transformation" of rainfall to runoff is the prediction problem in small watershed hydrology.

The Rational Method

The technique known as the *rational method* originated almost a hundred years ago. It has been widely misused and is not well understood, in spite of its popularity. Because of its limitations, some say it should be discarded. They ignore the fact that even the most sophisticated models have a rainfall-to-runoff transformation similar to the rational method. Thus, like other methods, the rational method can be very useful if properly employed.

A modern evaluation of the rational method was made by a technical advisory committee in the Denver area. The study recommended the rational method for watersheds up to 200 acres in size in the following form:

$$Q = CC_f IA \qquad (3-2)$$

where Q = peak runoff in cfs,
C = the runoff coefficient,
C_f = a frequency correction factor,
I = rainfall intensity in inches per hour, and
A = watershed area in acres.

The advantages, as well as the limitations, of the rational method are well known. Perhaps the most comprehensive discussion of the method was provided by McPherson.[4] He says that until improved methods are developed, the rational method is about as satisfactory as any other oversimplified empirical approach.

The equation above calculates discharge for a constant intensity rainfall of any duration, but the technique was developed for a rainfall of duration equal to the *time of concentration* of the basin. As rainfall intensity declines for longer duration storms, the indicated maximum peak runoff will result from the storm with duration exactly equal to the basin concentration times. Current practice seems to be to calculate time of concentration in terms of an inlet concentration time and a travel time from the inlet to a basin outlet. These times must be calculated on the basis of overland flow and channel or pipe flow hydraulics, respectively.

Three of the most important limitations reported by McPherson may be summarized as follows:

1. The method yields only a peak flow, not a hydrograph. (Triangular or dimensionless hydrographs can, however, be fitted to calculated peak flows.)
2. The rational method assumes that runoff is linearly related to rainfall. (If you double rainfall, you double runoff.) This is not really accurate, for many variables interact, examples being antecedent precipitation and soil moisture conditions.
3. The method assumes that a 10-year rain produces a 10-year runoff. This is not always the case due to other basin-related variations.

Runoff coefficients for urban areas may be determined from design tables such as are found in reference 5. These values are usually applicable for storms of 5-year to 10-year frequencies. Less frequent, higher intensity storms will require the use of higher coefficients because infiltration and other losses have a proportionally smaller effect on runoff. Where the drainage area is composed of several types of runoff surfaces, the runoff coefficient should be weighted according to the area of each type of runoff surface present.

The following example indicates the procedure in computing a weighted runoff coefficient:

Area (acres)	Type of Surface	C	CA
3.5	Concrete pavement	0.90	3.15
35.6	Suburban area	0.35	12.46
12.5	Apartment area	0.60	7.80
			23.11

$$\text{weighted } C = \frac{\sum CA}{\sum A} = \frac{23.11}{51.60} = 0.45$$

To account for the greater runoff occurring during rarer storms, the "frequency coefficient" can be used in conjunction with the runoff coefficient. The frequency coefficient C_f is normally taken as the following:

Return Period T (years)	C_f
2–10	1.00
25	1.10
50	1.20
100	1.25

We should note, however, that the product CC_f must not exceed 1.0.

Soil Conservation Service Method

The Soil Conservation Service has adapted the methods from their National Engineering Handbook[6] to urban areas. The methods are applicable to small and large catchments. Their applicability to large catchments is based on a summation of small basin hydrographs. They are well adapted to showing differences in runoff due to differences in land use, soil type, and soil cover. For most of the United States, they are based upon use of a Type II storm of 24-hour duration, which contains within it shorter periods of more intense rainfall. These SCS methods are far more comprehensive, and cover a far wider range of conditions than the rational method. In particular, they give volumes of runoff, and complete hydrographs rather than peak flow only.

When the entire hydrograph is desired, it is necessary to perform a *watershed routing*, using the subcatchment's runoff histogram and unit hydrograph. Space does not permit showing this calculation here. However, a significant contribution of the SCS are the *tabular method* hydrographs which result from computer calculated watershed routings. These tabular method hydrographs can be used to develop hydrographs for a variety of commonly occurring situations.

Table 3-3 is an example of one of the five pages of tabular method hydrographs presented by the SCS. For various subcatchment times of concentration, a family of hydrographs is presented. Each hydrograph represents a particular reach travel time (T_t). The hydrograph for $T_t = 0$ represents a point at the mouth of the subcatchment. The other hydrographs are for point T_t-hours downstream from the subcatchment mouth. This allows one to add the separate effects of each subcatchment to obtain the total hydrograph at a particular point of interest. More specifically the procedure is:

1. Determine the drainage area, time of concentration, and 24-hour depth of runoff for each subcatchment.
2. Calculate the travel time (T_t) from each subcatchment to the mouth of the watershed by adding the travel times of the reaches through which it travels.
3. For each subcatchment, select the tabular hydrograph for the appropriate combination of t_c and T_t (see Table 3-3).
4. Multiply these routed subcatchment hydrographs by the subcatchment's drainage area (in mi²) and 24-hour runoff (in in.).
5. Add the subcatchment hydrographs of step 4 to obtain the total watershed direct runoff hydrograph.

An application of this SCS procedure to an entire basin is given in the next section.

TABLE 3-3 Hydrograph Time in Hours (after SCS)

Time of Concentration = 0.3 hours

T_r	11.0	11.5	11.7	11.8	11.9	12.0	12.1	12.2	12.3	12.4	12.5	12.6	12.7	12.8	12.9	13.0	13.2	13.5	14.0	14.5	15.0	16.0	18.0	20.0
0	21	43	141	324	586	658	535	372	251	184	148	124	102	86	77	71	61	51	41	34	30	24	18	14
0.25	17	31	43	67	134	279	461	559	530	428	318	234	179	143	116	97	76	59	45	37	32	25	18	15
0.50	13	22	29	34	42	65	124	238	378	479	499	447	363	281	216	168	110	74	51	41	34	26	19	15
0.75	10	17	21	24	27	32	41	63	114	203	316	413	457	443	389	319	198	105	60	45	37	28	20	15
1.00	8	13	16	18	20	23	26	31	40	60	103	176	269	358	415	426	344	182	77	51	41	30	20	16
1.50	5	8	10	11	12	13	15	16	18	21	24	28	36	52	82	132	272	382	192	81	52	34	22	17
2.00	3	5	6	7	8	8	9	10	11	12	14	15	17	19	21	25	44	151	351	198	85	41	24	18
2.50	1	3	4	4	5	5	6	6	7	8	8	9	10	11	12	14	17	28	162	328	200	54	27	19
3.00	0	1	2	2	3	3	3	4	4	5	5	6	6	7	8	9	10	14	33	169	309	94	30	20
3.50	0	0	1	1	1	1	2	2	2	3	3	3	4	4	5	5	6	9	14	38	172	294	35	22
4.00	0	0	0	0	0	0	1	1	1	1	1	2	2	2	3	3	4	5	9	15	43	281	42	24

Time of Concentration = 0.4 hours

T_r	11.0	11.5	11.7	11.8	11.9	12.0	12.1	12.2	12.3	12.4	12.5	12.6	12.7	12.8	12.9	13.0	13.2	13.5	14.0	14.5	15.0	16.0	18.0	20.0
0	20	39	103	224	419	558	575	451	331	247	190	155	127	105	90	80	66	53	42	35	30	24	18	14
0.25	15	28	38	54	98	196	343	467	508	464	380	295	228	180	145	119	87	64	47	38	32	26	19	15
0.50	12	20	26	30	37	53	92	172	286	395	462	453	402	332	266	211	137	84	54	42	35	27	19	15
0.75	10	16	19	22	25	29	36	51	85	150	242	338	407	429	406	356	241	128	65	47	38	29	20	16
1.00	8	12	15	17	19	21	24	28	34	49	78	132	208	292	362	403	368	220	88	55	42	30	21	16
1.50	5	8	9	10	11	12	14	15	17	19	22	25	31	43	65	102	220	365	224	93	56	35	22	17
2.00	3	5	6	6	7	8	9	9	10	11	13	14	16	17	20	23	37	119	338	225	99	43	24	18
2.50	1	3	3	4	4	5	5	6	6	7	8	9	10	11	12	13	16	25	132	317	225	58	27	19
3.00	0	1	2	2	2	3	3	3	4	4	5	5	6	7	7	8	10	13	28	140	300	107	31	21
3.50	0	0	1	1	1	1	1	2	2	2	3	3	3	4	4	5	6	8	13	32	146	286	36	22
4.00	0	0	0	0	0	0	0	1	1	1	1	1	2	2	2	3	3	5	8	14	36	275	44	24

LARGE BASIN METHODS

Calculation of runoff in large basins is usually performed by modeling or by the use of hydrographs. Models are covered in Chap. 5. They usually involve the summation of some kind of hydrograph that is routed from the point of origin to the point of interest. The use of hydrographs is traditional in hydrology and depends for validity on the quality of the calibration data available.

Unit hydrographs are often employed to introduce the unique runoff characteristics of a watershed into the analysis. The use of synthetic unit hydrographs has become especially popular in urban areas in recent years.

As part of this presentation, two basic methods will be explained: the use of the synthetic unit hydrograph and the SCS methods. Most current hydrology texts go into more detail concerning basic methods.

The Synthetic Unit Hydrograph Approach

For watersheds larger than 200 acres, the Denver group recommended the "Colorado Urban Hydrograph Procedure" (CUHP) method. It is simply a version of the Snyder Unit Hydrograph Approach and can be implemented very simply with or without a computer. In this method, the parameters of the unit hydrograph are given by the following equation:

$$t_p = C_t(LL_{ca})^{0.3} \qquad (3\text{-}3)$$

where $t_p =$ basin lag, the time interval from the center of mass of the rainfall excess to the hydrograph peak (hours);

$L =$ total length along the longest water course to the catchment boundary in miles;

$L_{ca} =$ distance from the study point along the stream to the centroid of the basin in miles; and

$C_t =$ a coefficient reflecting the time to peak, and is a function of the runoff terrain.

Then, we have

$$q_p = \frac{640C_p}{t_p} \qquad (3\text{-}4)$$

where $q_p =$ peak rate of runoff of the unit hydrograph, in cfs/square miles; and

$C_p =$ a coefficient related to peak rate of runoff.

The following relations for C_t and C_p have been recommended for use in the Denver region:[7]

$$C_t = \frac{7.81}{(I_a)^{0.78}} \qquad (3\text{-}5)$$

and $$C_p = 0.89(C_t)^{0.46} \qquad (3\text{-}6)$$

where $I_a =$ fraction of basin which is impervious multiplied by 100. Although the generalized equations for predicting C_t and C_p may find wide application in many urban areas, the specific coefficients in the equations must be determined for each area. The above coefficients are applicable only in the Denver area.

The parameters used for sketching the unit hydrograph (Fig. 3-8) are Q_p, T_{50} W_{50}, and W_{75}, and estimated by the following equations:

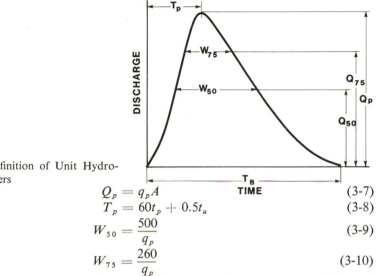

Figure 3-8 Definition of Unit Hydrograph Parameters

$$Q_p = q_p A \qquad (3\text{-}7)$$
$$T_p = 60 t_p + 0.5 t_u \qquad (3\text{-}8)$$
$$W_{50} = \frac{500}{q_p} \qquad (3\text{-}9)$$
$$W_{75} = \frac{260}{q_p} \qquad (3\text{-}10)$$

The parameter T_B is usually adjusted to ensure that the volume of the unit hydrograph results in a one-inch runoff. The parameter t_u is simply the chosen incremental time for runoff computation. A guide for selecting t_u is $t_p/5.5$. The parameters W_{50}, and W_{75} are hydrograph widths, in hours, at 50 and 75% of Q_p.

An innovation has recently been introduced by Espey through the regionalization of unit hydrograph parameters.[8] Espey found that unit hydrographs resulting from rainfall durations of 10 minutes could adequately describe most urban watersheds, subject to local validation with observed data. He thus developed generalized equations. Values for the watershed conveyance factor ϕ are given in Fig. 3-9.

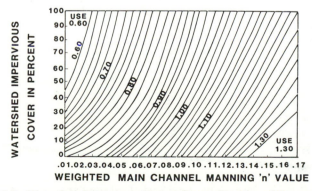

Figure 3-9   Watershed Conveyance Factor, Φ, as a Function of Percent Watershed Impervious Cover and Weighted Main Channel Manning "n" Value (after Espey)

CALCULATION PROCEDURES FOR SMALL AND LARGE BASINS

Although there are a number of available procedures for calculating runoff, most are based on the same principles and have the same objectives. Here we present some brief examples demonstrating the application of these methods.

Consider the case study basin shown in Fig. 3-10. This is a large urbanizing catchment of 1070 acres containing 9 subcatchments, each of which is 50 to 200 acres in size. The basic data for the subcatchments and for the channel reaches are given in Table 3-4.

The objective of the following problems is to calculate the 25-year peak flow rate for subcatchment 6.

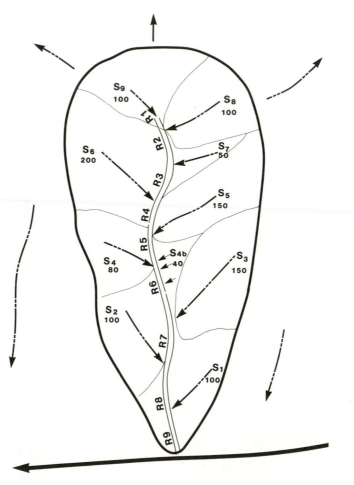

Figure 3-10 Case Study Drainage Basin

TABLE 3-4   Subcatchment and Reach Data

Subcatchment Data[a]

Number	Drainage Area (acres)	Length (ft)	Slope (ft/ft)	Surface	Diameter (in.)	Length	Slope (ft/ft)	Diameter (in.)	Length (ft)	Slope (ft/ft)
		Overland Flow			**First Sewer**			**Second Sewer**		
1	100	200	.030	forest	18	2256	.015	60	855	.010
2	100	200	.030	forest	18	2256	.015	60	855	.010
3	150	200	.030	fallow	10	3264	.015	66	760	.010
4	120	150	.030	meadow	10	1320	.015	60	427	.010
5	150	200	.030	fallow	10	3264	.015	66	760	.010
6	200	250	.030	lawn	10	3995	.015	72	776	.010
7	50	150	.030	meadow	12	1563	.015	48	472	.010
8	100	3313	.030	pasture						
9	100	3313	.030	pasture						

[a] All single family residential, 38% impervious, except 8 and 9.

Reach Data

No.	Length (ft)	Slope (ft/ft)	Type of Rectanglular Channel	Width (ft)	Depth (ft)
1	500	0.0100	Winding, some pools and shoals, clean, fair cond.	6.7	3.3
2	1900	0.0063	Straight bank, no deep pools, some weeds, fair cond.	8.6	4.1
3	2400	0.0044	Clean, straight bank, fair cond.	9.2	4.3
4	1800	0.0037	Same as 3	11.5	5.1
5	1600	0.0034	Same as 3	12.5	5.5
6	2400	0.0034	Same as 3	12.6	5.6
7	1800	0.0033	Same as 3	13.2	5.7
8	2400	0.0018	Earth ditch, straight, fair cond.	13.4	5.8
9	2300	0.0018	Same as 8	13.4	5.8

1. *Rational method.* Using the Rational Method, the equation

$$Q = CC_f iA$$

is used. Let the runoff coefficient $C = 0.5$. For the 20-minute time of concentration our rainfall analysis yields $i = 5.14$ inches for a 25-year storm hour. Therefore,

$$Q = 0.50(1.1)\ (5.14)\ (200) = 565\ \text{cfs}$$

2. *SCS graphical method.* The calculations reveal
   a. Precipitation for 24-hour, 25-year in Atlanta

$$P_{24} = 6.4 \text{ in.}$$

   b. For single family residences, 38% impervious, soil group C, AMC II,

$$CN = 83; \; S = \left(\frac{1000}{83} - 10\right) = 2.05 \text{ in.}$$

   c. $T_c = 20$ minutes
   d. $A = 200$ acres $= 0.312$ sq. miles
   e. From Fig 3-11, Peak $Q = 640$ CSM/in.

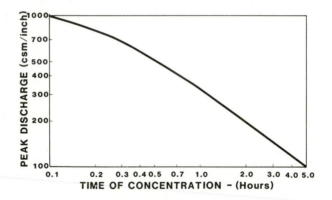

Figure 3-11   SCS Graphical Method Peak Discharge

   f. $Q_{24} = \dfrac{(P_{24} - 0.2S)^2}{(P + 0.8S)} = \dfrac{(6.4 - 0.2 \times 2.05)^2}{(6.4 + 0.8 \times 2.05)} = 4.46 \text{ in.}$

Therefore,

$$\text{peak flowrate} = 640(4.46)\,(0.312) = 890 \text{ cfs}$$

Examples using methods from Espey and the SCS basic approach were also given in.[9] The final results from all four methods were:

Method	Calculated Discharge
Espey	742 cfs
SCS	875 cfs
SCS graphical	890 cfs
Rational	565 cfs

The wide divergence in calculated peak discharge is not uncommon. The general trend is for SCS to overpredict on very small basins and for the rational method to overpredict on large basins.

SCS Tabular Method for Total Watershed Hydrograph

Suppose that it is necessary to calculate the 25-year direct runoff hydrograph for the entire case study watershed.

1. Drainage area, t_c and 24-hour runoff for each subcatchment are as follows:

Subcatchment	A (mi²)	t_c (h)	Q (in.)	QA (mi² in.)
1	0.1562	0.25	4.46	0.697
2	0.1562	0.25	4.46	0.697
3	0.2344	0.30	4.46	1.045
4	0.1875	0.22	4.46	0.836
5	0.2344	0.30	4.46	1.045
6	0.3125	0.33	4.46	1.394
7	0.0781	0.20	4.46	0.348
8	0.1562	0.95	3.52	0.550
9	0.1562	0.95	3.52	0.550

2. The travel time from each subcatchment to the mouth of the watershed is as follows:

Subcatchment No.	Reach No.	Reach Travel Time (min)	T_t (min)	T_t (h)	t_c (h)
	9	6.4			
1			6.4	0.11	0.25
	8	6.7			
2			13.1	0.22	0.25
	7	5.0			
3			18.1	0.30	0.30
	6	6.7			
4			24.8	0.41	0.22
	5	4.5			0.30
5			29.3	0.49	0.30
	4	5.2			
6			34.5	0.58	0.33
	3	7.2			
7			41.7	0.70	0.20
	2	5.8			
8			47.5	0.79	0.95
	1	1.6			
9			49.1	0.82	0.95

3. The routed hydrographs expressed in csm/in. are as follows:

Time (h)

Sub.	11.5	12.0	12.1	11.1	12.3	12.4	12.5	12.6	12.7	12.8	12.9	13.0	13.5	14.0
1	47	641	424	245	170	138	125	104	85	75	71	68	49	40
2	34	419	603	627	486	341	235	173	138	114	96	83	55	43
3	31	279	461	559	530	428	318	234	179	143	116	97	59	45
4	24	87	181	341	490	545	497	397	296	219	167	133	67	49
5	22	65	124	238	378	479	499	447	363	281	216	168	75	51
6	22	65	124	238	378	479	499	447	363	281	216	168	75	51
7	18	36	49	84	161	284	409	491	481	422	340	263	89	56
8	11	20	25	33	46	67	94	128	165	202	233	256	236	140
9	11	20	25	33	46	67	94	128	165	202	233	256	236	140

Note: The values tabulated here are for the closest listed combination at t_c and T_t. No interpolation was attempted. This will not introduce serious error in the total watershed hydrograph.

4. The routed hydrographs are converted to cfs by multiplying by the QA column of step 1.

Time (h)

Sub.	11.5	12.0	12.1	12.2	12.3	12.4	12.5	12.6	12.7	12.8	12.9	13.0	13.5	14.0
1	33	447	295	171	118	96	87	72	59	52	49	47	34	28
2	24	292	420	437	339	238	164	121	96	79	67	58	38	30
3	32	292	482	584	554	447	332	245	187	149	121	101	62	47
4	20	73	151	285	410	456	416	332	248	183	140	111	56	41
5	23	68	130	249	395	501	522	467	379	294	226	176	78	53
6	31	91	173	332	527	668	695	623	506	392	301	234	105	71
7	6	13	17	29	56	99	142	171	168	146	118	92	31	20
8	6	11	14	18	25	37	52	70	91	111	128	141	130	77
9	6	11	14	18	25	37	52	70	91	111	128	141	130	77

5. The total watershed direct runoff hydrograph is the sum of these.

Time (h)	11.5	12.0	12.1	12.2	12.3	12.4	12.5	12.6	12.7	12.8	12.9	13.0	13.5	14.0
ro[a] (cfs)	181	1298	1696	2123	2449	2579	2462	2171	1825	1517	1278	1101	664	444

[a] Runoff.

Example using different methods and schemes for subdividing the total watershed are presented in reference 10. Final results of these are as follows:

Method	No. of Subcatchments	Discharge
SCS	1	1501 cfs
Espey	1	1930 cfs
SCS	3	2458 cfs
SCS	9	2579 cfs
Espey	9	2546 cfs

The agreement is suprisingly good among the multi-subcatchment analyses. The single subcatchment analyses predict much lower peaks. Single subcatchment analyses implicitly assume that varied land use is evenly distributed throughout the watershed. However, in the case study example, the urbanized areas were nearest the mouth of the watershed. This would yield higher peak flows than an "equivalent" but evenly distributed land use.

EFFECTS OF URBANIZATION

One of the most common objectives of hydrologic studies is to estimate the hydrologic effects of urbanization in a watershed. It should be clear that urbanization will significantly increase the volume of excess precipitation. Furthermore, the time of concentration will be reduced and, therefore, the peak of the unit hydrograph will be increased. In other words, the peak flowrate would be increased even for equal volumes of runoff, but the volume of runoff is usually also increased. Conditions before development and after development may be designated respectively as pre-D and post-D conditions. The procedure according to SCS methods for estimating the future condition hydrograph in a previously undeveloped basin can be summarized as follows:

1. Determine the "future condition" curve number.
2. Determine the future condition 24-hour runoff.
3. Calculate t_c using the future condition curve number.
4. Compute the "percent of hydraulic length modified lag factor." When natural waterways are replaced with sewers, lined channels, etc., t_c and lag are reduced. SCS TR-55 quantifies this, reproduced here as Fig. 3-12.
5. Compute the "percent impervious lag factor." Similarly, t_c and lag are reduced because of increased imperviousness. This is shown here as Fig. 3-13.

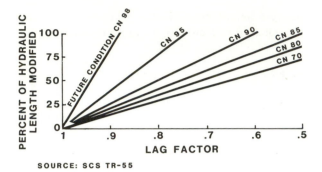

SOURCE: SCS TR-55

Figure 3-12   Hydraulic Length Modified Lag Factor

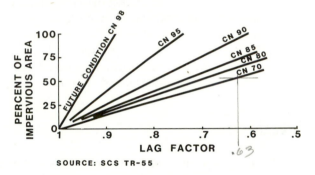

SOURCE: SCS TR-55

Figure 3-13   Percent Impervious Lag Factor

6. Predict future condition t_c as the product of t_c per step 3 times the factors from steps 4 and 5.

7. Compute the future condition direct runoff hydrograph. This is accomplished by multiplying the tabular method values (based on future condition t_c) by future condition runoff (step 2) and drainage area.

The procedure is illustrated in the following sample problem:

Undeveloped versus Developed Subcatchment Hydrograph

Compare the "before" and "after" development direct runoff hydrographs for subcatchment 8 (Fig. 3-10).

1. Determine undeveloped hydrograph. Subcatchment 8 drainage area = 100 acres = 0.156 mi², lag = 3313 ft, and $Y = 3\%$. Subcatchment 9 in its natural state has a $CN = 74$, $S = 3.51$ in., and $t_c = 0.95$ h. The 25-year, 24-hour runoff is calculated as follows:

$$Q = \frac{(P - 0.2S)^2}{(P + 0.8S)} = \frac{(6.4 - 0.2 \times 3.51)^2}{(6.4 + 0.8 \times 3.51)} = 3.52 \text{ in.}$$

Interpolation between tabular method hydrographs (for $T_t = 0$) and conversion from csm/in. to cfs is as follows:

Time (h)	Tabular Hydrograph $t_c = 0.75$ h (csm/in.)	Tabular Hydrograph $t_c = 1.0$ h (csm/in.)	Interpolated for $t_c = 0.95$ h (csm/in.)	Subcatchment 8 before Development (cfs)[a]
11.0	15	13	13.4	7
11.5	29	24	25.0	14
11.7	57	45	49.0	27
11.8	98	66	72.4	40
11.9	163	107	118.2	65
12.0	248	155	173.6	96
12.1	329	211	234.6	129
12.2	375	258	281.4	155
12.3	388	301	381.4	175
12.4	369	313	324.2	179
12.5	325	316	317.8	175
12.6	276	301	296.0	163
12.7	232	277	268.0	148
12.8	195	247	236.6	130
12.9	165	217	206.6	114
13.0	142	188	178.8	98
13.2	107	146	138.2	76
13.5	76	102	96.8	53
14.0	51	64	61.4	34

[a]Previous column times 0.156 mi^2 times 3.52 in.

2. Determine developed hydrograph.
   a. Assume same conditions as the developed subcatchments. Therefore, $CN = 83$ and $S = 2.05$ in.
   b. $Q = \dfrac{(6.4 - 0.2 \times 2.05)^2}{(6.4 + 0.8 \times 2.05)} = 4.46$ in.
   c. $t_c = \dfrac{l^{0.8}(S+1)^{.7}}{1140Y^{0.5}} = \dfrac{3312^{0.8}(3.05)^7}{1140(3)^{0.5}} = 0.72$ h
   d. Figure 3-12 with future $CN = 83$ and assuming 90% of hydraulic length modified yields

   $$\text{hydraulic length modified lag factor} = 0.51$$

   e. Figure 3-13 with future $CN = 83$ and percent impervious $= 38$ yields percent impervious lag factor $= 0.79$
   f. $t_c = 0.72 \times 0.51 \times 0.79 = 0.29$ h $= 0.3$ h $= 18$ min
   g. Multiplying the tabular values for $t_c = 0.3$ h by $A = 0.156$ mi^2 and $Q = 4.46$ in. yields

t (h)	Developed Q (cfs)	Undeveloped Q (cfs)
11.0	15	7
11.5	30	14
11.7	98	27
11.8	226	40
11.9	409	65
12.0	459	96
12.1	373	129
12.2	259	155
12.3	175	175
12.4	128	179
12.5	103	175
12.6	86	163
12.7	71	148
12.8	60	130
12.9	54	114
13.0	50	98
13.2	43	76
13.5	36	53
14.0	29	34

Note that volume of runoff was increased 27% while peak discharge was increased 156%

CONCLUSION

The reader can conclude from the variability of the results shown that storm hydrology is not an exact science. Existing methods can be used with confidence for engineering design; however, as with many hydrological calculations, the basic problem in storm hydrology is usually of predicting the impact on a facility of changing land use or expected storm events. The key to success is to gain facility with existing methods and to apply them with checks and balances to ensure that final calculations are adequate for design.

NOTES—CHAPTER 3

1. Stifel W. Jens, "Design of Urban Highway Drainage. The State-of-the-Art," U.S. DOT, Federal Highway Administration, Aug. 1979.
2. R. K. Linsley, M. A. Kohler, and J. L. Paulhus, *Hydrology for Engineers*, New York: McGraw-Hill, 1958.
3. Jens, 1979.
4. M. B. McPherson, "Some Notes on the Rational Method of Storm Drainage Design," ASCE Urban Water Program TM No. 6, New York, January 1969.

5. American Society of Civil Engineers, "Design Manual for Storm Drainage," New York, 1960.

6. U.S. Soil Conservation Service, "Urban Hydrology for Small Watersheds," TR 55, Jan. 1975.

7. Wright-McLaughlin Engineers, "Urban Storm Drainage Criteria Manual," 2 vols., Urban Drainage and Flood Control District, Denver, Colo., 1969.

8. W. H. Espey and D. G. Altman, "Nomographs for Ten-Minute Unit Hydrographs for Small Urban Watersheds," ASCE Urban Water Program TM No. 32, July 1977.

9. Bruce H. Bradford, Neil S. Grigg, and L. Scott Tucker, *Stormwater Management, Vol. I Urban Hydrology*, Atlanta, Ga.: Water Management Science Inc., 1979.

10. Bradford, 1979.

4

Runoff Pollution

CLIFFORD W. RANDALL

THOMAS J. GRIZZARD

BASIC CONCEPTS

When planning stormwater management programs, there is a strong tendency to consider only the quantity of stormwater runoff and its effects such as flooding, and to ignore the quality impacts. The long-term effects of polluted stormwater, however, can be very significant, and in some cases may be the most critical aspect of stormwater management.

The Occoquan Reservoir of northern Virginia is an example of such a situation. It is an indispensable supply of drinking water for approximately 650,000 persons located in the Virginia suburbs of Washington, D.C.; but it is unfortunately located downstream from some rapidly urbanizing areas of those same suburbs. During the 1960s it was observed that the water quality in the reservoir was rapidly deteriorating, and an extensive program of point source pollution control was developed by the State Water Control Board to improve the quality of water in the reservoir and to preserve this essential supply of water, As the program progressed, however, it was observed that, although the amount of pollution from the point sources had greatly decreased, the concentration of pollutants in the reservoir had continued to increase and the quality of the water had continued to worsen. Extensive monitoring showed that the nonpoint sources of pollution, i.e., stormwater runoff, were the main cause of water quality changes in the reservoir.

An interesting aspect of the Occoquan experience is that when the first assessment of reservoir water quality was made during the late '60s, point sources were dominating the condition and were responsible for most of the deterioration. The change in the primary source of pollution occurred for two reasons: (1) urbanization in the upstream area of the watershed significantly increased, thereby increasing the amount of stormwater runoff and the loads of pollutants reaching the streams, and (2) pollutants from point sources, which had previously masked nonpoint effects, had been reduced to less significant levels.

The Occoquan experience points out two inportant principles. One is that nonpoint sources of pollution are always present and must be considered in water quality management plans. The second is that urbanization greatly increases the loads of pollutants that reach the streams and other bodies of water in the area, and this impact of urbanization should be considered when developing land use plans and stormwater management strategies.

Major Types of Runoff-Borne Pollutants

Urban stormwater runoff may transport many undesirable pollutants, some of which will deplete the oxygen budget of the stream or body of water reached, sone of which will accumulate and exert toxic effects on aquatic plants and animals, and others which may stimulate the growth of microorganisms and plants such as algae and rooted aquatics. These undesirable components are composed of both organic and inorganic matter as well as soluble and insoluble material. The pollutants present, and their concentrations, are a function of the degree of urbanization, the type of land use, the densities of automobile traffic and animal populations, and the degree of air pollution just prior to rainfall. The major types of pollutants may be classified as follows:

1. Suspended sediment;
2. Oxygen-demanding substances;
3. Heavy metals;
4. Toxic organics—pesticides, PCBs;
5. Nutrients—nitrogen, phosphorus;
6. Bacteria and viruses;
7. Petroleum-based substances or hydrocarbons;
8. Acids; and
9. Humic substances—precursors for trihalomethanes.

Measurement of Pollutants

It is usually unnecessary or too difficult to measure the specific pollutants that are in stormwater runoff, such as the actual bacteria present or the exact type of organic compound that is oxygen-demanding or toxic; so water quality parameters that group similar pollutants are used to classify the strength or degree of contamination of the runoff. A list of the commonly used parameters and the types of pollutants they measure follows:

1. Biochemical oxygen demand (BOD). Measures oxygen-demanding substances that can be metabolized by bacteria. A measure of biodegradable organic matter if properly performed.
2. Chemical oxygen demand (COD). Measures oxygen-demanding substances that react with an oxidizing chemical in a heated acid bath. Designed to measure organic matter but also includes reduced inorganic chemicals, which may be present in significant concentrations in precipitation and runoff in urban areas.
3. Total organic carbon (TOC). Measures oxygen-demanding substances that are organic. Measures the carbon released from substances after combustion at a high temperature. Because a correction is made for inorganic carbon present, it is an excellent measure of total organic matter.
4. Suspended solids, both total and volatile. Measures the insoluble material. Total suspended solids (TSS) is usually a good approximation of the suspended sediment present in runoff.
5. Settleable solids. Measures the suspended solids that will rapidly settle out of the water.
6. Acidity. A measure of the amount of acid in the water and therefore its tendency to cause corrosion.
7. Alkalinity. A measure of the capacity of the water to neutralize acids.

8. pH. A measure of the amount of acid or base in the water.
9. Total dissolved solids (TDS). A measure of all soluble material in the runoff, both organic and inorganic. Determined by evaporating all of the water from a sample and measuring what is left.
10. Coliform bacteria. A test that indicates the degree of animal and human waste contamination. Indicates the likelihood of the presence of disease-causing bacteria and viruses.
11. Oil and grease. A measure of a specific group of organic materials. An indicator of the amount of petroleum-based material plus other fatty substances.
12. Metals such as lead, copper and cadmium.

All of the above tests are thoroughly described in *Standard Methods for the Examination of Water and Wastewater*.[1] In addition to these tests, more specific measurements are used for pesticides, such as chlorinated hydrocarbons and organophosphates, for polychlorinated biphenyls (PCBs), and for some of the toxic organics, particularly solvents.

Origin of Runoff-Borne Pollutants

The principal pollutant in stormwater runoff, i.e., the pollutant present in the largest amount, is nearly always suspended sediment. Tons of eroded soil may be transported from an area of just a few acres during a single storm if effective control measures are not used. Conditions that could cause such an occurrence are: (1) denuded and loose soil such as would be present during construction; (2) intense rainfall, i.e., with large droplets, that deposits a large amount of water in a short time; (3) pre-existing saturated moisture conditions in the soil; and (4) steep slopes from the site to the receiving water. An additional aspect of erosion is that the suspended soil particles may also carry heavy loads of other pollutants, particularly phosphorus, sorbed to their surfaces. An interesting aspect of the phosphorus-suspended solids relationship is that suspended solids from many sources, either rural or urban, may carry approximately the same phosphorus load. Data from six different land use sites in Northern Virginia, which included a highly impervious commercial area, a medium density residential section, a pasture, and a conventionally tilled farm, showed that the total phosphorus load in the runoff was approximately 3% of the total suspended solids load. Data collected by Novotny et al.[2] in Wisconsin also illustrated the similarity of urban and rural sediment-phosphorus loads. Other pollutants that particles tend to adsorb are petroleum-based organics, or hydrocarbons, heavy metals, and oxygen-demanding organics. Many of the most important pollutants in urban runoff occur in particulate form.

Soil erosion during the precipitation event is the major source of suspended solids pollution, but it is not the only source, particularly for urban areas. Particles may be transported and dispersed by wind and automobiles and deposited on impervious surfaces, such as streets and parking lots, and also on pervious areas. Other pollutants originate from many types of industrial and commercial activities. Stormwater runoff may then wash the particles off of the surfaces. Pollution also comes from the particles of rubber that are abraded from tires. Each year more than one billion pounds of tire matter is worn off in the United States. Ninety-four percent of this matter is in the form of large particles that do not become airborne.[3] The materials abraded from tires consist of more than just rubber particles. They also contain pollutants such as zinc, oil, and oxygen-demanding organic polymers. The buildup of solids on impervious surfaces in urban areas has been described by Sartor and Boyd,[4] as shown by Fig. 4-1.

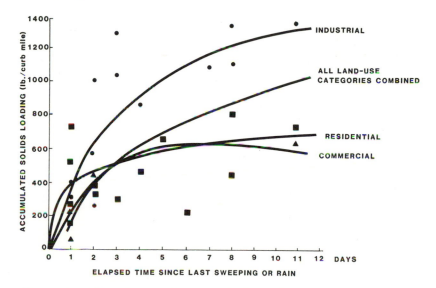

Figure 4-1 Pollutant Accumulation for Different Urban Land Uses (Sartor and Boyd)

Automobiles are the source of many other pollutants that find their way into urban runoff. Oil, which contains pollutants such as zinc and phosphorus, originates from vehicles and numerous other places. Copper and chromium worn from parts are deposited on surfaces. Lead contaminates the atmosphere, as do other components of exhaust emissions such as nitrous oxides, hydrocarbons, and phosphorus. These materials may undergo chemical change while in the atmosphere and form more noxious compounds such as nitric acid. The various forms of pollutants then settle or are washed out of the atmosphere during the early stages of rainfall events, and they become part of runoff pollution.

A tabulation of major pollutants found in urban runoff and the principal sources of these pollutants is given in Table 4-1. Of course, the list is not exhaus-

TABLE 4-1 Origins of Urban Runoff Pollutants

Pollutant	Soil Erosion	Automobiles		Industrial By-products	Fossil Fuels	Lawn and Garden Chemicals[a]	Birds and Pets
		Wear	Exhaust				
Suspended solids	M	M			m		
Organic matter	M	M	m				M
Nutrients							
Nitrogen	m		M		M	M	M
Phosphorus	M		m			M	M
Petroleum substances		M	M	M			
Bacteria and viruses							M
Heavy metals							
Iron	M						
Manganese	M						
Zinc	m	M		m		m	
Lead			M	m			
Copper		M		M			
Chromium		M		M			
Nickel		m		M			
Cadmium		m		M			
Sulfur			m		M		
Acids							
Nitric			M		M		
Sulfuric					M		
Pesticides						M	m

M = major source   m = minor source
[a]Fertilizers, herbicides, insecticides.

tive, and other pollutants may be present in high concentrations, depending on local conditions. The importance of the sources also varies with local conditions. Whether the source is typically major or minor for the specific pollutant is also indicated in the table.

In a fully developed urban area, where most of the land surface is impervious because of paving and roof tops, actual soil erosion during storm events may be minor. Under such conditions, the washoff of deposited particles and their transport to water courses become the important mechanisms. Since washoff may be nearly complete for impervious areas, and since storm sewers are designed for virtually complete transport, the controlling mechanisms, if storm sewers are present, become those that deposit the pollutants. An understanding of suspended solids transport mechanisms, therefore, becomes important in the development of control strategies.

The relationship of imperviousness to the quantity of some pollutants that will be washed from an urban land use site is further illustrated by Fig. 4-2.

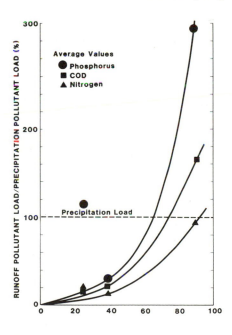

Figure 4-2 Effect of Imperviousness on Urban Runoff Pollution[5]

Impervious areas accumulate pollutants during dry periods, and these pollutants are washed off of the surfaces during rainfall events, thus adding to the quantities of pollutants washed out of the atmosphere. The large increase in the fraction of pollutants transported by the runoff when the imperviousness increases from 40% to 90% graphically illustrates the potential impact of urbanization on water quality.

The high phosphorus load for sites with 25% imperviousness, shown in Fig. 4-2, was the result of erosion, and underscores the importance of control even in supposedly stabilized urban areas, since no construction sites were included in the data.

Air Pollution and Washout

The importance of air pollution and subsequent washout for certain pollutants is illustrated by Fig. 4-3. This figure compares the pollutant loads of nitrogen, phosphorus, and COD in rainwater collected at specific sites, with the loads of the same pollutants in the stormwater runoff from the same site. Interestingly, for all land use sites, the nitrogen load in the precipitation was greater than the observed load in the runoff. Furthermore, for three of the land use sites, the loads of all three pollutants were greater in the precipitation than in the runoff. Only the highly impervious (90%) commercial site and the easily erodable tilled farm site had greater loads of phosphorus and COD in the runoff than were deposited with the precipitation for the observed storm events. However, in New Jersey it was found that only a small proportion of the heavy metals in urban runoff could be attributed to precipitation input. For the highly impervious commercial area, the runoff load included the pollutants that were washed out of the atmosphere by the precipitation, plus the previously deposited pollutants washed off of the surfaces by the runoff. At the tilled farm site, which would be comparable to a construction site, the runoff eroded the soil and transported high loads of suspended solids with their adsorbed pollutants loads. The other three sites had significant grassed areas, and each of them performed as a net sink for the pollutants in the precipitation. This shows the potential of using grass strips or swale drainage for urban runoff pollution reduction.

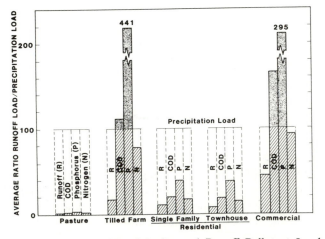

Figure 4-3 Comparison of Precipitation and Runoff Pollutant Loads for a Variety of Land Uses[5]

In a study performed in the Washington, D.C. area, dry weather atmospheric fallout was found to be negligible for nutrients but significant for metals. Even in highly impervious areas, the results indicated it would take thousands of days of dry weather fallout to account for the nitrogen and phosphorus loads in a single runoff event. However, studies in other areas have shown that dry weather fallout may be a significant source of urban runoff nutrient pollution. An inspection of data published by the EPA, shown in Table 4-2, indicates that values from other parts of the United States go from a little

TABLE 4-2   Average Annual Dustfall Values for Various
Water Resources Regions[a]

Area	Geometric Mean (metric tons/km^2)	Range (metric tons/km^2)
New England	2.9	0.2 – 53
Mid Atlantic	1.9	0.1 – 84
South Atlantic	1.8	0.4–104
Great Lakes	11.2	0.7 – 72
Ohio	0.98	0.6 – 2.1
Tennessee	1.5	0.4 – 6
Upper Mississippi	4.4	0.1 – 11
Lower Mississippi	21.7	6.3 – 95
Missouri Basin	12.2	2.1 – 36
Sonris—Red Rainy	8.2	1.0 – 26
Texas Gulf Region	11.4	2.8 – 41
Upper Colorado	50.2	24.0 – 98
Rio Grande Region	10.3	4.2 – 94
Great Basin	5.2	1.8 – 20
Lower Colorado	11.9	5.6 – 24
Pacific Northwest	2.5	0.1–111
California	5.9	0.4 – 13

[a]From EPA National Aerometric Data Bank, Environmental Monitoring and Support Lab., EPA, Research Triangle Park, N.C.[6]

more than one to as much as 70 times greater than the dustfall rate near Washington, D.C., where the average observed value was 0.71 metric tons/km^2 per month. Even for the largest of these values, however, it would take nearly two months of dry weather fallout to account for the load observed in a typical runoff event.

Erosion

Erosion of soil or other materials from pervious surfaces is first initiated by raindrop impact. Particles are dislodged from the surface by the transfer of kinetic energy at impact. Following detachment from the surface, sediment particles may be carried by the runoff. Further detachment of soil particles may occur as a result of the action of water flowing over the surface. Delivery of this suspended load to a receiving water is a function of the ability of the overland flow to maintain sufficient energy to carry the suspended load and, in defined channels, to promote bed load movement. This entire process may be viewed schematically in Fig. 4-4, after Foster.[7]

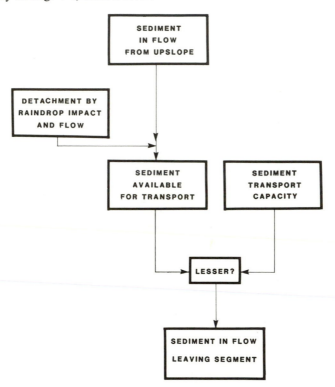

Figure 4-4 Sediment Flux, Schematic

The Universal Soil Loss Equation (USLE) is an empirical relationship derived from field plot work conducted at Purdue University in the 1950s.[8] The equation is based on some 20,000 plot years of natural runoff data, and has been used to predict annual soil losses from fields. It should be emphasized that the equation was never intended to be used in predicting sediment yields from single storm events. The equation is as follows:

$$A = RKLSCP \qquad (4\text{-}1)$$

where A = annual loss in tons per acre,
       R = rainfall factor,

$K =$ soil erodability factor,
$L =$ slope length factor,
$S =$ slope gradient factor,
$C =$ crop management factor, and
$P =$ erosion control practice.

A detailed discussion of USLE and the estimation of its parameters is beyond the scope of this text, but the reader will find ample treatments in the literature,[9,10] It should also be noted that modifications have been applied to the equation to allow it to predict sediment yield from watersheds rather than fields (sediment delivery ratio), and to enable it to predict transport of other sediment-related pollutants (enrichment ratios).[11]

Washoff

The removal mechanisms of particulate pollutants residing on impervious surfaces include detachment and incorporation into overland flow. The kinetic energy requirements for maintenance of materials in suspension may be seen to be similar to those of eroded sediment transport.

The modeling of pollutant washoff from impervious surfaces will be treated in the next chapter.

Soluble Material Transport

Following the incorporation of particulate and dissolved phase pollutants into runoff flow, many constituents may be transferred from one phase to another. Such changes may have significant impacts on potential control strategies and on ultimate receiving water quality. For instance, those pollutants likely to remain largely in the soluble phase cannot be successfully removed by solids separation. On the other hand, those pollutants entering a receiving water system attached to sediment may not be carried further by streamflow. If pollutants are deposited, subsequent biological and chemical interactions may serve to increase their water quality impacts.

A few materials of water quality significance, such as nitrate, remain almost exclusively in the dissolved phase. Most materials, however, can be divided, or partitioned, between the dissolved and particulate phases. Some researchers have investigated the use of theoretical isotherms to compute partition coefficients for runoff pollutants.[12] Some observations of the distribution of nitrogen and phosphorus between dissolved and particulate phases have been reported for a number of urban land uses.[13] Summaries of these data are reproduced in Table 4-3. As may be seen, sizable fractions of both nitrogen and phosphorus have been observed to remain soluble. This has some interesting control measure implications.

TABLE 4-3   Percentage of Plant Nutrient Loads
in Dissolved Form[a]

(after Grizzard and Randall[13])

Land Use	Dissolved N (%)		Dissolved P (%)	
	Mean	S.D.	Mean	S.D.
Large-lot single family residence (0.1—2.0 DU/Acre)	72.5 (18)	±16.4	54.8 (18)	±23.8
Medium density single family residence (2.0—8.0 DU/Acre)	57.7 (24)	±18.6	50.3 (24)	±24.6
Townhouse garden apartments (8—22 DU/Acre)	57.4 (51)	±16.8	41.9 (51)	±17.9
High rise residential (22 DU/Acre)	69.9 (11)	±11.1	47.2 (11)	±10.2
Suburban shopping center	73.4 (27)	±14.1	46.9 (27)	±17.7
Central business district (CDB)	57.9 (14)	±16.7	31.3 (14)	±19.2
Construction site	84.6 (19)	±13.9	43.3 (19)	±20.1

Note: Reported values for stabilized urban land uses are based on mean ratios of total loads. Reported values for transitional urban land uses are based on mean ratios of instantaneous concentrations.

[a]Number of observations is shown in parentheses on the second line of each cell.

DU = dwelling units

First Flush

At the time washoff commences from an impervious surface, there are often large quantities of loosely attached materials on that surface. These loosely bound and easily transported materials are usually incorporated largely into the initial part of the storm flow.[14,15] The first flush effect concentrates pollutant loads in the first part of the runoff waters, and it too has some interesting control measure implications. The essentials of this phenomenon are illustrated in Fig. 4-5(a–c). In Fig. 4-5(a) and (b), the phenomenon can be observed in terms of a hypothetical hydrograph and pollutant loading curve. A rather small runoff volume, taken as the hatched area beneath the hydrograph (a), can be seen to be associated with a large fraction of the total pollutant load, taken as the hatched area beneath that curve (b). Another, more useful way to observe the phenomenon has been reported by Griffin et al.[16] A plot

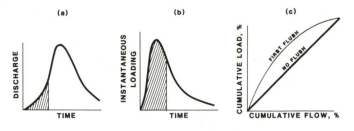

Figure 4-5 Essentials of the First Flush Phenomenon

of cumulative flow versus cumulative load is produced for a single event, as illustrated schematically in (c). If the data plot above the 45° no-flush line, then first flush has occurred, because, for a given fraction of the total flow, a greater fraction of the total load has been generated.

Figure 4-6 illustrates the occurrence of the phenomenon for a number of constituents during a runoff event occurring in a Northern Virginia townhouse development.[17] As can be seen, extractable metals exhibited the greatest propensity towards the first flush effect, followed by total nitrogen and total phosphorus. Soluble phosphorus exhibited the least tendency towards the effect, but it too preceded the flow during the middle stages of the storm runoff event. It may be seen that, for the storm described, capturing or removing approximately 23 % of the runoff flow (the initial portion) would result in a 65 % removal of heavy metals.

Settleability of Urban Runoff Pollutants

The association of many of the pollutants in urban runoff with the suspended solids makes the reduction of pollution by sedimentation a feasible means of water quality control. Because detention basins are a primary method of controlling flood flows and already exist in many areas, the conversion of these basins from single to dual purpose basins, to include the removal and storage of particulate pollutants, presents a readily available, economical, and potentially effective solution to urban runoff pollution problems. Clearly, it is important to understand the potential effectiveness of this approach, and this requires knowledge of the settleability of the suspended solids and other pollutants in urban runoff.

Trap efficiency of detention basins for sediment has been studied and has been correlated with laboratory determinations of grain size and particle settling velocity in still water.[18-21] However, these results cannot be satisfactorily translated into pollutant settleability results because of differing specific gravities of the grains of the various particles, and because of the association of several pollutants with particles of other materials. In fact, very little information is available regarding the actual settleability characteristics of urban runoff pollutants. Such a study has been conducted by Whipple and Hunter[22] and the average results are summarized in Table 4-4.

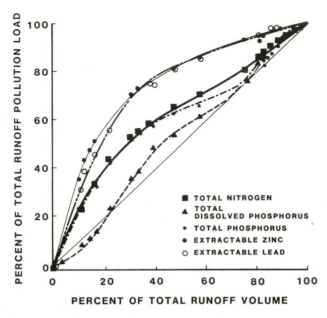

Figure 4-6 Runoff Pollution Timing Curves

TABLE 4-4 Settleability of Urban Runoff Pollutants[a]

(after Whipple and Hunter[22])

Pollutant	No. of Observations	Avg. Removal (%)	Removal Range (%)	16 Hour Removal as % of 32 Hour Removal
Suspended solids	4	68	62–73	80
Hydrocarbons	4	68	61–73	95
BOD$_5$	3	40	20–55	95
Total phosphorus	4	50	30–67	98
Lead	4	65	55–84	85
Zinc	4	30	17–36	98
Copper	4	42	31–58	70
Nickel	4	30	20–42	—

[a]32 hours of settling in a 1.83-meter high, 22.9-cm diameter column. Removals are the composite of samples from 0.46- and 1.37-meter depths.

The results given in Table 4-4 show the close association of hydrocarbons with suspended solids. The percent removals were the same for a 32-hour settling period, and the range of values were very nearly the same. Lesser removals of other pollutants were obtained, with lead and phosphorus having the next highest removals, respectively. Even though less than 50% of the other pollutants were removed by sedimentation, the removals were significant and would be beneficial in efforts to control the water quality effects of urban runoff.

It is also of interest to note, as shown in column five, that most of the removal for all pollutants was accomplished during the first 16 hours of settling.

The average results, as summarized in Table 4-4, varied considerably from site to site, and would very likely be different for different regions.

Information on settleability, combined with consideration of the first flush phenomenon, provides the basis for the strategy for control of runoff pollution by dual-purpose detention basins described in Chap. 7.

FIELD STUDIES

It is important to distinguish between types of field studies conducted for different purposes. Stormwater management is a rapidly developing field and is in a formative stage; accordingly, not only research institutions but also planning agencies may have to make field studies of a rather complex nature. As will be explained later, stormwater management techniques are often implemented by means of standard criteria that are applied over large areas, and field studies of pollutant occurrence and settleability may be needed as a basis for establishment of the criteria. Such studies can profit from research findings and use simplified approaches which eliminate much of the detail required for research purposes. Where criteria have been accepted for general application, it may be unnecessary to obtain any site specific flow or water quality data prior to construction.

Because the occurrence of stormwater runoff in urban systems is a random process, the acquisition of reliable data on pollutant export requires a more sophisticated sampling program design than that which might be employed in ambient water quality assessments. When rainfall events occur, especially in small urban catchments with short times of concentration, the peak loading of pollutants borne by stormwater may take place before personnel are able to occupy sites and commence manual sampling. For this reason, it may be desirable to design a data acquisition program to incorporate the use of automatically functioning flow measurement and sampling equipment. If manual sampling methods are used, their greater simplicity and flexibility are balanced by failures to obtain data when rainfall occurs other than as predicted. In any case, it should be assured that the methods employed produce flow data and samples that adequately represent the quantity and quality of runoff flows.

Sampling Methods

In the past, conventional receiving water quality surveys have relied upon the retrieval of grab samples. This approach allows the description of quality at a number of sites over a period of time. However, because of the transient nature of urban runoff phenomena, the random collection of grab samples does not allow a true representation of pollutant transport to be constructed. Even if grab sampling programs are modified to concentrate on storm events, the potential for error still remains quite high because of the large variations in pollutant concentrations which occur during runoff events.

One attempt to address the deficiencies of grab sampling has been the use of simple composite sampling. In this method, aliquots of equal volume are withdrawn at regular time intervals during a runoff event, and composited into a single volume for analysis. The flow used to compute pollutant load with this method is the mean of instantaneous flows at the times of sample collection. This method assigns equal weight to each aliquot of the composite; consequently samples taken during periods of high flow affect the final composite concentration less than they should, while the reverse is true for low flow samples. Depending upon the changing relationship between concentration and flow, the true event load may be over- or underestimated.

Flow-weighted composite samples may be collected either by hand sampling methods or appropriate automatic instrumentation. In general, either the volume of each aliquot taken or the time between aliquots is varied to enable the construction of a truly flow-weighted composite from many samples. The analysis of such a composite sample and the use of synoptic flow data allow the computation of an excellent estimate of runoff pollution loads if the intervals between samples are short. The method, however, does not lend itself to the determination of the shape of the pollutant loading curve, because the instantaneous variations of concentration and flow cannot be discerned. Under this restriction, phenomena such as the so-called first flush effect cannot be identified However, where the objective is to determine the total pollution loading during a storm event, such methods are adequate.

When, in addition to total pollution loading, it is necessary to investigate load variations during a storm event, the sequential discrete procedure must be adopted. This option is generally the most expensive to utilize in field studies because it entails the analysis of multiple samples. Briefly, a series of samples is retrieved during the runoff event monitored, either manually or by automatic methods. Following laboratory analysis of each of the collected samples and analysis of synoptic flow data, the runoff hydrograph and a curve of pollutant concentration or loading as a function of time may be plotted, as shown schematically in Fig. 4-7. By determining the area under the curve, a very accurate estimate of the total pollutant load for an event may be determined.

Figure 4-8 shows the results of utilizing the sampling strategies discussed to monitor a runoff event at a multiple family housing catchment in 1977.[13] The phosphorus loading plot and summary data readily show the efficacy of the flow-weighted composite and sequential discrete sampling methods compared to the other methods used. Comparisons were made to a load estimated from a smooth curve integration of the loading curve.

As may be seen, the single grab sample method has the greatest potential for producing erroneous loading estimates, with estimated errors ranging from −62% to +219%. A simple composite made from samples retrieved at the

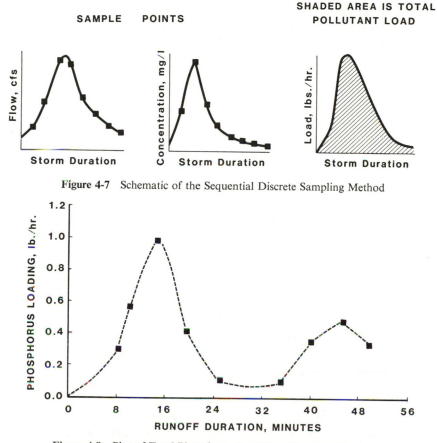

Figure 4-7 Schematic of the Sequential Discrete Sampling Method

Figure 4-8 Plot of Total Phosphorus Loading at Irongate Catchment

indicated locations produced an error of 27%. The sequential discrete and flow-weighted composite methods produced an estimated error of only 8%. This error could be further reduced merely by taking more samples.

A summary of methods that have been utilized in urban stormwater sampling and comments on each has been prepared by Shelley.[23]

In urban catchments where base flow exists between runoff events, a procedure must be adopted for selecting the point at which the recession limb of the hydrograph terminates. In many instances, the selection of this point is obvious; in others, the process may be more arbitrary. Linsley et al.[24] have described a procedure for such separation.

Flow Measurement

The most often neglected, yet one of the most important, aspects of designing an urban runoff data collection program is the measurement of flow. No data collection effort will be capable of achieving its goals if the precision and accuracy of the flow data required for load calculations are not considered.

In general, open channel flow measurements are made by making some direct measurement of the free surface level of the water and converting that measurement to discharge with some previously determined relationship. There exists, however, an entire range of methods for the measurement of flow, and the selection of one should be based upon a combination of factors, such as: (1) accuracy required, (2) period of study, and (3) budget available. In general, the types of measurement techniques employed in stormwater management studies may be found in the following groups:

Float velocity	Current meter
Tracer velocity	Flumes
Tracer dilution	Weirs

Recent publications of the United States Geological Survey,[25] the Bureau of Reclamation,[26] and the Agricultural Research Service[27] provide excellent discussions of flow measurement techniques.

Sometimes the data collection program for an urban stormwater management study will be able to take advantage of existing flow measurement stations. These are often operated by federal, state, or local agencies charged with the collection of surface water data on perennial streams. To the extent that such streams drain the urban catchments to be studied, these flow data may be used quite effectively to augment pollutant transport data collection. In fact, several investigators have discussed the interfacing of automatic sampling equipment to the flow recording devices used at such stations.[28,29,30]

In recent years, however, studies of urban stormwater pollution have focused mostly on small catchments of single land use. Experience has shown that seldom does one find an existing program of discharge data collection on such sub-basins, draining as they do areas of usually less then a thousand acres. In such situations, the investigator is left to the installation and maintenance of his own flow measurement stations. Often, such measurements must be made in the confines of an existing storm sewer or at an outfall. Such studies generally take place in a much shorter time frame than surface water supply studies, and therefore the time required for development of reliable rating curves may not be available. Techniques employed, then, should be adaptable to short-term studies and, in addition, should be usable in existing drainage works with a minimum of modification to the structure.

Because of the general limitations of budget and time in performing field studies of this type, there appears to be an almost universal temptation to utilize steady state flow equations such as the widely employed Manning Formula:

$$V = \frac{1.49}{n}(R)^{2/3}S^{1/2} \tag{4-2}$$

By applying this estimated mean velocity to the cross-sectional area of flow at a given depth, one is able to compute a discharge in cfs:

$$Q = \frac{1.49}{n} AR^{2/3} S^{1/2} \qquad (4\text{-}3)$$

where Q = discharge in cfs;

n = roughness coefficient, dimensionless;

A = cross-sectional area of flow, ft²;

R = hydraulic radius, ft; and

S = slope of energy line.

In most cases, the quality of the flow data required for urban storm-water pollution studies renders the Manning Formula unreliable, because of the uncertainty associated with the estimation of the roughness coefficient, n. For this reason, investigators should be extremely wary of using such equations as the sole means of flow estimation unless some independent verification of conduit roughness can be made.

Calibration of a channel reach may be accomplished by using dilution techniques with continuous injection of a tracer solution. With such a tracer system, it is possible to obtain numerous direct flow measurements during storm events with station monitoring equipment. These may be used to back-calculate a Manning n from available discharge and conduit physical data. In fact, if sufficient measurements are made over a large range of flows, the empirical approach may be abandoned in favor of the construction of an observed stage-discharge relationship.

Figure 4-9 is a schematic of the tracer injection dilution system recom-

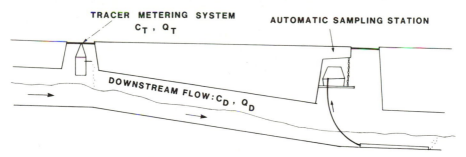

Figure 4-9 Flow Determination Using Continuous Tracer Injection

mended, and also shows the nomenclature for the calculations necessary to compute flow. Constructing a mass balance around the upstream manhole, it may be seen that Eq. 4-4 results:

$$\frac{Q_U C_U + Q_T C_T}{Q_U + Q_T} = C_D \qquad (4\text{-}4)$$

where Q_U = flow upstream,

C_U = tracer concentration upstream,

Q_T = tracer input flow,

C_T = tracer input concentration,

Q_D = flow downstream, and

C_D = tracer concentration downstream.

Equation 4-4 may be simplified in the following manner:

1. Note that the value of $C_U = 0$ (if appropriate tracer is used).
2. Note that $Q_D = Q_U + Q_T$ and $Q_T \ll Q_U$, $\therefore Q_D \simeq Q_U$.

Rewriting Eq. 4-5 yields:

$$Q_D = \frac{Q_T C_T}{C_D} \tag{4-5}$$

A simple technique using lithium chloride as a tracer has been described by Grizzard and Harms.[31] Dyes and other materials may also be used.

Where budget and time permit, it is generally desirable to make use of some primary device to measure flow. Primary flow devices generally fall into the broad categories of weirs or flumes, with at least one of the more functional devices being a hybrid of the two.

In general, weirs are damlike structures built across a watercourse. For a given set of conditions of weir and channel geometry, only a single value of head on the device may exist for each discharge under a free-flow, steady state regime. The existence of such a relationship makes it a simple task to construct a rating curve of head versus discharge. Indeed, for most common configurations, such ratings are available in the literature.[26,32,33] Weir installations, however, have had their historical application principally in studies of watershed hydrology, and they have a rather serious deficiency in their use for studies involving water quality measurements. Weirs, by definition, require a pool upstream of the crest; a pooled area implies a reduction of velocity in stormwater flow; and a velocity reduction will likely allow suspended materials to settle. Such a change in the character of the flow, besides making it impossible to obtain representative samples in the pool upstream of a weir, will necessitate periodic cleaning of the area in the vicinity of the crest if sediment-laden flows are common.[23] For these reasons, weirs should be used only under carefully controlled conditions, such as at detention basin outlets, where suspended solids concentrations are likely to be low. One advantage of weirs is that they do have a large relative measurement range.

Flumes, in general, do not suffer as badly from the previously mentioned deficiency of most weirs, but on the contrary have excellent cleansing characteristics. Most flumes function by creating a transition from subcritical to supercritical flow by providing (1) a restriction in channel area, (2) an increase in channel slope, or (3) a combination of the two. The transition in flow regime creates a differential in water surface elevation through the device, creating a situation where a unique rate of flow exists for any measured upstream depth as long as the discharge is not submerged. Rating curves for almost any critical flow flume geometry may be constructed from solution of the Bernoulli Equation at points upstream of and in the flume throat. While generally exhibiting excellent characteristics of self-cleaning, flumes unfortunately do not share the wide range of flow measurement characteristic of weirs. Several types of Venturi flumes are available for use, including Parshall and Palmer-Bowlus types. Specific discussions of each may be found in the literature.[26,33]

A third type of primary device, mentioned earlier as a hybrid of weir and flume, was developed by the Soil Conservation Service in the 1930s. Three versions designated HS, H, and HL flumes were designed to measure small, moderate, and large runoff flows, respectively. The devices combine the best features of both flumes and weirs, having wide ranges of measurement, good self-cleaning characteristics, small head loss, and relative insensitivity to submergence. Rating tables for flume sizes capable of measuring discharges up to 117 cfs have been published by the Agricultural Research Service.[27]

As mentioned previously, relative range is an important consideration in selecting a primary device for flow measurement. Grant[33] has published an analysis of available range for a number of devices.

Automatic Sampling Equipment

In order to obtain necessary flow measurements along with stormwater samples, two devices are usually required, one for sampling and one for flow metering, with an interconnection to insure synoptic collection of samples and flow data.

In general, the selection of automatic sampling equipment should be guided by one major goal: to obtain a device that will reliably extract truly representative samples from the environment. Experience has shown that adequate devices all share some common characteristics, some of which are summarized below:

Sample transport velocity $\geq$ 3.0 fps,

Minimum of 24 discrete sample bottles,

Capacity for cooling samples,

12 volt dc operation,

Constant sample size over full suction lift range,

Pre- and postsample purge of intake line,

Minimum intake diameter of 3/8 in.,

No solids deposition in sample train, and

Chemically inert surfaces in contact with sample.

A wide range of equipment from a number of manufacturers is currently available for use in unattended stations. In general, the devices having the best application to urban runoff pollution studies fall into the following general categories of pumping methods:

Positive displacement,
Peristaltic, and
Vacuum.

Positive displacement pumps are most often found as a part of permanent installation samples. In cold weather, problems may often be experienced with equipment damage from freezing. Submersible positive displacement pumps may be required in sampling applications where equipment installation is restricted to locations too high above the water surface to operate in a suction lift mode.

Peristaltic pump samplers function well in most applications, and do not have the problem of freezing mentioned above. The invesitgator should be assured that the device selected maintains adequate sample transport velocities at all suction lifts. In addition, it should be determined that reproducible sample volumes can be retrieved over the full range of suction lifts experienced.

Vacuum type samplers generally require frequent maintenance of the seals on the metering chamber. This is important because the integrity of the seal is critical to the proper functioning of the device.

Flowmetering Devices

The selection of a secondary device to make the continuous measurement necessary to convert stage to discharge is an extremely important facet of developing an automated monitoring program. As with sampling devices, there are certain general criteria that satisfactory secondary devices will incorporate:

Wide measurement range,
Accuracy and precision over entire range,
Minimal calibration loss with time,
Insensitivity to suspended solids in flow,
Capacity to internally convert stage to discharge,
Capacity to trigger an associated sampler, and
Unattended operation.

Commercially available automatic flowmetering devices generally fall into the following catagories:

Float-operated devices,

Ultrasonic devices,

Bubbler devices (manometric and transducer), and

Combination bubbler-magnetic devices.

Float-operated devices are perhaps the oldest method of maintaining stage records. In the simplest of designs, a float is connected to a strip chart or digital recorder via a flexible steel tape. Most commercially available float recorders are easy to maintain and are generally very reliable because of their simplicity of design. In most applications, however, float-type devices require a stilling well to damp out surges and rapid fluctuations in water surface elevation. In some cases, particularly on large streams, this may dramatically increase installation costs. In addition, most float-operated devices do not provide an internal stage-to-discharge conversion.

Ultrasonic devices have been available in portable flow measurement instruments for several years. This secondary device type relies upon the measurement of time of travel of an ultrasonic signal from a transponder to the water surface and back. The main advantage of this type of meter is that it functions in a noncontact mode, and therefore is free from the problems of clogging and freezing that plague other types. Some investigators have reported, however, that ultrasonics are sometimes subject to spurious signals from floating matter or foam. Some of the devices currently available have internal programmable read-only memories (PROMs) and microprocessor circuitry to perform the conversion of measured stage to discharge using the unique relationships of the primary device.

Bubbler devices come in essentially two types: (1) inclined manometer and (2) pressure transducer. In both types, gas is slowly bubbled from a fixed orifice, oriented to assure that only static head is encountered. The static pressure required to maintain a given bubble rate is proportional to the height of the water column above the orifice. The static pressure may be measured either by the inclined manometer or pressure transducer devices mentioned above. Some devices are available with internal PROMs for flow data reduction. Gas may be supplied from compressed tanks, continuous pumps, or intermittently operating pumps. In general, the transducer type devices are more portable and easier to install, because of the need for precise leveling of inclined manometer devices. All bubbler systems require only the orifice to be located in the streamflow, allowing the instrument to be located elsewhere.

A final type of flowmeter which has received increased acceptance requires no interface with a primary device. This instrument type relies on the use of velocity-area measurement to compute instantaneous flow rates. Briefly, stage measurements are made with a conventional transducer bubbler. These data are converted to area measurements by using a PROM which describes the geometry of the conduit in question. Measurements of flow velocity are made at the same time with an electromagnetic device located in a band attached to the conduit wall. By using the independently collected values of area and velocity, the device is able to compute discharge. See Figs. 4-10 and 4-11.

Rainfall Measurement

A number of rainfall measurement devices are available for runoff monitoring studies. Numerous publications have cited recommendations for rain gage density and placement based on basin size and morphology.[24,27] Measurement techniques include sight gages, weighing, and counting tips of a balanced dual cell bucket. The recording-type devices can be easily interfaced with flow-metering devices by recording the output from both devices on a common strip chart. This step assures the collection of truly synoptic data, and prevents problems associated with reconciling two or more charts running at slightly different speeds.

Typical Installations

Figure 4-10 shows a pair of schematics of runoff monitoring installation for (a) a perennial stream station and (b) a portable, urban storm sewer station. The schematic in Fig. 4-10(a) is for a semipermanent station used by the Occoquan Watershed Monitoring Program in northern Virginia. The equipment represented is a conventional stilling well-float recorder arrangement interfaced

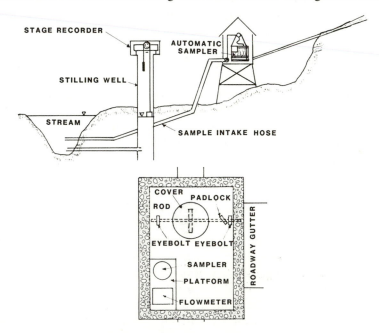

Figure 4-10(a)   Schematic Diagram of a Typical Storm Monitoring Station

with a separately housed automatic sampler. In Fig. 4-10(b), a portable installation in an urban storm sewer curb inlet is represented. This type of arrangement was used successfully by Virginia Tech in conducting field studies for the Metropolitan Washington Water Quality Management Plan Program conducted under Section 208 of P.L. 92-500.

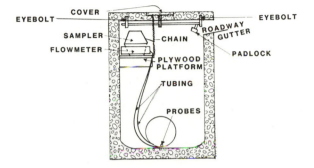

Figure 4-10(b)   Flowmeter/Sampler Installation (Plan View)

Figure 4-11 is a schematic of the monitoring equipment layout employed in the Nationwide Urban Runoff Program field studies being conducted by Virginia Tech in the National Capital Area. Major improvements of the station designs previously described may be seen in the use of portable data logging equipment to record synoptically collected rainfall, flow, and sampling event data. This is a major improvement of field study methods, especially if the collected data will be used in mathematical model calibrations.

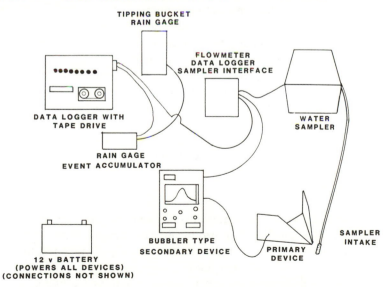

Figure 4-11   Schematic of Monitoring Station

ANALYSIS OF URBAN RUNOFF POLLUTION DATA

Urban runoff pollution data are highly variable and difficult to generalize. Because of the highly variable nature and timing of precipitation events, the data obtained from monitoring such events are also highly variable. Furthermore, data obtained in one geographic region are not equally applicable to another region, and data obtained at a site one year may not be representative of what is obtained at the same site the next year. Yet it is necessary that expected pollutant loads be estimated to some reasonable degree if the potential water quality impacts of such pollution are to be accounted for during planning and management. An objective, then, is to analyze the data so that they can be put into a form that can be used for predictive purposes. Of course, the techniques used must be based on sound principles and sound data or their utilization becomes a futile exercise.

When considering the significance of runoff pollutant contributions, both the concentrations and the total loadings must be examined. Concentrations in the receiving water are of prime concern, and in principle, if these concentrations do not exceed certain allowable maxima, detrimental effects caused by concentration will not occur. For example, concentrations of BOD are directly related to resultant deficiencies in dissolved oxygen, and certain definable levels of toxics may be related to the survival, or the capacity to reproduce, of certain biota. However, for many polluting substances allowable concentrations in the water are not known. Also, because of sedimentation, the accumulation in benthal deposits of pollutants such as phosphorus, hydrocarbons, and heavy metals may be more significant than concentration in the water column. Both receiving water column concentrations and benthal accumulation of sediment are much more a function of the mass loads of pollutants entering the receiving water than of the pollutant concentration in the runoff. Thus, while an estimate of the approximate range of runoff pollutant concentrations that can be expected is of interest, an estimate of the mass loadings of the principal pollutants is of much greater importance for planning and management purposes. The highest priority, then, is placed on obtaining a reliable estimate of the mass loadings of the pollutants that will enter a body of water because of urban runoff during a specific period of time, such as a year, and data collection efforts should be so designed.

Pollutant Mass Loadings

Any methods used must take into account the variable or "stochastic" nature of meteorological events producing runoff, and other changes both seasonal and long-term, which effect the amount of pollutant resulting from a given amount of rainfall. Pollutant mass loadings are necessary mainly for two purposes: first, to determine the mean annual pollutant loading characteristic of the site under present conditions, and second, to determine the characteristic loading under expected future conditions of land development. Other more specialized problems may need to be solved either for research or management purposes, such as the shock pollutant loading which might occur in the Delaware River due to a given storm in the Philadelphia Metropolitan area.

If actual data are very sparse, loading estimates can be made based on estimates of typical pollutant concentration in runoff, multiplied by anticipated flows. However, the estimation of typical concentrations is no easier or more reliable than the direct estimation of loadings for the same conditions, since concentration data without corresponding flow rates are statistically of little value.

For any large area, it is best to obtain data on actual pollution loadings from small areas of a single land use, determined under various seasonal and meteorological storm conditions, and to use such data in conjunction with data from the literature to apply to other areas of similar land use, either at the same time or in the future.

The most difficult analytical step in the above process is to use pollution loading data from a number of specific storm events to determine mean annual loading rates for the given watershed. This can be done by bi-variate regression of loading on flow rate, which assumes implicitly that loadings do vary reasonably closely with flow rate. In fact, experience shows that loadings for the larger storm events do not increase proportionately with flows, but at a lesser non-linear rate. Therefore, in this case, the mathematical perfection of regression analysis does not result in corresponding accuracy. More accurate results can be obtained in two ways. The first is by graphically eliminating the first flush effect, as described by Griffin et al.[17] The second is simply to use the aggregate loading and aggregate flow of the storms observed to obtain a mean concentration, and to apply this mean concentration to predicted aggregate flow for the year. If the data are taken from a representative group of storm events, the estimate made by this simple method should be reasonably accurate. If the data available are not representative of the total annual cycle of storms, no statistical process is apt to produce a reliable estimate.

Estimation of Loadings from Land Use Types

Once the mass loadings for a given land use type have been accumulated over a considerable period of time, the results can be expressed in terms that can be used to estimate loadings from that type of land use for the rest of the watershed(s) of interest. A variety of terms have been used for this purpose. The approaches below, or their metric equivalents, are commonly used.

1. Annual loading/area of given land use, lbs/acre (for a typical year);
2. Annual loading/curb miles of given land use, lbs/mile-yr;

3. Annual loading/traffic volume, lbs/vehicle-yr;
4. Annual loading/air pollution index, lbs/avg. index-yr;
5. Annual loading/runoff volume, lbs/million gallons;
6. Annual loading/precipitation amount, lbs/in. (for a specific area);
7. Pollutant loading/sediment load, lbs/ton SS, and
8. Loading/land area/precipitation amount, lbs/acre/in.

While the terms are developed to permit application of relationships from observed sites to unobserved sites, or to the same sites in the future, the pitfalls of such a procedure should be recognized.

Besides the possibilities of error due to nonrepresentative data, discussed above, each of the approaches implicitly assumes the accuracy of a specific relationship, which may not, in fact, be fully accurate. Number 1 assumes that pollution will vary according to land use. This is the most commonly used method of predicting loadings under future conditions, as indicated in Tables 4-6 and 4-7. Number 2 assumes that pollution loading varies in accordance with the number of miles of curb in various stages of development. Approaches 3,4, and 5 make similar assumptions regarding, respectively, sediment loading, automobile traffic, and air pollution. Numbers 6, 7, and 8 are approaches used in the preliminary stages of analysis, designed to convert loading data from specific storm events to annual average loadings, which are then usually converted to relationships with land use for predictive purposes. Since the runoff and the precipitation from any storm event are quantitatively related, and since both vary from year to year, it should be possible to make a good estimate based upon either one. The principal advantage of using amount of precipitation rather than amount of runoff, is that a more nearly proportionate relationship with loading is apt to be encountered for the former, which is important if regression analysis is to be used. On the other hand, unless the area is small or a network of rain gages is available, the precipitation data may be inaccurately represented by a single rain gage. If a mathematical model is used, the selection of approach to estimate loadings is influenced by the type of model, as discussed in Chap. 5.

Typical Values

In recent years, local, state, and federal programs have resulted in a dramatic increase in the collection of nonpoint pollution loading data on a national basis. Most notable of these programs have been those sponsored under Sections 208 and 314 of P.L.92-500. The former data collection programs were undertaken for the preparation of areawide water quality management plans; the latter, for diagnostic and feasibility studies for lake restoration.

More recently, the EPA has funded a series of 30 prototype projects under the auspices of its Nationwide Urban Runoff Program (NURP). These projects are all part of an effort to make a 1983 report to the Congress regarding the water quality impacts and control requirements of urban runoff pollution.

It is apparent, then, that the data base of urban runoff characterizations has been continuing to expand rapidly. Many of the better studies in recent years have produced site and land use specific monitoring data, enabling investigators to make runoff load characterization as a function of single land uses.

Nutrients

Table 4-5 is a summary of recently reported data on the annual export of nitrogen and phosphorus forms in stormwater from a variety of urban land uses. As many be seen, even within general land use categories, wide ranges

TABLE 4-5   Phosphorus and Nitrogen Export in Urban Stormwater

Land Use	Ortho P	TP (kg/ha/yr)	$NO_2 + NO_3 - N$ (mg/l)	TKN (mg/l)	TN (mg/l)	Ref.
Single family		0.21			1.48	34
residential		0.77–1.44			4.9–7.1	34
(large lot)		0.17–0.67			1.8–7.1	34
Multi-family		1.29–1.61			6.7–8.4	34
residential		8.39				35
High rise		1.96–2.18			8.7–9.7	34
residential						
General	0.2	0.4 –1.3			5.0–7.3	27
residential	0.32	0.89	0.51	0.30		6
Commercial		2.09–2.85			18.9–30.5	25
	0.02–0.08	0.1 –0.9			1.9–11	37
	3.8	7.6	14.1	7.4		6
Industrial	0.3	0.9 –4.1			1.9–14	37
General urban		2.0			8.5	6
	0.05–0.30	0.3 –2.1			6.2–10.0	37

of variation exist for most constituents. This points up the need to consider factors other than general land use classification in predicting annual nutrient export.

Oxygen-Demanding Materials and Suspended Solids

Table 4-6 gives a summary of data reported in the literature on annual yields of solids, BOD, and COD in stormwater from urban land uses. Although none of the studies cited have reported synoptic data on BOD and COD, it

TABLE 4-6   Suspended Solids and Oxygen Demanding Materials
Export in Urban Stormwater

Land Use	TSS	BOD	COD	Ref.
		(kg/ha/yr)		
Single family			22.5	34
residential			253–474	35
(large lot)			59–233	35
Multi-family			335–420	35
residential	76.8			36
High rise residential			685–761	35
General residential	620–2300			37
	420	35		6
Commercial			1000–1029	35
	50–830			37
	840	87		6
Industrial	400–1700			37
General urban	210–1750			37
	450	50		

may be seen that there are likely to be large differences between the two measures of oxygen demand. It is unfortunate that more data are not available for
BOD on urban stormwater. The presence of toxic materials which inhibit
bacterial action, and of refractory organic compounds, as well as the inability
to obtain acclimated seed bacteria, contribute to the current uncertainty about
ultimate impacts on the oxygen budgets of receiving waters.

Heavy Metals

Table 4-7 is a summary of reported heavy metals yields in urban stormwater. It may be seen that reported yields are generally positively related to the
density of urban land use. Such a relationship is not surprising, in view of what
is known about the principal mechanisms of deposition and transport of metals
in urban catchments. Atmospheric and direct deposition sources are more
likely to achieve complete transport to receiving waters if they occur on impervious surfaces. As urban use becomes more dense, so does the percentage of
impervious cover, as does the load from the previously mentioned sources,
particularly those associated with transportation.

Microbial Contamination

Many studies in recent years have reported fecal coliform densities in
urban stormwater that exceed receiving water standards. Table 4-8 shows a
summary of some recent literature in this area.[17] The wide range of the avail-

TABLE 4-7 Heavy Metals Export in Urban Stormwater

Land Use	Cd	Cr	Cu	Fe	Mn	Pb	Zn	Ref.
				(kg/ha/yr)				
Single family residential (large lot)						0.12–0.23	0.10–0.20	35
Multi-family						0.06–0.12	0.07–0.24	35
		0.10				0.68–0.84	0.31–0.39	35
						1.15	2.05	36
High rise residential			0.51			1.72–1.91	1.03–1.15	35
General residential			0.03			0.06	0.02	37
Commercial						2.72–6.84	2.99–3.24	35
			0.07–0.13			0.17–1.10	0.25–0.43	37
Industrial			0.29–1.3			2.2 –7.0	3.5–12.0	37
General urban			0.53–0.13			0.14–0.50	0.90–0.60	37
		1.80	1.80	114	5.50	3.26	2.25	38
		0.12	0.52			2.69	1.40	39
						1.46–3.30		40

TABLE 4-8 Mean Fecal Coliform Concentrations Observed During NVPDC/VPI&SU Field Study of Nonpoint Pollution Loadings

Land Use	No. of Observations	Mean Concentration (MPN/100 ML)	Standard Deviation (MPN/100 ML)	Maximum Concentration (MPN/100 ML)	Minimum Concentration (MPN/100 ML)
Large-lot single family residential (0.1–2.0 DU/Ac)	19	15,800	33,000	150,000	2,800
Medium density single family residential (2.0–8.0 DU/Ac)	25	11,700	13,000	43,000	—
Townhouse/garden apt. (8–22 DU/Ac)	38	137,200	427,500	2,400,000	—
Suburban shopping center	41	101,300	379,600	2,400,000	—

Source:: Reference 17.
DU = Dwelling Units

able data show that few generalizations regarding the incorporation of indicator organisms into urban stormwater are currently possible, except that levels are high.

It should also be noted that the receiving water quality standards for indicator organisms have generally been based upon the assumed relationships between their occurrence and that of pathogenic species. Although generally accepted in the United States, this assumption has been challenged in Great Britain, where research has failed to provide any direct evidence of a connection between coliform counts and disease. This has led to the spectacle of the British public bathing freely in such apparently unsuitable waters as the Thames at Oxford and the Serpentine, a shallow pond in Hyde Park in the heart of London. There is, however, sufficient epidemiological evidence of water-borne disease in the United States that coliform counts should not be taken lightly.

It seems probable that urban stormwater containing no sanitary sewage is not highly contaminated, except by animal populations, which probably have a less direct relationship to human disease than do similar coliform counts of human origin.

In the most complete study to data of microorganisms in urban aquatic systems, Olivieri et al.[41] consistently found high densities of indicator organisms in both urban streams and urban stormwater. The authors also reported high densities of such pathogens as *P. aeruginosa*, *Staphylococcus aureus*, and *Salmonella* (as well as the presence of enteric virus), but they could observe no consistent correlation between these and indicator organisms in stormwater. The study results led the authors to conclude that, although they were unable to identify specific sources of pathogens in urban catchments, it was likely that most were due to some kind of sanitary sewage contamination. This seems very probable since most urban sewers leak, and also overflow during heavy rains. The results of Olivieri et al. from stormwater and urban streams are shown in Table 4-9.

Summary

Non-point sources of pollution are always present and must be considered in comprehensive water quality management plans. The long-term impacts of stormwater runoff pollution can be very significant and, in some cases, may be the most critical stormwater management aspect. Techniques for characterizing and monitoring stormwater pollution have been developed. Pollutants originate from erosion, air pollution, impervious surface washoff, and birds and animals. Suspended particulate matter, such as sediment, is always the pollutant present in the greatest quantity in stormwater runoff, and can be particularly insidious because it transports many other pollutants such as phophorus, heavy metals, and hydrocarbons. Thus, sedimentation may be an effective way to treat stormwater runoff. Automobiles are a major source of runoff pollution, particularly in

TABLE 4-9 Pathogens to Indicator Microorganisms

(after Olivieri[41])

Microorganisms	Ratio
P. aeruginosa to TC	1:45
P. aeruginosa to FC	1:14
P. aeruginosa to FS	1:18
P. aeruginosa to ENT.	1:5
Staph. aureus to TC	1:4,780
Staph. aureus to FC	1:1,410
Staph. aureus to FS	1:2,000
Staph. aureus to ENT.	1:630
Salmonella to TC	1:141,000
Salmonella to FC	1:105,000
Salmonella to FS	1:147,000
Salmonella to ENT.	1:45,500
Enteric virus to TC	1:151,000
Enteric virus to FC	1:50,000
Enteric virus to FS	1:85,500
Enteric virus to ENT.	1:40,700

urbanized areas. Urbanization greatly increases the quantities of pollutants that reach the streams and other bodies of water, and this impact of urbanization should be considered when developing land use plans and stormwater management strategies. The pollutants in runoff, and their concentrations, are determined by the degree of urbanization, the type of land use, the densities of automobile traffic and animal populations, and the degree of air pollution just prior to rainfall. While literature values can be used to estimate runoff pollution, specific monitoring provides much more reliable information.

NOTES—CHAPTER 4

1. *Standard Methods for the Examination of Water and Wastewater, 15th Ed.* American Public Health Association, 1980.

2. V. Novotny et al., "Mathematical Modeling of Land Runoff Contaminated by Phosphorus," *Journal of the Water Pollution Control Federation*, 50, No. 10, 1978.

3. L. L. Hoover-Siegel, "Where the Tire Meets the Road," Search 15, No. 4, General Motors Research Laboratories, Warren, Mich., July–Aug. 1980, pp. 1–2.

4. J. D. Sartor and G. Boyd, "Water Pollution Aspects of Street Surface Contaminants," EPA-R2-72-081, USEPA, Washington, D.C., 1972.

5. C. W. Randall et al., "A Comparison of Pollutant Mass Loads in Precipitation and Runoff in Urban Areas," Proceedings, 2nd International Conference on Urban Storm Drainage, IAWPR, Univ. of Illinois, Urbana, 1981.

6. M. P. Wanielista, *Stormwater Management Quantity and Quality*, Ann Arbor, Mich.: Ann Arbor Science Publishers, 1978, p. 190.

7. G. R. Foster, "Soil Erosion Modeling: Special Considerations for Nonpoint Pollution Evaluation of Field-Sized Areas," *Environmental Impact of Nonpoint Source Pollution*, M. R. Overcash and J. M. Davidson, eds.; Ann Arbor, Mich.: Ann Arbor Science Publishers, 1980, pp. 213–240.

8. W. H. Wischmeier and D. D. Smith, "Predicting Rainfall Erosion Losses from Cropland East of the Rocky Mountains," USDA Agricultural Handbook No. 282, 1965.

9. G. R. Foster and W. H. Wischmeier, "Evaluating Irregular Slopes for Soil Loss Prediction," *Transactions of the American Society of Agricultural Engineers*, 17, No. 2, 1974, pp. 305–309.

10. W. H. Wischmeier and D. D. Smith, "Predicting Rainfall Erosion Losses: A Guide to Conservation Planning," USDA Agricultural Handbook No. 537, 1978.

11. A. D. McElroy et al., "Loading Functions for Assessment of Water Pollution from Nonpoint Sources," EPA-600/2-76-151, U.S. EPA, Washington, D.C., 1976.

12. L. A. Mulkey and J. W. Falco, "Sedimentation and Erosion Control Implications for Water Quality Management," *Proceedings of National Symposium on Soil Erosion and Sedimentation*, American Society of Agricultural Engineers, Chicago, Ill., 1977.

13. T. J. Grizzard and C. W. Randall, *Occoquan/Four Mile Run Runoff Pollution Field Study—Final Report*, Department of Civil Engineering, Virginia Tech, Blacksburg, Va., 1978.

14. J. W. Kluesener and G. F. Lee, "Nutrient Loading from a Separate Storm Sewer in Madison, Wisconsin," *Journal of the Water Pollution Control Federation*, 46, No. 5, 1974, pp. 920–936.

15. D. M. Griffin et al., "Analysis of Nonpoint Pollution Export from Small Catchments," *Journal of the Water Pollution Control Federation*, 52, No. 4, 1980, pp. 780–790.

16. D. M. Griffin, C. W. Randall, and T. J. Grizzard, "Efficient Design of Stormwater Holding Basins Used for Water Quality Protection," *Water Research*, 14, Elmsford, N.Y.: Pergamon Press, 1980, pp. 1549–1554.

17. *Occoquan/Four Mile Run Nonpoint Source Correlation Study—Final Report*, Northern Virginia Planning District Commission and Virginia Polytechnic Institute and State Univ. 1978.

18. C. Chen, "Design of Sediment Retention Basins," *Proceedings, International Symposium on Urban Hydrology and Sediment Control*, pp. 285–293 Univ. of Kentucky, Lexington, Ky. 1975.

19. C. Chen, "Evaluation and Control of Soil Erosion in Urbanizing Watersheds," *Proceedings, International Symposium on Urban Rainfall and Runoff and Sediment Control*, pp. 161–174, Univ. of Kentucky, Lexington, Ky., 1974.

20. J. A. Bondurant et al., "Some Aspects of Sedimentation Pond Design," *Proceedings, International Symposium on Urban Hydrology and Sediment Control*, pp. 117–121, Univ. of Kentucky, Lexington, Ky., 1975.

21. A. J. Ward, C. T. Haan, and B. J. Barfield, "Simulation of the Sedimentology of Sediment Detention Basins," *Proceedings, International Symposium on Urban Hydrology and Sediment Control*, pp. 309–316, Univ. of Kentucky, Lexington, Ky. 1977.

22. W. Whipple and J. V. Hunter, "Settleability of Urban Runoff Pollution," Report, Water Resources Research Institute, Rutgers Univ., New Brunswick, N.J., 1980.

23. P. E. Shelley, "Monitoring Requirements, Methods, and Costs," Areawide Assessment Procedures Manual, EPA-600/9-76-014, Water Planning Division, U.S. EPA, 1976.

24. R. K. Linsley, M. A. Kohler, and J. L. H. Paulhus, *Hydrology for Engineers*, New York: McGraw-Hill, 1975, pp. 230–232.

25. "Techniques of Water-Resources Investigations of the United States Geological Survey—Book 3: Applications of Hydraulics," U.S. Geological Survey, Reston, Va., 1967–1969.

26. *Water Measurement Manual*, United States Department of the Interior, Bureau of Reclamation, Denver, Colo., 1975.

27. *Field Manual for Research in Agricultural Hydrology*, United States Department of Agriculture, Agricultural Research Service Handbook No. 224, 1962.

28. T. J. Grizzard, C. W. Randall, and R. C. Hoehn, "Data Collection for Water Quality Modeling in the Occoquan Watershed of Virginia," *Proceedings of the Environmental Modeling and Simulation Conference*, EPA-600/9-76-016, Office of Research and Development, U. S. EPA, 1976.

29. P. B. Bedient and C. B. Amandes, "Monitoring, Modeling and Management of Nonpoint Sources in Houston, Texas," *Proceedings, International Symposium on Urban Stormwater Management*, Univ. of Kentucky, Lexington, Ky., 1977.

30. M. D. Smolen and C. Heatwole, "A Dual-Interval, Stage Actuated Water Sampler Control," *Proceedings, National Conference on Quality Assurance of Environmental Measurements*, Information Transfer, Inc., Silver Spring, Md., 1978.

31. T. J. Grizzard and L. L. Harms, "Flow Measurement by Chemical Gaging," *Water and Sewage Works*, 121, No. 11, 1974, pp. 82–83.

32. Stevens Water Resources Data Book, 2nd Edition, Leupold and Stevens, Inc., Beaverton, Oregon, 1975.

33. D. M. Grant, *Open Channel Flow Measurement Handbook*, Instrumentation Specialties Co., Lincoln, Nebr., 1979.

34. H. C. Mattraw and C. B. Sherwood, "Quality of Stormwater Runoff from a Residential Area, Broward County, Florida," *Journal of Research U.S. Geological Survey*, 5, 1977, p. 823.

35. J. P. Hartigan et al., "Calibration of Urban Nonpoint Pollution Models," *Proceedings, ASCE Specialty Conference on Verification of Mathematical and Physical Models*, College Park, Md., 1978.

36. International Reference Group on Great Lakes Pollution from Land Use Activities," Environmental Management Strategy for the Great Lakes System," *Final Report to the International Joint Commission*, Windsor, Ontario, Canada, 1978.

37. W. Whipple, J. V. Hunter, and S. L. Yu, "Runoff Pollution from Multiple Family Housing," *Water Resources Bulletin*, 14, No. 2, 1978, pp. 288–301,

38. N. V. Colston, "Characterization and Treatment of Urban Land Runoff," EPA-670/2-74-096, 1974.

39. W. Whipple and J. V. Hunter, "Nonpoint Sources and Planning for Water Pollution Control," *Journal of the Water Pollution Control Federation*, 49, No. 1, 1977, pp. 15–23.

40. E. H. Bryan, "Quality of Stormwater Drainage from Urban Land," *Water Resources Bulletin*, 8, No. 2, 1972, p. 578.

41. V. P. Olivieri et al., "Microorganisms in Urban Stormwater," EPA-600/2-77-087, Municipal Environmental Research Laboratory, Cincinnati, Ohio, 1977.

5

Stormwater Models

ROBERT P. SHUBINSKI

LARRY A. ROESNER

INTRODUCTION

Stormwater models first came into use in the late 1960s when researchers began to apply computer technology to the solution of storm drainage problems. The field has since developed into a complex array of models ranging from the very simple, single purpose program to quite elaborate modeling systems. This chapter describes some of the more useful models. It provides an outline of the kinds of data that the programs require and points toward the situations where such programs are practical. The frontiers of modeling have been omitted from the discussion as they are of a research nature.

It is interesting that stormwater modeling has evolved generally from complex models to simple ones. The first method to receive widespread attention was the EPA Storm Water Management Model, usually denoted by the acronym SWMM, and the Stanford Watershed Model, better known now as the Hydrocomp Simulation Program (HSPF). Both are very large computer programs intended to be universal in their coverage of stormwater problems. A major distinction between the two models is that SWMM was originally developed to simulate runoff from a design rainstorm applied to a highly urbanized watershed, whereas the Stanford Watershed Model was designed to simulate a continuous time trace of watershed drainage from predominantly rural watersheds. In their infancy both of these models could be used only by experts in computer technology and engineering. Today, derivatives of SWMM and the Stanford Watershed Model are in use rather widely, but they still rank among the more complex of the available models.

Movement during the 1970s was clearly toward more specialized models. Today, a large number of programs exist. Users can select programs to do the particular jobs they want done.

Why Use a Model?

Engineers designed drainage systems for decades before models were available. Why is it necessary, or even useful, to work with models now? The answer to this question lies in an examination of what models will *do* for the engineer—and perhaps it also lies in what they will *not* do.

First, it should be stated emphatically that models are not a substitute for field-gathered data or knowledge of hydrologic/hydraulic and water quality processes on the part of the user. No model (or any other analytic technique, for that matter) can predict how a physical/chemical/biological system behaves as dependably as direct measurements of the system itself. Nor is any model sufficiently comprehensive to represent accurately every physical/chemical/biological prototype situation that the user may desire to simulate. Failure to heed these obvious truths has resulted in a good deal of model misuse.

The principal use of models is in situations where direct measurements are either impossible or impractical. When a drainage system is under design, for example, a model will let the designer look at many alternative configurations. The designer can project several population growth patterns and answer the "what if" questions that planning for the future demands, and can do so in a reasonable framework of time and costs. Models also permit a more accurate hydraulic analysis of complex drainage systems where backwater, split flows, and surcharging occur. The advent of models has changed the engineer from a cookbook artist who relied heavily on judgement to a serious analyst.

Models permit the inclusion of water quality in the design and management of stormwater systems. At one time, drainage was considered to be the art of getting rid of stormwater as quickly as possible. Now it is recognized that this practice is generally inferior to retaining water in or on the system for some period of time. Water quality has become as important a factor as flood control in many instances. Models are an essential part of this new approach.

Selecting a Model

Many potential model users are bewildered by the number and complexity of the models available. Not only are there many programs, there are many versions of the same program. Moreover, the several comparative tests that have been conducted to determine the relative accuracy of the better known models, while informative, were inconclusive. The fact is that all of the major models, those described here and several others, are useful. Each is based on well-known and acceptable flow relationships. Their water quality sections are much less well defined than their hydrologic and hydraulic sections; but, even so, they are valuable tools.

It is more important that a model be used intelligently than it is that a particualr model be used. The user's first consideration should be to define the problem. Is the problem one of predicting overall changes in runoff due to urban development? Is it to design pipes to carry flow from point A to point B? Or is it to simulate the effects of detention basins on nutrient discharges to a stream? No single program will address all of these problems, and several programs are available to address each of them. The user must understand the problem before an attempt is made to model it. Then the proper model can be selected and used to its best purpose, as a tool.

This chapter first presents a general discussion of the kinds of processes that are modeled in surface runoff, transport systems, and water quality. It is useful before entering upon this discussion to study the model names and their abbreviations, listed in Table 5-1. This list is just a sample of the many models available.

TABLE 5-1   Model Sponsors, Model Names, Abbreviations

1. U.S. Army Corps of Engineers: STORM (Storage, Treatment, Overflow, Runoff Model).[1,2,3]
2. U.S. Environmental Protection Agency: HSPF (Hydrocomp Simulation Program—Fortran).[4]
3. U.S. Environmental Protection Agency: SWMM (Storm Water Management Model); submodels under the names RUNOFF, EXTRAN, RECEIV and others.[5,6]
4. Illinois State Water Survey: ILLUDAS (Illinois Urban Drainage Simulator).[7]
5. Southeast Michigan Council of Governments: RUNQUAL (Runoff and Quality Model).[8]
6. Massachusetts Institute of Technology: MITCAT (M.I.T. Catchment Model).[9]
7. U.S. Soil Conservation Service: TR-20 (Flow Frequency Model).[10]
8. U.S. Environmental Protection Agency: HVM-QQS (HVM-Quantity-Quality Simulator).[11]

SURFACE RUNOFF MODELING

Surface runoff, as the term is generally used in stormwater modeling, is a broad term that includes both surface and some subsurface runoff elements. It is customary to group the runoff from fields, lawns, roofs, parking lots, drainage ditches, and some small pipes in this category. The usual characteristic of surface runoff is that although it is the drainage from a geometrically complex area, it is not necessary to represent each element (roof, sidewalk, lawn, etc.) of the drainage system in a great deal of detail.

Most surface runoff models simulate flow as a series of simple hydrologic/hydraulic processes. Both the rational method and the Soil Conservation Service method of translating rainfall into runoff have been used successfully. (See Chap. 3 for a discussion of these methods.) Flow routing is accomplished by Manning's equation or a similar technique. Computer programs typical of this approach are the RUNOFF Block of EPA SWMM, STORM, ILLUDAS, and TR-20.

Figure 5-1 shows a 386-acre area in the City of San Francisco as it was set up for the EPA SWMM.[12] The surface runoff system is composed of four sub-areas, each of which contains roofs, yards, streets, gutters, and minor sewer pipes. For computational purposes, each sub-area is conceptualized as a single plane surface discharging at a single point, as illustrated in Fig. 5-2.

The sub-area shown in Fig. 5-2 may contain any mixture of land uses, each having a characteristic percentage of this area being impervious.[13] The model treats the sub-area as three units connected in parallel. The first unit contains the aggregate of all impervious land uses that share a feature called "depression storage," a means of accounting for minor losses of water due to such phenomena as parking lot ponding and surface adhesion to buildings and plants. Depression storage captures what would be a small initial runoff. Although physically based, it must be determined empirically.

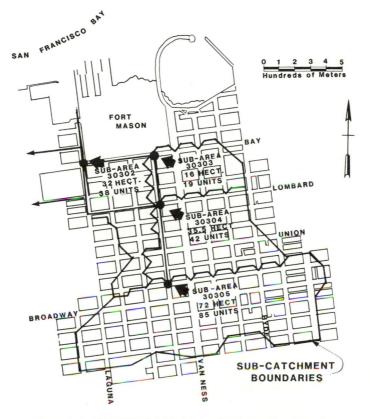

Figure 5-1 EPA SWMM Model Application to San Francisco

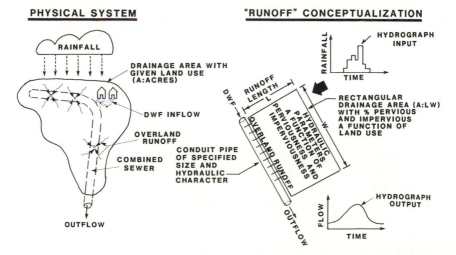

Figure 5-2 Conceptualization of a Physical System for the Model "Runoff"

The second unit of the three parallel units is defined as impervious area that has no depression storage at all. It produces runoff at the very beginning of the storm. The user must determine the part of the total impervious area that fits this category. This decision should be based on field data from the area if such data exist or from general knowledge of the area and its runoff characteristics.

Pervious land uses are aggregated to form the third unit of the simulation. Infiltration of rainfall into the groundwater is accounted for in this unit. In the EPA SWMM this infiltrated water is dropped from the simulations. Some other models such as SEMSTORM (a variant of STORM) and HSPF continue to account for infiltration and permit it to reenter the surface system at a later time. In many urban cases where the impervious area is significant (more than 10% of the total area) this is an unnecessary complication, not germane to the problem being examined. Surface water/groundwater interaction is always a data intensive operation.

As Fig. 5-2 indicates, small pipes and open drainage channels may be a part of the surface runoff modeling. It is almost always to the user's advantage to include as much of the pipe and channel system in the surface runoff model as can be done reasonably. The alternative, placing these pipes and channels in the sewer transport model (see the next section), is more costly; it requires both more user time and more computer time.

Pipes and channels may be kept in the surface runoff model whenever the kinematic wave approximation is an adequate representation of their hydraulics. Physically, this means that there must be no backwater, or, stated differently, pipe friction must control the flow in each pipe or channel. This restriction precludes looped or network sewers and flow control devices such as weirs, orifices, dropouts, and pump stations.

There is enough flexibility in the various programs that the user can represent the flow regime of any urban drainage situation. However, it is evident from the above discussion that surface runoff modeling is not a trivial activity that one undertakes in an afternoon. It should also be clear that the user must understand the basic behavior of the system before beginning. Otherwise, the array of parameters to be adjusted will result only in confusion.

Basic Computations

Space does not permit a detailed discussion of the mathematics of surface runoff computations; each model will differ slightly. However, a simplified exposition of the techniques used in the EPA SWMM can provide a useful introduction to the topic.

Figure 5-3 shows an idealized view of the surface runoff plance conceptualized in Fig. 5-2.[14] Rainfall, R, is the sole input to the element. EPA SWMM does not permit cascades of surface elements as some other models do. Water leaves the element either as outflow, Q, or as infiltration from the pervious area, I.

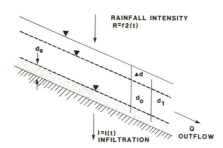

Figure 5-3 Idealized Side View of a
Surface Runoff Plane

Infiltration is computed from the simple Horton equation:

$$I = f_c + (f_0 - f_c)e^{-kt}$$

where f_c, f_0 and k are constants defining the exponential decay curve describing I. The outflow is computed by Manning's equation, which can be written in this case as:

$$Q = \frac{1.49}{n} S^{1/2} w \left(\frac{d_0 + d_1}{2} - d_s \right)^{5/3}$$

where S is the average slope of the catchment and w is its average width. The Manning coefficient is designated n, and d_0 and d_1 are the depth of water on the element at times t_0 and t_1 respectively. The depth of depression storage, d_s, where applicable, is subtracted to obtain the effective depth for flow computation.

Mass continuity, or the storage equation, provides the final relationship necessary to compute the flow hydrograph:

$$\frac{\Delta d}{\Delta t} = R - I - \frac{Q}{A_s}$$

where A_s is the surface area of the plane. These three equations, applied on a step by step basis in time, transform the rainfall hyetograph into an output hydrograph for the element.

Open channels and pipes can be handled in a very similar manner. No rainfall needs to be considered, nor are infiltration losses (or gains) permitted. Inflow from an upstream channel or pipe is included, subject to the restriction that only three branching systems are allowed. The cross-sectional shape and slope of open channels and pipes must also be accounted for.

TRANSPORT SYSTEM MODELING

The design and analysis of large trunk sewers, storm drains, and interceptor sewers involve more sophisticated hydraulics than were considered in surface runoff computation. The form of the motion equation used in EXTRAN is:

$$\frac{\partial Q}{\partial t} = -gAS_f + 2V \frac{\partial A}{\partial t} + V^2 \frac{\partial A}{\partial x} - gA \frac{\partial H}{\partial x}$$

101

where Q = discharge through the conduit,
  V = velocity in the conduit,
  A = cross-sectional area of the flow,
  H = hydraulic head, and
  S_f = friction slope.
  g = gravitation constant
The frictional slope is defined by Manning's equation,

$$S_f = \frac{n^2}{(1.49)^2 R^{4/3}} |V| V$$

where n = Manning's coefficient, and
  R = hydraulic radius.
Use of the absolute value sign insures that the frictional force opposes the flow.

Numerical treatment of the motion equation continues to be a difficult problem, but EXTRAN and HVM-QQS, which use different solution techniques, are able to produce valid solutions for most hydraulic conditions. On occasion the model will produce either numerical instabilities or an invalid solution, and the user is cautioned to examine all solutions very carefully. Transport system models constitute one of the most difficult areas in modeling today. Many people consider this to be a still-developing field. These models can yield very valuable results, but they should be approached with care.

SURFACE RUNOFF QUALITY MODELING

A number of stormwater models have attached to them some kind of water quality routine. Often, one of the main reasons for considering modeling in the first place may be the need for water quality control. Two points should be emphasized before a detailed look at modeling stormwater quality is begun. First, many practical problems concerning water quality can be solved by modeling only the flow. For example, a combined sewer overflow problem may be eliminated by reducing the frequency and magnitude of overflows, without regard to the actual modeling of the overflow quality. Second, surface runoff quality modeling is not nearly as advanced as is hydrologic/hydraulic modeling. The basic principles of hydrology and hydraulics are well known; but the basic principles of water quality are only partly understood.

Two mechanisms discussed in Chap. 4 are of primary interest to the modeler of the stormwater quality. The first is the way in which pollutants accumulate on the land surface. For pollutants found on pervious urban areas and on rural lands, the assumption that there is an infinite supply of pollutant available for washoff seems to work best for modeling purposes. For impervious surfaces, pollutants seem to accumulate on the land surface during dry weather and to wash away during rainfall events. The way in which the dry weather buildup occurs and the rate of buidup is a much debated subject.

Present opinion seems to be that the rate of accumulation is most rapid during the first few days after a significant rain storm. Why this is so is not well understood.

Also of interest is the way in which pollutants on the land surface are dislodged and carried by the storm flow to create a stormwater pollution problem. This also is a point of debate. Some pollutants are associated with sediments and seem to be controlled by or related to sediment washoff rates. Others are dissolved and may be unrelated to sediment washoff rates. At issue, too, are questions of whether a "first flush," or initial period of high concentration, is to be expected. Models have been proposed and developed for a wide variety of water quality mechanisms. The user should study each problem on a site specific basis, and the way a model works should be consistent with the user's knowledge of that problem.

Pollutant Accumulation

Some of the earlier surface runoff quality models, including EPA SWMM and STORM, used a linear relationship for pollutant buildup. Experience with the models and field data showed this assumption to be inadequate, and both of these models now have a buildup rate that decreases with time. Typical forms of the commonly used relationships are shown in Fig 5-4, in which solids accumulation rates are plotted as functions of time from last rainfall and land use.[15] These curves are generally useful, but they demonstrate some of the questions that arise as well. For example, how important is the magnitude of the previous rain? It seems apparent that a one-inch rainfall may wash the streets and sidewalks quite clean, but what about a 0.03-inch rain? Where should the line be drawn that connects several storm events into a single event?

The figure shows three classes of land use. It implies that all residential lands accumulate pollutants in the same way, and in the example shown, residential and commercial properties are quite similar. When should a property

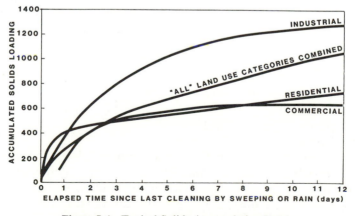

Figure 5-4 Typical Solids Accumulation Rates

be classified industrial instead of commercial, thus qualifying for a much higher accumulation rate? How can a planning agency that carries 15 or 20 land uses in its records use these three curves with any degree of reliability?

The answer is that, as shown in Chap. 4, there are no generally reliable guidelines for pollutant accumulation rates.

It is extremely unwise to attempt to model pollutant accumulation (and washoff) without site specific data. Perhaps the state of the art will advance to this point in the future. For the present, the more data, the better.

To conclude, most available models now use a decreasing rate of increase for pollutant accumulation through time. This is consistent with the present level of knowledge. Site specific field data are very important, and great care should be exercised in transferring data from one region to another.

Pollutant Washoff

Several types of pollutant washoff models have been used somewhat successfully. The forms of these models vary widely. Their "success" is a comment on the lack of definitive data that would permit them to be checked. In the discussion that follows, the different modeling techniques will be categorized by their principal features. Model names or acronyms often will not be given. It has frequently happened that different versions of the same named model have quite different pollutant washoff equations. These equations are easily changed in most programs, and many users have tailored a program to a specific application. While not technically wrong, this is a practice that has resulted in no little confusion about how a package model really works.

Solids Washoff From Urban (Impervious) Areas

Most models consider suspended solids either as the primary indicator of pollutant washoff or as at least one of the main factors. Thus all pollutant washoff models contain suspended solids as a constituent. The most widely used form of solids washoff is that of an exponential decay. It can be written:

$$\frac{\partial P}{\partial t} = -kRP$$

where P = total amount of solids remaining on the catchment after a period t of rainfall,

k = an empirical coefficient, and

R = runoff rate.

When this is applied sequentially through a storm, as it is in the models RUNOFF and STORM, the resultant washoff function or pollution loading is as shown in Fig. 5-5.[16] For a moderate storm the pollution loading will resemble the hydrograph. For a more intense storm the rate will decrease as the amount of pollutant remaining on the watershed becomes smaller.

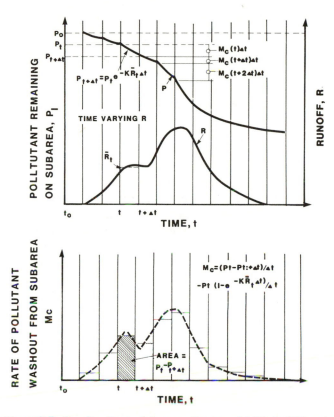

Figure 5-5 Loading Derived from an Exponential Washoff Function

The original EPA SWMM work used a value of k of 4.6; this value has been picked up incorrectly as a "true value" by several subsequent studies. The coefficient 4.6 will result in 90% of the pollutant being removed in one hour with a constant runoff rate of 0.5 inches per hour. It is not a sacred value in any sense. A range of k between 1.0 and 6.0 appears to be normal. This is another case where field data are required. It should be noted that stormwater data are expensive to collect and subject to significant error. Literature values, when used very cautiously, can be an acceptable expedient in some areas.

Availability Factor for Urban Areas

In a low intensity storm, much of the solids mass on a urban catchment is not available for washoff because there is insufficient energy in the runoff to suspend and/or transport it. The exponential washoff equation can be modified by adding an availability factor, A, so that:

$$\frac{\partial P}{\partial t} = -kRP \times A$$

In the EPA SWMM, A has the form:

$$A = a + bR^c$$

where a, b, and c are empirical coefficients. The availability factor is usually limited to a maximum value in the range 0.75 to 1.0.

Rural or Undeveloped (Pervious) Areas

Most of the foregoing discussion pertains to developed or developing areas. These are areas where a substantial fraction of the land is impervious, and most of the runoff comes from impervious areas, at least in small to medium-sized storms. The concept of pollutant accumulation is then a supportable one.

When most of the land is pervious, the prior assumptions break down. Farmlands in particular, and most undeveloped lands in general, have an unlimited source of sediment, and for practical purposes, the same can be said of other pollutants. It is popular to use a modified form of the Universal Soil Loss Equation to estimate the mass rate of sediment removal from these areas:

$$A = R \times K \times L \times C \times P$$

where A = soil loss per unit area,
$\quad R$ = rainfall factor,
$\quad K$ = soil erodibility factor,
$\quad L$ = slope-length gradient ratio,
$\quad C$ = crop management factor, and
$\quad P$ = erosion control practice factor.

A detailed exposition of the Universal Soil Loss Equation was presented in Chap. 4. It is an equation for which the coefficients can be obtained fairly quickly from publications. Its form is generally good, or at least supportable, and it enables the model user to study the transition from undeveloped land use to developed land use.

Washoff of Other Pollutants

As stated earlier, most models consider suspended solids either as the primary indicator of pollutant washoff or as at least one of the main factors. Other constituents are related to suspended solids by one of two relationships. In the most case, it is:

$$C_x = f(C_s)$$

where C_x = concentration of constituent x, and
$\quad C_s$ = concentration of suspended solids.

The function f in most cases is a simple liner one, i.e., C_x is directly proportional to C_s. This does not imply that other constituents are attached to the suspended solids. Instead, it says that suspended solids is an indicator constituent. It is analogous to using coliform bacteria as an indicator of disease organisms. It provides a single, easily measured parameter that points to the probable presence of other substances. Studies of field data have shown this to be a valid approach for pollutants that have an ionic affinity to soil (clay) particles.

In some cases the relationship has been stated in a slightly more complex form:

$$C_x = f(C_s) + g(Q)$$

where g is a function representing a dissolved fraction not related to suspended solids concentrations.

Data in Chap. 4 will show the great range of ratios between suspended solids and other constituents in different cases. No typical values can be relied upon.

Some models have used the simplest of all equations:

$$C_x = K$$

where K is an empirically determined constant. This may be useful in computing total pollutant load under some conditions, but is has happily vanished from modern models.

CONTINUOUS SIMULATION

Most stormwater models simulate a single storm event. This was illustrated in Fig. 5-2, which indicated the transformation of a single rainfall hyetograph into an outflow hydrograph. There is another class of models that works on a long-term rainfall record—months or years instead of a single event. They are called continuous simulation models. STORM and HSPF are the best-known continuous simulation models.

Continuous simulation always uses measured rainfall records for its hydrologic input. This eliminates the need for design storms. If a fairly long period, say 10 to 30 years, is being simulated, it is useful and customary to perform a frequency analysis on the runoff record. This will inform the user as to the spectral characteristics of the runoff record.

Antecedent conditions are handled automatically by the program in continuous simulation. Of course it is necessary for the user to specify management techniques, such as street sweeping and catch basin cleaning.

It is advantageous to use continuous simulation in large planning studies. It enables the user to examine the relative usefulness of control measures on a broad scale and eliminates the need to select a design storm before the "design" conditions have been determined. The cost of continuous simulation would be exhorbitant if it were applied at the facility design level. Many people have used continuous simulation as a first pass to set general system requirements, then switch to an event model with the appropriate design storm for detailed analysis and design.

SPECIFIC MODELS

The list of models and versions of models available to the potential user seems endless. Documentation ranges from very detailed to cursory. There is, however, a handful of programs that have evolved as a useful foundation for the field in general. These programs are fairly well documented, and they are available to the public. Most of them are under continuing sponsorship by a governmental agency. They have been tested by many users, not just one user, and these tests have been real-world tests. This chapter presents an overview of these models.

STORM (Storage, Treatment, Overflow, Runoff Model)

This model is one of the more widely used planning level models. It is sponsored by the Hydrologic Engineering Center (HEC) of the U.S. Army Corps of Engineers. HEC provides ongoing updating of STORM, and limited assistance in its use is sometimes available.

A conceptual sketch of a form of STORM is given in Fig. 5-6.[17] The drainage area is defined by land use type, each of which has a specified percentage of impervious cover. The user also specifies a storage capacity, which may include both off-line and in-line storage, and a "treatment rate." Treatment rate is really only the rate at which storage empties. It may or may not include pollutant removal. STORM routes flow first to treatment, then to storage when the treatment rate is exceeded, and finally to overflow into the receiving waters

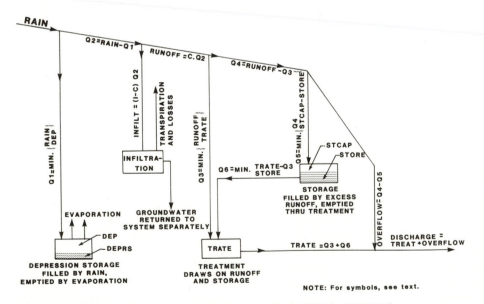

Figure 5-6 Conceptual Sketch of the Model "SEM—STORM"

when storage capacity is exceeded. The abbreviated terms shown in Fig. 5-6 are as follows:

> MIN.—minimum of quantities in
> DEPRS—maximum available depression storage
> DEP—available depression
> TRATE—treatment rate
> STCAP—storage capacity
> STORE—amount in storage
> DISCHARGE—equal to sum of treated and overflow quantities

Developed and nondeveloped land uses are both considered. The rational method is used to compute runoff from developed areas. Pollutant buildup and washoff are based on the exponential decay functions described previously. For undeveloped land uses, the SCS method is used to produce flows, and the Universal Soil Loss Equation to produce suspended solids loads. The water quality constituents included in STORM are suspended solids, settleable solids, BOD, total nitrogen, and orthophosphate.

STORM operates on a one-hour time step, an interval chosen to be consistent with rainfall tapes available from the National Weather Service. Most of the model's output is statistical in nature. It reports rainfall duration, runoff values, frequency and magnitude of overflows, and quality of the overflows. It also gives annual totals for these quantities.

Figure 5-7 shows a set of frequency curves developed from STORM output.[18] It indicates how the frequency of overflows can be changed by the addition of treatment and storage for the City of San Francisco. They can be used to develop general planning guidelines for treatment and storage needs. Similar curves can be drawn for all of the other parameters reported by the model.

HSPF (Hydrocomp Simulation Program—Fortran)

HSPF is the latest version of the Stanford Watershed Model, one of the earliest stormwater models. It also is the first version of that model in the public domain; all prior versions were proprietary. HSPF is sponsored by the Athens Laboratory of the U.S. EPA.

This is a model that includes a complete water balance within the study area. It accounts for both surface water and groundwater and for exchanges and interactions between them. The kinematic wave method is used for all surface water routing.

The water quality section of HSPF gives special emphasis to the kinetics of the nutrient cycle and the lower forms of plant and animal life. This is illustrated in Fig. 5-8, which shows the water quality parameters considered

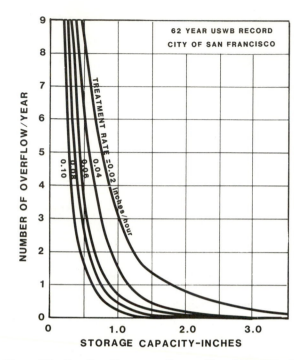

Figure 5-7 Overflow Frequency Curves, City of San Francisco

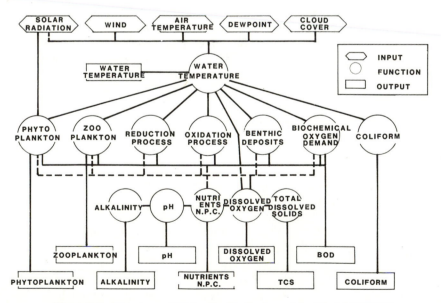

Figure 5-8 Structure of Water Quality Section of the Model "HSPF"

and the main lines of mass and energy transfer.[19] HSPF is particularly useful in studying the long-term effects of nonpoint source control programs, including agricultural management practices.

It is not suprising that HSPF is expensive to operate. It requires an extensive data base for proper calibration. Individual runs of the program can be costly, although some users have held these costs down. Where the detail offered by this model is needed, it can be an excellent choice.

SWMM (Storm Water Management Model)

SWMM is not a single model but a package of models linked together by an executive program. It was originally developed under sponsorship of the U.S. EPA with the ambitious objective of being a complete stormwater model. The EPA has countinued its support of SWMM through a University of Florida program of updating, documentation, and user assistance.

Most users of SWMM do not run the entire model; they work only with the module or block of the program that meets their needs. There are seven blocks: RUNOFF, INFILTRATION, and DRY WEATHERFLOW; TRANSPORT and EXTENDED TRANSPORT (EXTRAN); STORAGE/ TREATMENT and RECEIVING WATER. The names are self-explanatory.

No attempt is made here to describe in detail the workings of the SWMM blocks. Portions of RUNOFF and EXTRAN were dealt with in earlier paragraphs. Let it suffice to say that SWMM translates rainfall hyetographs into complete hydrographs and pollution loadings throughout the runoff/drainage/ sewer/receiving water system. There are many regular users of SWMM, but it is not a model for the fainthearted. It requires a major commitment of time to learn the requirements of the model. Its cost would be expected to be significantly greater than the cost of STORM, but less than the cost of HSPF.

RUNQUAL (Runoff Quality)

RUNQUAL is a blend of two well-known models.[20] It is composed of the hydraulic portion of the SWMM RUNOFF block and the water quality routing algorithms of the QUAL-II stream water quality model. It is an event model that generates runoff and pollutant washoff for 12 land use categories. It routes these through the drainage system, which can consist of both pipes and receiving stream channels. Its kinship to RUNOFF dictates that flow conditions not represented by kinematic wave theory are outside the model's scope. RUNQUAL can be thought of as a version of RUNOFF in which the water quality section has been greatly expanded.

A schematic of the model structure is shown in Fig. 5-9. The flow and quality sections have been kept separate; data are transferred back and forth by tape. This would facilitate the model's use by persons familiar with the parent models.

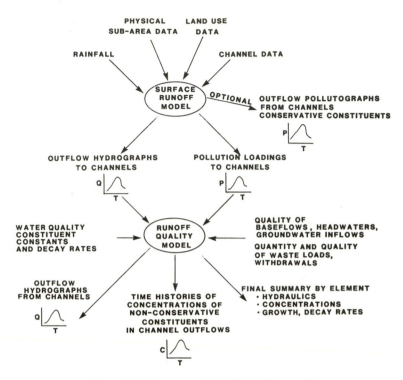

Figure 5-9 Structure of the Model "Runqual"

RUNQUAL is available from the Southeast Michigan Council of Governments in Detroit, the agency that sponsored its development. Complete documentation also is available, but the agency does not provide ongoing support.

MITCAT (M.I.T. Catchment Model)

This model was developed at M. I. T. in the early 1970s as a runoff quantity model. It has no water quality section. Its basic structure is similar to RUNOFF. It uses the kinematic wave approximation to simulate overland flow and a linearized form of the motion equation for channel routing. Although available from M. I. T., the model does not have current support.

ILLUDAS (Illinois Urban Drainage Simulator)

This model is an American adaptation of the Road Research Laboratory (RRL) model developed in Britain in the late 1960s. RRL assumed no contribution to flow from pervious areas. This has been added in ILLUDAS. ILLUDAS is an event model with some unique or unusual features. It contains the ability to develop its own design storm based on rainfall depth and duration, using the Illinois State Water Survey method. The present version has no water quality section, but this capability is being added. ILLUDAS is supported and updated by the Illinois State Water Survey.

TR-20

TR-20 uses the Soil Conservation Service (SCS) curve number technique to predict flow frequency curves. It is very easy to use and has attracted a fairly widespread following. The curve numbers used in TR-20 are derived from a sparse data base. They may not be reliable when applied to changing land use situations where measured data are not available. Also, the unit hydrograph that is internally programmed in the model is not universally applicable, and the user may have to modify it. TR-20 is sponsored and supported by the SCS, but complete documentation and a user's manual have not been published.

HVM-QQS (HVM-Quantity-Quality Simulation)

It is likely that HVM-QQS is the most sophisticated model available. It was developed in Germany where it has been used in several studies, and it has been applied also in Canada and the United States. It is a continuous simulation model like STORM that contains the hydraulic sophistication of EXTRAN.

Until a short time ago, HVM-QQS was a proprietary model. It recently was acquired by the U.S. EPA, which is placing it in the public domain and providing documentation. At present little detail can be given as to how it works, and no widespread experience in its use can be cited.

CALIBRATION (AND VERIFICATION)

Most modelers realize that programs must be calibrated against field data if confidence in the model results is to be established. In practice, many different exercises have passed for calibration. The purpose of this section is to give some guidance about what should be sought in the calibration process.

First, some definitions are in order. *Calibration* is the exercise of changing model coefficients until the model simulates measured results with satisfactory accuracy. *Verification* is checking a calibrated model against a data set not used in the calibration process. For best results, a model should be both calibrated and verified. In practice, this is seldom possible because of the scarcity of data.

Most stormwater models have an overabundance of coefficients that can be adjusted to produce desired results. Some of the parameters usually determined during calibration are: (for flow) Manning's n, the rational formula C, and the percent impervious land cover; (for water quality) pollutant accumulation rates, pollutant washoff rates, and kinetic relationship rates between constituents. In a typical case the modeler may have more than a dozen parameters for each element, and for a large system there may be literally hundreds of coefficient values that could be changed during calibration.

Taken at face value, this appears to be an absurd situation. Most field data would not support this number of independent coefficients even if a person capable of sorting through such a multidimensional problem could be found. Some efforts have been made to let the model calibrate itself via an optimization routine. This has been successful only in a very limited sense, not on the large scale described here.

The first rule in rationalizing calibration is to reduce the dimension of the problem. The model may permit a different value of Manning's n for each element. The user can decide to use a single value throughout or at least to use a single value in zones. This approach is also more defensible physically. It is important to remember that the model is only a tool, not Truth.

Keeping coefficients within a meaningful range is another essential tactic. If it is necessary to set the percent imperviousness of single family residences on quarter acre lots at 98 % to match calibration data, there is a serious problem somewhere else in the model or in the data. Where a direct physical (or chemical or biological) meaning attaches to a coefficient, be sure it stays within tolerable limits. When no such physical significance can be drawn, find out what other users have done in similar circumstances. A good example of the latter is the exponential pollutant washoff coefficient, k. A good range is between 1.0 and 6.0. Other values may conceivable be valid at times, but they lend uncertainty to the model.

Finally, learn to interpret the field data. The modeler should know the circumstances under which data were collected. It is important to estimate the probable error in the data themselves, and a judgement should be made about whether or not the data are typical of the study area. Where it is feasible, the modeler should help plan the data collection program, and even participate in it, to insure its suitability for the modeling. One should recognize that the best data include errors, and all of the conditions extant at data collection time cannot be known. Thus, calibration consists of adjusting the model coefficients until a reasonable agreement with data has been obtained. It does not entail matching the model results completely with field data.

An added complication is that most of the calibration parameters cannot be measured directly. They must be inferred from measurement of another quantity. Rainfall intensity can be measured, as can flowrate and the concentration of pollutants in the flow. Many physical characteristics such as area and pipe size are amenable to precise measurement, but percent imperviousness is not. Flow and concentration can only be measured at discrete points in time and space. Thus, mass emission rates, Manning's n, pollutant washoff exponents, and the host of other factors needed in a model are inferred quantities.

The most satisfactory results are obtained when field measurements are made at collection points in the system. Concentrations in the receiving stream, or in a collecting sewer, are greatly superior to street sweepings in determining pollutant buildup rates.

MINICOMPUTERS AND PROGRAMMABLE CALCULATORS

Most computer users are aware of the tremendous strides now taking place in the computer industry. The models discussed here all were designed for large, conventional hardware, and efforts to use the minicomputers and programmable calculators now arriving on the market are in their infancy. It is likely that such usage will increase dramatically. Some will develop new programs specifically for the new hardware. Others will simplify or adapt the older models to the new computer systems.

A preliminary report issued by the University of Ottawa[21] describes one of the better early attempts to develop a simple program for an HP-67 or HP-97 calculator. It notes that caution is warranted at this time in using model results. However, readers are encouraged to keep abreast of this rapidly growing field. It certainly will be a major tool in tomorrow's stormwater modeling package.

SOME CASE STUDIES

A typical example of a fairly successful calibration is shown in Fig. 5-10.[22] It compares computed and measured values for the 386-acre Laguna Street

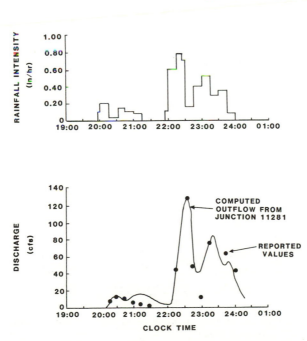

LAGUNA STREET
STORM OF 15 MARCH, 1967

Figure 5-10 Comparison of Computed and Measured Hydrographs, City of San Francisco

watershed in San Francisco that was shown in Fig. 5-1.[23] The storm of 15 March 1967 was simulated using predecessor versions of the current SWMM RUNOFF and EXTRAN programs. The agreement between computed and measured flow is excellent in every respect—peak flow, time to peak, and hydrograph shape. The mass emmission rate comparison is not as good, but it is an acceptable fit. The measured data are not complete, but they are fairly typical of the kind of data usually obtained. The first flush indicated by the model is greater than that measured, but the overall agreement is quite good.

Figure 5-11 shows good results obtained with the model RUNQUAL.[24] The area is the Rouge River Basin in Southeast Michigan, a region undergiong fairly steady urbanization. The total basin is large, some 464 square miles, and data from only 6 to 12 stations were available for calibration. Much of the

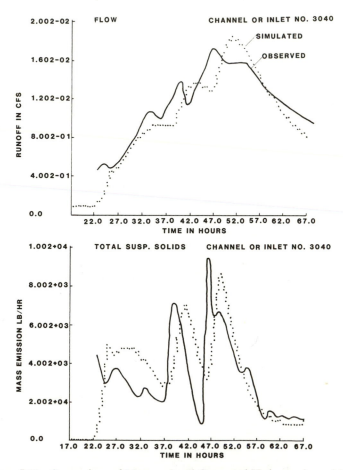

Figure 5-11   Comparison of Measured and Computed Hydrographs and Pollution Loadings, Rouge River Basin

upper basin is still agricultural. The figure indicates good agreement between measured and computed values for both flow and total suspended solids. To be sure, the agreement is not as good as the Selby Street results, at least for flow. The paucity of data on the basin characteristics is a large factor in declaring this calibration to be a satisfactory one.

A less acceptable case is shown in Fig. 5-12.[25] This is another location in the Rouge River Basin, and the same model was used. Flow values are fairly good, but inferior to the preceding location. The suspended solids prediction from the model is less than half the measured total. The shape of the modeled pollution loading does not show the oscillations of the measured data. It was suspected that the problem lay both in the model and in the data. Crop management factors in the model and been estimated on a very large scale, and it

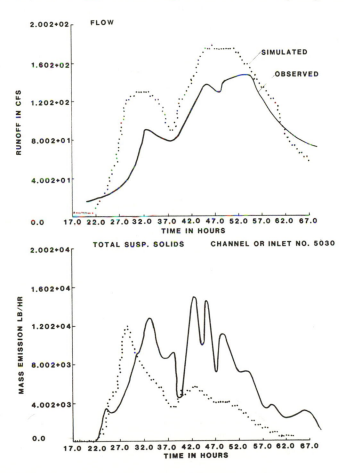

Figure 5-12 Comparison of Measured and Computed Hydrographs and Pollution Loadings, Rouge River Basin

was believed that some observed erosion was not being modeled. On the other hand, the oscillations in the pollution loading are not matched by oscillations in the measured hydrograph, so there is some mystery in the data.

This example illustrates a common occurrence. The field program was poorly funded, and a thorough program of model calibration could not be completed. The result is a model suitable only for large-scale planning without further calibration.

A different approach was required for the next example, an application of STORM to the City of Philadelphia. Actually, the model used was SEM-STORM, a variant, but this does not affect the example here. STORM is a continuous simulation model, and it was the intent of the study to use it with 10 or more years of rainfall data. Calibration data existed for less than a dozen storms for a few homogeneous land use basins and for six storms on larger sub-basins. A two-step procedure was followed to calibrate and verify the model on the available data.

First, the model was run for single storm events on each of the homogeneous land use areas. Flow and quality coefficients were adjusted to obtain the agreement shown in Table 5-2. It is important to note that the same coefficients were used for each storm. This set of coefficients was locked in place for the verification.

The verification storms were then run, utilizing the larger sub-basins, which have a mixed land use. The results are plotted in Fig. 5-13. Agreement for the total set was quite satisfactory, although some were high and some were low.[26]

No attempt was made to fit the shape of the hydrograph or pollutograph. STORM calculates hourly values of these quantities, but the simplicity of the model really precludes such a detailed approach. The objective here was to calibrate the model for the computation of long term loads, and it is believed that this objective was accomplished.

From this chapter it may be seen how hydrologic modeling and prediction evolved from very simple empirical approaches involving quantities of runoff

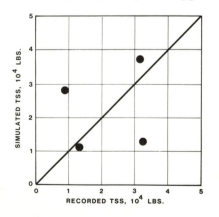

Figure 5-13 Verification Results — Mixed Land Use Basin, City of Philadelphia

TABLE 5-2 Comparison of Measured and Computed Flow and Water Quality Parameters—City of Philadelphia

Basin	Storm	Storm Date	Rainfall (in.)	Observed Runoff (in.)	Runoff Coefficient	Simulated Runoff (in.)	Error (%)
Poquessing Creek	1	3/22/77[a]	2.020	1.032	0.51	0.924	−10
	2	4/2/77[b]	0.850	0.165	0.19	0.289	+75
Drainage area =	3	4/24/77[b]	0.450	0.069	0.16	0.104	+51
10,445 acres	4	5/4/77[a]	0.420	0.076	0.19	0.090	+18
				$\sum = 1.342$		$\sum = 1.407$	
Pennypack Creek	1	3/22/77[a]	2.020	1.029	0.51	0.930	−10
	2	4/2/77[b]	0.850	0.293	0.34	0.305	+4
Drainage area =	3	4/24/77[b]	0.450	0.228	0.51	0.114	+50
7,616 acres	4	5/4/77[a]	0.420	0.154	0.36	0.099	−36
				$\sum = 1.704$		$\sum = 1.448$	
Wissahickon Creek	1	3/22/77[a]	2.020	0.945	0.47	0.923	−2
	2	4/2/77[b]	0.850	0.175	0.20	0.298	+70
Drainage area =	3	4/24/77[b]	0.450	0.059	0.13	0.110	+86
6,656 acres	4	5/4/77[a]	0.420	0.121	0.29	0.096	−21
				$\sum = 1.300$		$\sum = 1.427$	

[a] Local—gages near uniform land use sub-basins.
[b] Philadelphia International Airport gage.

and flow to highly complex dynamic models involving physical, chemical and biological changes in pollutants as well as physical movements of the water itself. Although technology has been improved, this evolution should be regarded as a proliferation, in which many widely different alternative approaches may be most valuable depending upon the circumstances.

NOTES—CHAPTER 5

1. Hydrologic Engineering Center, U.S. Army Corps of Engineers, "Storage Treatment, Overflow, Runoff Model, STORM," *User's Manual*, Davis, Calif., 1976.

2. R. P. Shubinski et al., "Computer Program Documentation for the Continuous Storm Runoff Model SEM-STORM," Report to Southeast Michigan COG by Water Resources Engineers, Inc., 1977.

3. R. P. Shubinski and R. J. Chernik, "Computer Program Documentation for the Continuous Storm Runoff Model DEL-STORM," Report to the Delaware Valley Regional Planning Commission, Philadelphia, Pa., 1980.

4. R. C. Johnson et al., "User's Manual for Hydrologic Simulation Program— FORTRAN-" EPA-600/9-80-015, Report by Hydrocomp Inc. to U.S. EPA, 1980.

5. Metcalf & Eddy, Inc., University of Florida and Water Resources Engineers, Inc., "Storm Water Management Model," Vol. I, Water Pollution Control Research Series 11024DOC10/71, U.S. EPA, October 1971.

6. L. A. Roesner, R. P. Shubinski, and J. A. Aldrich, "Storm Water Management Model User's Manual Version III: Addendum I EXTRAN," Report to the Univ. of Florida, Gainsville, 1981.

7. M. L. Terstriep and J. B. Stall, "The Illinois Urban Drainage Area Simulator, ILLUDAS," Bull. 58, Illinois State Water Survey, Urbana, 1974.

8. L. A. Roesner, P. R. Giguere, and L. C. Davis, "User's Manual for the Storm Runoff Quality Model RUNQUAL," Prepared for Southeast Michigan Council of Governments, Detroit, July 1977.

9. CDM/Resources Analysis, "MITCAT Catchment Simulation Model, Description and User's Manual," Version 9, 1980.

10. Soil Conservation Service, "Urban Hydrology for Small Watersheds," T. R. No. 55, 1975.

11. W. F. Geiger and H. R. Dorsch, "Quantity Quality Simulation (QQS), A Detailed Continuous Planning Model for Urban Runoff Control," EPA-600/2-80-011, U.S. EPA, Cincinnati, ohio, 1980.

12. D. F. Kibler, J. R. Monser, and L. A. Roesner, "San Francisco Stormwater Model, User's Manual and Program Documentation," Water Resources Engineers, Walnut Creek, Calif., (about 1974).

13. Camp Dresser and McKee Inc., "Report to the Metropolitan District Commission, Boston, MA, on Combined Sewer Overflows in Dorchester Bay Area," Vol. I, 1980.

14. Metcalf and Eddy, 1971.

15. J. D. Sartor and G. B. Boyd, "Water Pollution Aspects of Street Surface Contaminants, Environmental Protection Technology Series, Environmental Protection Agency," Report No. EPA-R2-081, Nov. 1972.

16. L. A. Roesner et al., "A Model for Evaluating Runoff Quality in Metropolitan Master Planning," ASCE TM No. 23, April 1974.

17. Shubinski, 1977.

18. Kibler, Monser, and Roesner, 1974.

19. Geiger and Dorsch, 1980.

20. Roesner, Giguere, and Davis, 1977.

21. E. P'ng et al., "Preliminary Assessment of a Simplified Linear Reservoir Model for Programmable Calculators," IMPSWM Progress Report No. 11, Univ. of Ottawa, 1980.

22. D. F. Kibler and L. A. Roesner, "The San Francisco Stormwater Model for Computer Simulation of Urban Runoff Quantity and Quality in a Combined Sewer System," Report to the City and County of San Francisco by Water Resources Engineers, Walnut Creek, Calif., 1975.

23. Kibler and Roesner, 1975.

24. L. C. Davis et al., "Model Calibration and Validation: QUAL-II SEM-STORM, and RUNQUAL," Environmental Background Paper No. 68, Southeast Michigan Council of Governments, Detroit, Nov. 1977.

25. Davis, 1977.

26. Shubinski and Chernik, 1980.

6

Erosion and Stormwater

WILLIAM WHIPPLE

GEOMORPHOLOGY

Throughout the ages, precipitation, freeze-thaw cycles, and other material causes have moved or leached portions of rock and soil, which are then transported into channels and streams by flowing water. The water and accompanying solids in the stream wear away or move downstream additional materials of the banks and the bed of the stream. Prior to the onset of civilization, these processes were extremely slow, and conditions were relatively stable; so that with rare exceptions, even though erosion never ceased, the slopes and depths of stream channels and the erosion of the slopes and uplands remained relatively constant. Even highly erodible soils were protected by their configuration and by vegetation; and steeper channels were armored by rocks, or had slopes consistant with the amounts of bed load brought in from above by natural processes.

BABBLING BROOKS AND LEAFY GLADES

In relatively humid and well-vegetated parts of the country, such as most of the United States east of the Mississippi, and in mountainous areas generally, the stable streams in their natural condition were clear and attractive, with shade, fish in the deeper water, and an irregular alternation of rapids, riffles, and pools which most people find agreeable. Some of the western areas were less pleasant, where natural alkali, parched and arid soils, treeless plains, burnt over vegatation, and dry stream beds struck a harsher note; but even then many of the small streams had a narrow valley of bushes and small trees to shade and help to stabilize the channel

It is important to keep in mind this original state of small streams, because it is important to have environmental quality and provide amenities when we can. The fact that the natural beauty of an unspoiled stream cannot be reduced to a mathematical formula is no excuse for ignoring it.

DEVELOPMENT AND LAND EROSION

With development by man, much of this erosional stability is disappearing. Construction of logging roads, cutting down of forests, and tilling of land for agriculture have rendered vast areas many times more vulnerable to erosion. Fortunately, techniques have been developed and applied in national programs to control land erosion in normal agriculture and silviculture. Although there are difficulties of implementation, and particular vulnerability during droughts, these programs are reasonably successful.

Influences of other forms of economic development upon erosion and sedimentation were recognized somewhat later. During building construction, the rate of erosion may be two or more orders of magnitude higher than during the relatively stable conditions which precede or follow it. Since in rapidly developing areas there is always some construction underway, sediments eroded from construction sites are characteristic of the process of urbanization. From fully developed areas, whether residential, commercial, or industrial, erosion is relatively unimportant. Stormwater runoff from such areas contains abundant particulates; but its origin is quite different. Some particles in urban runoff descend as atmospheric dust, but others are residues from human activities. Sanding of streets, remnants of leaves from trees, and detritus from various industrial and commercial sources, including construction, all are included. There may also be appreciable erosion of the land in established facilities, but only when planning is poor, new construction is undertaken, or when caused by some unusual circumstance.

SOIL AND WATER CONSERVATION

The U.S. Soil Conservation Service is charged with land erosion prevention in agricultural areas through a national network of Soil Conservation Districts. The U.S. Forest Service and other federal agencies, on land that they manage, conduct protective programs to minimize erosion to the extent practicable. In some states, legislation has given power to Soil Conservation Districts to require all developers to install temporary detention facilities and protective coverings of all exposed earth, until such time as grass is well established. The techniques are well known and effective, but construction sites are frequently neglected.

The land developers and their contractors are more difficult for the Department of Agriculture to control than are farmers, because there is no "carrot" corresponding to the various agricultural benefits to farmers; but progress is being made. It is certainly important for the condition of the streams that upstream erosion be controlled, preferably at source. However, in the long run, the safeguarding of the fertility of the soil and the preservation of the land surface against destructive gullying are probably of even greater concern.

STREAM EROSION AND BED LOAD

The sediment and erosion regimen of streams has been studied from a scientific viewpoint, although with much less attention than has been given soil erosion from the land. Engineering approaches to controlling stream erosion have been devoted mainly to short-range or localized analysis, leading mainly to bank protection and channel lining, and to protection of structures from undermining.

Sediment in streams is usually classified as suspended and bed load, the former of which moves freely with the water, while the latter moves along or near the bottom. In most streams, sand and fine gravel remain on the bottom during low flow, move as bed load during higher stages, and may or may not be moved as suspended sediment during floods, depending upon the velocity of the water. Within very wide limits, suspended sediment is transported by a stream in any quantities which are available; but bed load material can be moved only in quantifiable amounts, depending upon the size of particles, velocity and depth of flow, and other variables. The movement actually occurs mainly at high stages, and the mean value of bed load movement depends upon frequency of floods of various magnitudes.

In any reach of a stream, if the quantity of bed load which can be moved by a stream is less than that which enters the reach, the excess will gradually build up, or the bed of the stream will aggrade. If, on the other hand, the mean bed load carrying capacity exceeds the mean amounts which are available, the bed of the stream will degrade, or erode itself deeper, as long as bed load material of suitable size remains available.

Erosion of the bed, or channel degradation, is accompanied by increased bank erosion, often including erosion on the convex banks of streams, and also pronounced channel widening over a period of time. Bank erosion is also very characteristic of the meandering streams of very flat plains, where bed load carrying capacity is confined to relatively fine sediments; but in such cases there is no definite trend toward channel enlargement or deepening.

URBANIZATION AND STREAM EROSION

As explained in Chap. 3, the process of urbanization greatly increases the peak flow and somewhat increases the total runoff which results from a given rainstorm. It has now been realized that the increased flows of stormwater from urbanization increase the bed load carrying capacity of the stream, above what it was in a pre-development state, During the construction process, the quantity of bed load introduced into a stream may be increased; but this is a temporary effect, whereas the increase in bed load carrying power resulting from urbanization is permanent. A number of analysts have noted that streams in urban areas generally have a tendency towards channel degradation and enlargement.[1,2,3] Streams in their pre-development condition had slopes that had adjusted over hundreds and thousands of years to the geology, the flow regimen, and other climatic influences, and were relatively stable; some with very steep slopes and large-sized bed load particles and others with flatter slopes and small-sized bed load particles. In either case, the onset of development increased the bed load carrying capacity and resulted in an increased tendency towards erosion. In some cases, of course, the bed and banks resisted erosion because of exposed rock, cohesive materials, or tree roots; but in general an increase in bed load carrying capacity also resulted in increased capacity to displace or erode other substances.[4] The evidence that this is so is found in correlation between degree of development, as measured by runoff curve number (of the Soil Conservation Service),[5] and the severity of the stream erosion tendency.

INFLUENCE OF BUFFER STRIPS

It was also noted that erosion is greatest in areas where there are only thin fringes of natural wooded areas, if any, left on the edges of the stream,[6] as seen in Fig. 6-1. Streams where broad, wooded buffer strips were left on both sides have less tendency to erode than watersheds with similar degree of development overall but inadequate buffer strips. Good and poor buffer strips are illustrated in Fig. 6-2. By adding consideration of this factor, even better correlation with stream erosion tendency is obtained, as shown in Fig. 6-3. The modified curve number plotted in this figure is the regular CN of the Soil Conservation Service, increased by 6 for a poor buffer and diminished by 6 for a good buffer. These results indicate that, outside of very flat plains, the processes of land development, particularly those creating high percentages of impervious surfaces and eliminating wooded areas adjacent to streams, will almost inevitably result in an erosive disequilibrium, characterized by tendencies to stream bed lowering and channel enlargement and deepening. These processes, once started, are not self-corrective. Channel degradation started at any point tends to move upstream and into minor tributaries. If not restrained, some very destructive and unacceptable results may occur.

Figure 6-1   Poor Buffer Strip on an Urban Stream

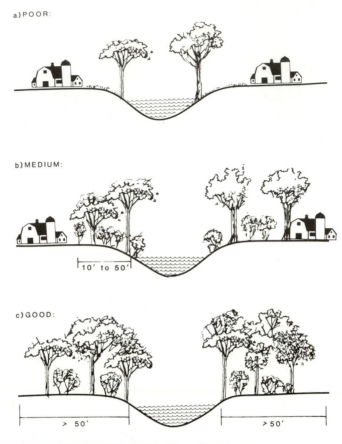

Figure 6-2   Buffer Zone Classifications

BED LOAD ANALYSIS

Modeling Bed Load Movement

Because of the difficulty of obtaining quantitative data on the movement of bed load, and the inherent complexity of the relationships involved, the engineering profession, despite many years of effort, has been unable to agree on a single best bed load movement algorithm or formula. A good summary of the state of the art is given by Simons and Senturk.[7] One of the most admired formulas is that of Einstein, which is, however, too complex for general use. Of the simpler formulas, those frequently used include those of Meyer-Peter,[8, 9] Inglis-Lacey,[10, 11] Laursen,[12] Blench,[13] and Shoklitsch.[14] The Shoklitsch formula is based on the concept that there is a certain discharge up to which no bed load of a given size moves, and that beyond that discharge the quantity of bed

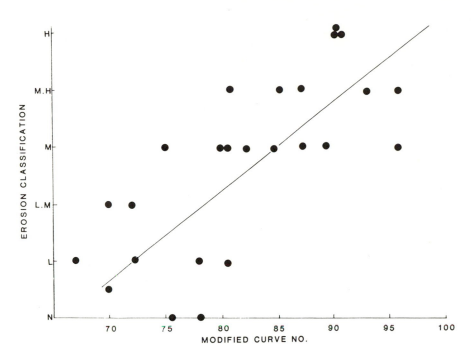

Figure 6-3 Variation of Erosion with Modified Curve Number

load moving increases proportionately to the increased flow. Besides older verification, studies in Oregon have recently confirmed that this is the case.[15] Because of its simplicity, and because its data basis included movements of bed load of the sizes locally encountered, this formula was adopted to evaluate stream erosion tendencies on two streams in Princeton Township, New Jersey.[16]

The Shoklitsch formula in metric units is as follows:

$$G = \frac{2213}{\sqrt{d}}S^{1.5}B(q - q_o)$$

where G = bed load in kg/sec,

 d = grain diameter in centimeters,

 S = hydraulic slope,

 q = instantaneous discharge per meter of width, in m³/sec/m,

 B = width of channel in meters, and

 q_o = 0.000194 $d/S^{4/3}$ = critical discharge to begin movement (in m³/sec/m).

To evaluate quantitatively the complete regimen of bed load carrying capacity of any stream would be task of enormous complexity, as application would have to be made separately to each different size flood for past, present, and future conditions, and to each different reach, taking into account the different sizes of rock and gravel found in different bars. The study of the two Princeton streams obtained a measure of relative erosive tendency by comparing the impact of a 15-year flood on past, present, and future conditions, using the largest size gravel found in bars showing evidence of recent movement. The runoff model used to obtain flood hydrographs for original undeveloped conditions, present conditions, and future conditions of full development was the TR-20.[17,18] The less developed of the two watersheds, Mountain Brook, was estimated to have peak discharges during a 15-year storm about twice those which occurred for the same storm prior to development. In spite of the allowance for reduction on account of overbank flows, the bed load carrying capacity was estimated also to have doubled. If development were to be completed for the watershed under present zoning, further increases of 26% to 46% would occur. In the more developed watershed, Harry's Brook, bed load carrying capacity has already increased to two or three times the pre-development level for different reaches studied, and on the lesser developed major tributary about 30% further increase is expected. Harry's Brook has extensive commercial development on one tributary; but further planning is for residential areas.

In summary, this study showed that at the peak of a 15-year frequency flood, the bed load carrying capacity of each stream would be about three times as great after full development as it had been before. With such a disparity, it is not to be wondered at if serious erosion is now occurring in the basin that is the more developed.

Road-Crossing Culverts

The accentuation of flood heights by urbanization has resulted in the inadequacy of many existing culverts and small bridges to carry flood flows. During floods, it is frequent for water to back up at small culverts and to overflow the road, resulting in a temporary impoundment of stormwaters, sometimes to depths as much as 12 feet. Inhabitants of the communities sometimes become indignant at the poor planning of past administrations, which built inadequate culverts, not realizing that at the time the culverts were built, they were adequate to pass flood flows. Current design criteria call for culverts to pass a large flood, usually a 15-year to 100-year mean frequency flood, with a head loss of only a few inches. Therefore, if for any reason it becomes necessary to rebuild a road-crossing in a developed area, a much larger culvert opening, perhaps three times as wide, is apt to be specified. However, such an increase should not be accepted without full knowledge of the consequences.

Studies have shown that the impoundment of water by "undersized" culverts, while small in each case, may contribute to a considerable effect of flood water retardation in the aggregate.[19,20] Moreover, each culvert anchors the stream bed level at that particular point, so that channel erosion, moving upstream, can proceed no further. The slope of the flood profile between culverts is reduced by the amount of head loss at the culverts, and there may be some bed load deposition upstream of the culvert. See Fig. 6-4. A much wider culvert, built at the same elevation under existing criteria, would have the same effect of limiting the progress of channel erosion upstream, but would not assist otherwise. It would provide no appreciable detention of stormwaters, no reduction in flood slopes, and no retardation of the bed load movement from upstream.

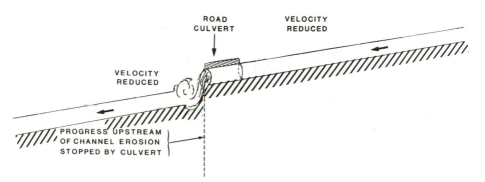

Figure 6-4   Local Effect of Culvert During Flood

SUMMARY AND CONCLUSIONS

In almost all environments, except very flat plains, the development of a watershed brings with it an erosional disequilibrium, with increased bed load carrying capacity sufficient to initiate a channel erosion and channel enlargement process of long duration, called channel degradation. Once started, this process will continue indefinitely, until restrained by exposure of more resistant material in the bed, or by channel control measures. The increased channel erosion tendency is greater for the more intensive forms of development, with their high proportions of impervious surfaces, and for streams without adequate wooded buffer strips.

Channel and land erosion in the headwaters may result in undesirable sedimentation and aggradation further downstream.

Wise land use planning can reduce potential stream erosion problems by favoring the location of intensive development on the flatter land, and by encouraging or requiring adequate stormwater management and soil conservation measures. However, special channel management measures may also be used to reduce effective stream slope at flood stages, or to reduce the vulnerability of bed or banks to erosion from high flows. These channel management measures are described in Chap 8.

Present culvert design criteria accentuate channel erosion tendencies; and they should be revised to favor the construction of small-sized culverts, which will back water up during time of flood and allow part of it to flow over the road. These small culverts should be considered for use on all land other than flat plains, except where overflow over heavily traveled roads or unacceptable damage would result.

NOTES—CHAPTER 6

1. D. A. Rickert and G. L. Beach, "Assessing Impacts of Land Management Activities on Erosion-Related Nonpoint Source Problems," *Journal of the Water Pollution Control Federation*, Nov. 1978, pp. 2439–45.

2. Harold P. Guy, "Sediment Problems in Urban Areas," Geological Survey Circular 601-E, U.S.G.S., Washington, D. C., 1970.

3. T. S. Hammer, "Effects of Urbanization on Stream Channels and Stream Flow," Completion Report, Regional Science Research Institute, Philadelphia, Pa., Nov. 1973, p. 272.

4. William Whipple, Jr., James M. DiLouie, and Theodore S. Pytlar, Jr., "Erosional Potential of Streams in Urbanizing Areas," *Water Resources Bulletin*, 17, No. 1, Feb. 1981, p. 36.

5. "Urban Hydrology for Small Watersheds," U.S. Department of Agriculture, Soil Conservation Service, Technical Release #55, Jan. 1975, pp. 2–5.

6. Whipple, DiLouie, and Pytlar, 1981.

7. D. B. Simons and F. Sentürk, *Sediment Transport Technology*, Ft. Collins, Colo.: Water Resource Publications, 1977.

8. V. A. Vanoni, ed., "Sedimentation Engineering," ASCE Manuals and Reports on Engineering Practice, No. 54, 1975, p. 192.

9. Task Committee on Preparation of Sedimentation Manual, "Sediment Discharge Formulas," *Journal of the Hydraulics Division*, ASCE, 97, No. HY4, April 1971, p. 525.

10. C. C. Inglis, "Discussion of 'Systematic Evaluation of River Regime,'" *Journal of the Waterways and Harbor Division*, ASCE, 94, No. WW1, Feb. 1968, p. 111.

11. Vanoni, 1975.

12. Task Committee, 1971.

13. T. Blench, "Mobile-Bed Fluviology," Dept. of Technical Services, University of Alberta, Alberta, Canada, 1966, p. 96.

14. S. Shulits, "The Schoklitsch Bed-Load Formula," *Engineering, Vol. 139*, June 21, 1935, pp. 644–46, 687.

15. W. L. Jackson and R. L. Beschta, "A Two Phase System of Bedload Transported in an Oregon Coast Stream," Annual Conference, American Water Resources Assoc., Oct. 1980.

16. William Whipple, Jr., James M. DiLouie, and Theodore S. Pytlar, Jr., "Erosional Aspects of Managing Urban Streams," Water Resources Research Institute, Rutgers Univ., New Brunswick, N.J., Jan. 1980.

17. "Computer Program for Project Formulation Hydrology," Technical Release No. 20, U.S. Department of Agriculture, Soil Conservation Service, May 1965.

18. "Urban Hydrology for Small Watersheds," Technical Release No. 55, U.S. Department of Agriculture, Soil Conservation Service, Jan. 1975.

19. H. R. Malcom, "Culvert Design and Channel Erosion," in *Water Problems of Urbanizing Areas*, William Whipple, Jr., ed.; New York: American Society of Civil Engineers, 1979, p. 298.

20. Whipple, DiLouie, and Pytlar, 1981.

7

Detention and Flow Retardation Devices

WILLIAM WHIPPLE

CLIFFORD W. RANDALL

STORMWATER MANAGEMENT TECHNIQUES

Stormwater management programs in urbanizing areas retard storm runoff, and in this way counter the rapidity of runoff from impervious surfaces. This detention of flow limits flood damages downstream. Detention basins and other measures of flow retardation are used for this purpose. When designed appropriately, with more prolonged storage (which may be referred to as retention), these structures also partially settle out the particulate pollution contained in urban runoff and reduce tendencies for channel erosion.

Other objectives may be achieved by detention basins, such as provision of permanent ponds, or groundwater recharge.

As far as larger rivers are concerned, stormwater detention programs, even if very extensive, have little effect, since any decrease in flood peak caused by detention diminishes as the flood passes downstream, while the increase in total runoff caused by development swells the total mass of flood wave. Unless retention is provided over a prolonged period, the cumulative effect downstream of any number of detention basins in a large river basin is mainly to delay the arrival of the flood crest by a few hours, while having little or no effect on reducing the peak discharge. The increase of runoff caused by development may be considerable. For example, if a well-managed wooded area is converted to quarter-acre housing, a storm of two inches of rainfall will have total runoff more than doubled, from 0.24 to 0.70 inches.[1] Good programs of stormwater management may be implemented to prevent future increases in peak flood discharge on small streams, but the effects of urbanization on large rivers will generally be to increase flood discharges, in spite of stormwater management programs. Such increases can be partially controlled, but only through coordinated, extensive planning prior to development. Zoning to preserve undeveloped areas and the promotion of natural infiltration wherever possible in the developed areas are essential measures for such control.

Preventive Programs

With rare exceptions, stormwater management programs are being applied in a preventive mode, by requiring developers to provide detention at the time a development is initiated.

Stormwater management programs are most successful in areas just starting to develop. They may be administered as part of the land use planning process. This local orientation does not always result in technically sufficient and uniform criteria, but it does provide a very solid legal and institutional basis. If flow provisions are incorporated into the plans at the time of construction, the cost and incovenience will be minimized. Equally as important is the possibility of defining a specific obligation that may be both equitably and legally placed upon developers. This obligation is the requirement to make provisions through detention so that adverse flood and water quality effects on streams will not be accentuated by the development. If such an obligation is imposed, the cost of preventive measures is placed upon the owners or purchasers of the land developed; and if these measures are very costly in some particular case, the costs will be taken into account in deciding whether or not the particular land in question is the best suited for the particular purpose.

Remedial Programs

The use of stormwater management in a remedial mode, to correct stream deterioration resulting from previous development, is an altogether different matter. It would be impracticable, and doubtless also illegal, to apply land use controls retroactively for such a purpose. In remedial situations, there is no alternative to a government program, either financed by government or mandated by government edict. In the case of remedial programs, the costs will be much greater, as is evidenced by the enormous costs of Chicago's tunnel and reservoir plan (TARP). The EPA, which undoubtedly has legal power to do so, under the Clean Water Act,[2] has considered requiring the issuance of an NPDES permit for each storm sewer, which would mandate compliance with specified levels of pollution in drainage from virtually all urban areas. However, it is not clear to what extent detention/retention programs would be applicable in such cases, since the source of urban runoff pollution, and the practicality of various alternatives, have not been sufficiently studied.

An interesting program of general stormwater management is that of Fairfax County, Virginia,[3] in which storm drainage plans are being prepared for each watershed; and at least a start has been made towards general implementation. However, in this case also, a general ordinance requires that detention be provided for each new development. While originally enacted for flood control through the use of detention basins and other measures of flow retardation, the ordinance was amended in July 1980 to require modification of these facilities from single purpose to multiple purpose use. The amendment required the implementation of retention "Best Management Practices" in the Occoquan Reservoir watershed to protect the quality of the county's water supply, and specified that such practices would be applied to all pending preliminary plats whether residential, commercial, or industrial. A design manual has been developed to provide designers with some guidance as to how to meet this new requirement, and also to encourage developers and their design engineers to seek new, better, and more economical methods to achieve the goals of the stormwater runoff quality control program.

The general design guidelines emphasize the use of volume controls, i.e., controls which depend on infiltration, and the utilization of suspended solids settling processes in detention and retention ponds. Outlet controls must be designed to provide a 40-hour drawdown time for released water. Impervious areas are to be minimized through the preservation of natural wooded cover, open spaces, and greenways. If existing developments upstream do not have specified retention facilities, a compensating design controlling the upstream runoff pollution can be used instead. Pervious surfaces such as modular pavements, porous pavement, and gravel may be accepted.

Types of Flow Retardation Devices

Small impoundments used to detain storm flows over short periods of time are referred to as *detention basins*. These structures are much smaller than the "small dams" of the Soil Conservation Service; most detention basins built by developers are from one to 10 acre feet in capacity. Somewhat larger detention basins may be built as "regional" or "master basins." Detention basins are characterized by ungated outlets. Detention basins in a housing development are shown in Fig. 7-1.

Figure 7-1   Detention Basins in Housing Development near Hightstown, New Jersey

Detention basins are usually designed to control short, high-intensity local storms, since these cause the most frequent flooding on small streams: and the basins release the retained water over a period of a few hours. The effect on reducing flood peaks is greatest just below the structure, and diminishes rapidly downstream. Figure 7-2 shows the large effect of a single detention basin at site, with mean time of retardation X, as compared to the cumulative effect of many similar detention basins covering a large watershed, with lag time about four times as great. In the latter case, the effect of detention basins upon peak flow would be negligible, even if the entire watershed were controlled by conventional detention basins. Of course, if detention basins are designed to retain part of their storage capacity for a longer period of time, a greater effect

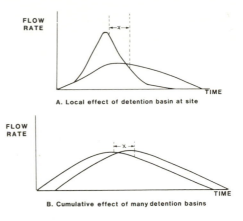

A. Local effect of detention basin at site

B. Cumulative effect of many detention basins

NOTE: X is retardation of mass of the flood wave.

Figure 7-2 Effects of Detention Basins

downstream can be produced. Basins designed to release stored water at slower rates, may be called *retention basins* if release is effected by means of outlets, or *infiltration basins* or *recharge basins* if the stored water is simply percolated into the ground. The usual purpose of such percolation is groundwater recharge.

Basins can be classified as dry basins or wet basins, the latter having a permanent pool of water below the elevations at which flood waters are stored. This pool can be used for purposes such as recreation, fishing, or for aesthetic reasons, and less often for fire-fighting reserve or for cattle watering.

Detention of floodwaters can also be effected by means of *rooftop storage* on flat roofs. Necessary structural provisions need to be made, including consideration of possible clogging of drains. *Dry wells*, sometimes called French drains, are pits or trenches excavated in porous soil and backfilled with rock, served by small storm drains which lead into them. They may remain effective for years unless clogged by dust or debris. They are, or course, only useful where the water table is sufficiently low. *Porous pavement* for hard stands and streets can reduce the extent of runoff from these surfaces. The most usual application of porous pavement is simply to replace bituminous material with crushed rock or gravel of considerable depth. The gravel is rather pervious, and through its porosity, may provide 20–30% of its space as temporary storage for storm-water. In some cases open joint tile is used to distribute the storm waters through a thick gravel layer underneath bituminous paving. The use of porous bituminous material is sometimes recommended for the same purpose; but it poses a special design problem. A thick rock sub-base must be provided, in order to avoid pavement settlement and deterioration under influence of water and of frost heave in any but warm climates. Also the porous pavement is subject to clogging. Accordingly, although initially enthusiastically welcomed in some quarters, the porous bituminous pavement has not been much used.

A better solution for parking lots, access roads, and loading areas appears to be the utilization of *modular pavement*, which consists of a strucurally sound material, usually concrete, with regularly interspersed void areas filled with pervious material such as sod, gravel, or sand. Modular pavement systems include:

1. Poured-in-place reinforced concrete. For large parking areas where heavy loads are expected, reinforced concrete slabs are poured in place on ground covered with special forms used to shape the void areas.
2. Precast concrete grids. Concrete paving units which are precast and placed on the ground after it has been properly prepared. Two types are common:
    a. Lattice pavers. Generally fiat and gridlike in surface configuration. The exposed paved surface is continuous and more than 50% of the finished area is exposed concrete.
    b. Castellated pavers. A pedestal type of surface configuration. The pedestals or "merlons" are exposed but surrounded by pervious material, usually sod. Only about 25% of the surface is exposed concrete.

All of the pavers are placed on a prepared sand and gravel base, which overlays the subsoil. The voids of the pavers are then filled with either sand, gravel, or sod. Frost heave problems are minimal. Figure 7-3 shows some typical modular pavement designs.

LATTICE TYPE PAVERS

CASTELLATED TYPE PAVERS

Figure 7-3 Typical Modular Pavement Design

Swales or broad, gently sloping grassed channels are a useful stormwater management device. In Colorado, where retention of moisture is desired as a water conservation device, or where swelling clay soils make drainage away from houses desirable, lots may be laid out sloping away from the street to swales in back of the house. In this case, storm runoff is retained and may be absorbed in the swales. Swales or shallow broad ditches are also useful to provide detention in highway design. *Curbs and gutters* are used in urban storm drainage to avoid erosion and to expedite the disposition of unwanted stormwater; but in more dispersed suburban development they may unnecessarily accentuate peak flows. Where lot sizes and topography permit, the avoidance of curbs and gutters in favor of overland flow considerably reduces the adverse effects of the development upon flooding in the streams. This practice was favorably cited by technical societies as long ago as 1975.[4]

Although a number of the approaches mentioned above may be useful in stormwater management, a complete program, designed to prevent increases in peak rate of flows due to development, usually involves use of detention basins

Detention Basin Nomenclature and Details

From a construction viewpoint, basins can be created by damming a stream, gulley, or overland flow channel, by excavating a basin into the existing ground, or by a combination of cut and fill. In any case, a basin must have one or more normal outlets, and also an emergency spillway, which allows floodwaters to pass from floods greater than that for which the structure was designed. Oridinarily, in multiple outlet structures, the lower outlet is small and is used to retard minor floods and sometimes to encourage deposition of sediment. The upper outlet handles larger floods. The purpose of the spillway is dam safety; that is, to prevent a disaster due to the breaking of an impoundment during an extreme storm event. Sometimes a stilling basin is required below the dam outlets, or below the spillway, to avoid damaging erosion. In almost all cases, a trash rack is required to prevent the outlet from being plugged by leaves and rubbish. The trash rack should be of mesh small enough to hold back small objects such as leaves, that might plug the lower outlet. A much coarser rack may be provided across the upper outlet to keep out large objects such as branches, if it is not located within the small-mesh trash rack. Figure 7-4 shows nomenclature of the main parts of a detention basin.

Detention Basins for Flood Control

Unlike large reservoirs, which are planned individually to provide an optimal degree of control of storms, detention basins are designed to meet criteria set for a given geographic area, by ordinance or regulation. The usual concept is that future storms, occurring after development, should have no more adverse effects than would have occurred from similar storms, if they occurred without the development.

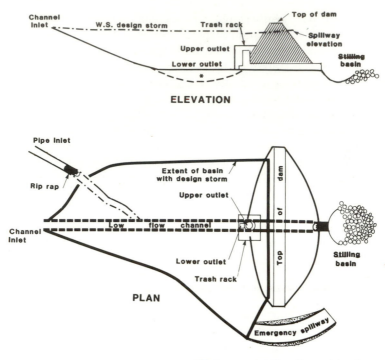

ELEVATION

PLAN

*Extra excavation for wet basin

Figure 7-4   Detention Basin Nomenclature

In applying this concept, many alternative approaches are possible. It is at once apparent that the same degree of control of outflow for each size of storm cannot be achieved by any detention basin. Therefore, the usual requirement is that peak flow of a given design storm, or storms, should not be increased; and this means peak flow at site. The design storm so specified may be anywhere from a 2 to a 100-year mean frequency flood. For example, Charlotte, North Carolina and Knoxville, Tennessee use a 10-year mean frequency storm. Sometimes the rule is stricter, requiring detention storage to reduce the post-development maximum flow from the design storm to less than the pre-development maximum flow from the same storm. For example, Princeton Township. New Jersey requires the post-development runoff from a 100-year one-hour storm to be 50% of that occurring pre-development from the same storm. Princeton also requires runoff from smaller storms to be reduced by an unspecified amount. Carroll County, Maryland requires the post-development maximum rate of runoff from a 5-year storm not to exceed the maximum pre-development rate from a 2-year storm. This approach is exemplified in a recent publication.[5]

Such requirements have raised the question as to whether it is equitable (and legal) to require a developer to contribute positively towards flood control.The justification which may be given is that it is impracticable to control all storms equally, and that the favorable effect of reducting damages from floods of less than the design storm frequency is counterbalanced by the damages from uncontrolled floods greater than the design storm flood, and by the flood and erosion damages further downstream, on account of the increased total volume of runoff, which is not reduced by the detention provisions. Of the criteria cited above, the Princeton ordinace requires more detention storage than the others. It has been in effect for several years and has not been tested in court.

Testing Detention Basin Design Alternatives
for Flood Control

A variety of design criteria were analyzed in Rutgers University in a series of comparative studies described below.[6] The area of the drainage basin was taken as 20 acres, with a pre-development condition of well-maintained woods, and a post-development condition of quater-acre single family housing. The slopes and soils selected are characteristic of the piedmont areas of northern New Jersey. The storm inflows used were from SCS Type II storms, with the ends of the hydrograph somewhat abbreviated in the interest of reducing computational detail. Main outlet pipes were sized to the nearest 2 inches. An emergency spillway of 25 feet in width was assumed.[7]

For each set of conditions, computations of routing were made by means of the usual routing equation.[8]

$$I_1 + I_2 + \frac{2S_1}{\Delta t} - O_1 = \frac{2S_2}{\Delta t} + O_2$$

where I_1 = inflow rate at start of time period
   I_2 = inflow rate at end of time period,
   Δt = duration of each time period,
   S_1 = storage at beginning of time period,
   S_2 = storage at end of time period,
   O_1 = outflow rate at start of time period, and
   O_2 = outflow rate at end of time period.

Computations were made on a Hewlett Packard 41c desk top computer with magnetic tape reader, extra memory modules, and printer. Necessary software was furnished by courtesy of Sasaki Associates of Boston. A time interval of 0.125 hour was used.

The first design criterion tested, designated 1A, required peak flow from the 100-year storm post-development not to exceed the peak rate of flow from the same storm, pre-development. (The designation "100-year storm" refers to the storm which, on a long-term average, will be equalled or exceeded once in 100 years, with no inference intended that any particular time will elapse before the next such storm.) To control the 100-year storm only, the economical design will consist of a single rather large outlet, as in Fig. 7-5(a). The quantity of detention storage required is not very great. The most obvious disadvantage of such a design is that it provides little reduction of flow from a 10-year storm and substantially no reduction for a 2-year storm, as shown in the following table.

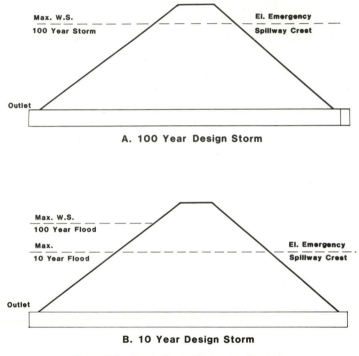

Figure 7-5   Single Outlet Detention Basins

DESIGN 1A   Single Outlet Basin Designed to Control 100-Year Design Storm to 100% Pre-development Flow

	100-Year Storm	10-Year Storm	2-Year Storm
Pre-D flow, cfs	57.0	32.3	14.1
Post-D flow, cfs	76.3	46.6	23.4
Controlled post-D flow, cfs	57.8	42.5	22.9
Storage, ft³	36,500	5,400	191

Since it does not materially reduce flow from the smaller storms, such a basin will not have much effect in limiting channel erosion downstream, and may even serve to increase it. Also, the flood control effect produced at site will be reduced further downstream much more rapidly than if a longer period of detention were provided. This effect is evaluated later in this chapter.

The second desgin criterion (1B) is to hold post-development peak flow from a 10-year storm to 100% of its pre-development rate. As compared to the 100-year design storm, the amount of storage required to control the 10-year storm is less. In this case also, a single pipe outlet will provide the most economical design, as in Fig. 7-5(b). The effect of this design on floods larger than the 10-year flood depends upon the width of the emergency spillway which was assumed to have its crest at the elevation required to contain the design storm. If the emergency spillway is not too wide, the effect of a basin designed to control a 10-year flood in controlling the 100-year flood may be appreciable, as shown in the table following. However, the total storage required is increased accordingly.

DESIGN 1B **Single Outlet Basin Designed to Control 10-Year Design Storm to 100% Pre-development Flow**

	100-Year Storm	10-Year Storm
Pre-D flow, cfs	57.0	32.3
Post-D flow, cfs	76.3	46.6
Controlled post-D flow, cfs	61.7	29.4
Storage, ft^3	53,600	31,400

In effect, the emergency spillway of 15-foot width is used as an additional outlet. Of course, in the interest of dam safety, the emergency spillway must be capable of handling much larger flows than that of the 100-year flood.

If a dual level outlet is provided, a detention basin can be made more effective in reducing the flood discharge from storms of various sizes. Figure 7-6 shows this type of design. The assumption was made that in each case the two outlets are of the same diameter. The following table shows the effectiveness of a dual outlet detention basin designed to control a 100-year design flood to 100% of its pre-development flow.

DESIGN 2A **Dual Outlet Basin Designed to Control 100-Year Design Storm to 100% Pre-development Flow**

	100-Year Storm	10-Year Storm	2-Year Storm
Pre-D flow, cfs	57.3	32.3	14.1
Post-D flow, cfs	76.3	46.6	23.4
Controlled post-D flow cfs	53.0	39.5	20.8
Storage, ft^3	49,400	17,900	3,980

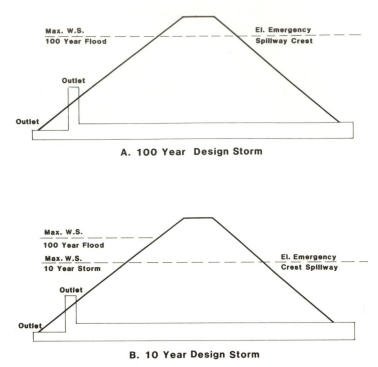

A. 100 Year Design Storm

B. 10 Year Design Storm

Figure 7-6   Dual Outlet Detention Basins

It is interesting to compare with the above the effectiveness of double-outlet detention basins designed to control the post-development outflows to 50% of the pre-development outflows from the 10-year storm.

DESIGN 2D   Dual Outlet Basin Designed to Control 10-Year Design Storm to 50% of Pre-development Flow[a]

	100-Year Storm	10-Year Storm	2-Year Storm
Pre-D flow, cfs	57.3	32.3	14.1
Post-D flow, cfs	46.8	15.2	11.7
Storage, ft³	110,300	77,800	27,600

[a]This design had a 25-foot spillway.

By comparison with results from other design criteria, it appears that the requirement to reduce the 10-year design storm outflow to 50% of the pre-development outflow requires about twice as much storage as a requirement that the design storm outflow not be exceeded. Note that when the 10-year design storm and a double outlet are used, the result is to reduce both the

2-year and the 100-year maximum discharges below their pre-development maxima.

In various ways, advanced design criteria now generally require that detention provisions be effective in reducing maximum flows from different sizes of flood. For example, Somerset County, New Jersey, requires that post-development flows not exceed pre-development for floods of estimated mean frequency of 2, 5, 10, 25, 50, and 100 years. Economical design to meet such requirements usually requires outlets at two or more levels below the crest of the emergency spillway, or a V-notch outlet. The following example illustrates the operation of a dual outlet detention structure, designed to hold post-development outflows from the 2, 10 and 100-year floods to the respective peak levels that would have existed for the same storms pre-development.

DESIGN 2E   Dual Outlet Basin Designed to Control the 2, 10, and 100-Year Design Storms to 100 % Pre-development Flow

	100-Year Storm	10-Year Storm	2-Year Storm
Pre-D flow, cfs	57.3	32.3	15
Post-D flow, cfs	17.7	15.2	11.7
Storage, ft^3	154,400	77,800	27,600

With this design criterion, and dual level outlets of equal size, considerably more storage is required than is needed to reduce outflows of the 10-year storm to 50% of their pre-development level (Design 2D). By more refined design, using outlets of different sizes, the difference would be reduced; but it would probably still be substantial. This finding helps to provide legal support for ordinances which require outflows below the pre-development outflow from a given design, since it can be shown that such a criterion may be less onerous than the alternative of providing for no increase in outflows of a number of alternative storms.

In conclusion, it is clear that if design is cost-effective for the criterion stated, the designation of a single design storm does not provide optimum results for control of storms of various magnitudes. If a 100-year storm is chosen, the effect upon reducing peaks of small storms will be relatively little. If a 10-year design storm is chosen, the 100-year storm may pass through the basin with a peak discharge considerably greater than would have been caused by the same storm pre-development. At first consideration, the ineffectiveness in controlling small floods may appear to be unimportant with respect to flood damages. However, the small floods do cause some damage and inconvenience and may be of prime importance as a cause of channel erosion. If only the small floods are controlled, the result is even worse. The marked effect of the detention structure in controlling small floods may mislead the public into believing that the floodplain is safe for all floods. A preferable design criterion is to require the developer to avoid increasing floods produced by either the 2, 10 or 100-year storm. This requires more storage, although the amount shown above for Design 2E could be reduced by optimal design of outlets. The added control of smaller floods also will have a somewhat better effect on flood heights downstream of the site, on account of the more gradual release rate in the latter portions of the hydrograph and the larger total storage provided.

A design criterion that shows up well in comparisons is Design 2D, which requires dual outlets, and a reduction of the 10-year storm to 50% of its pre-development peak. This criterion utilizes only three quarters of the storage of the preceding one, while still succeeding in holding all three sizes of floods below their pre-development peaks. It is the use of a lower level spillway that is largely responsible for this effectiveness. The computer printout showing a 100-year flood routed past this design is illustrated by Fig. 7-7.

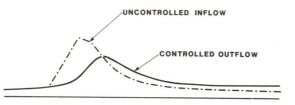

Figure 7-7   Routing of 100-year Flood Past Design 2D

However, it should not be inferred that engineering considerations alone can govern design criteria. In principle, a decision must be made whether or not the environmental and economic benefits of stormwater management warrant the imposition of controls on development. The maximum burden which appears to be equitable and legal to impose on developers on account of flood control appears to be the criterion described above (the 2, 10, 100-year require-ment). In sparsely settled areas, where some deterioration in the condition of streams would hardly be noticed, some lesser degree of detention, or no deten-tion at all may be warranted. However, as communities become increasingly urbanized, with manifest threats to the environment due to development, it will usually be found necessary and desirable to institute detention programs.

Locational Detention Basin Anomaly

It has frequently been said, and it is certainly true, that the effectiveness of detention basins varies greatly with the timing of storm rainfall and the location of the basins. In theory, it is desirable to plan the size and location of each detention basin with respect to these factors, including the location of flood damage centers.[9] However, such planning is seldom accomplished. The practical importance of locational aspects arises from the fact that detention requirements are usually imposed uniformly upon developments throughout a given area; and if development occurs mainly in the lower portion of a basin, there are some conditions in which the requirement for detention may increase the post-development flood peak downstream, rather than reducing it. The effect is more marked if the drainage basin is elongated.

In order to illustrate more clearly the possibilities of such a situation, a drainage basin is assumed in which the runoff from the upper, middle, and lower thirds of the basin are respectively identical and equally spaced in time and travel. Conditions are assumed under which the basin runoff from a given uniform rainfall hydrograph would be as shown in Fig. 7-8(a), with the three sectors' runoff shown combined with a relative peak of 4.5. A similar storm moving upstream would result in more widely spaced sector hydrographs, resulting in a combined hydrograph of 3.5 (Fig. 7-8(b).) In Fig. 7-8(c) is shown the result of a similar storm moving downstream, which would result in an accentuated combined peak of 7.2.

When a detention-modified hydrograph is substituted for the natural hydrograph in the approach to the entire basin, the results are those shown in Fig. 7-9. It is shown that for spatially undifferentiated rainfall, the result of the detention storage is to increase peak runoff from 4.5 to 5.0. With a storm moving

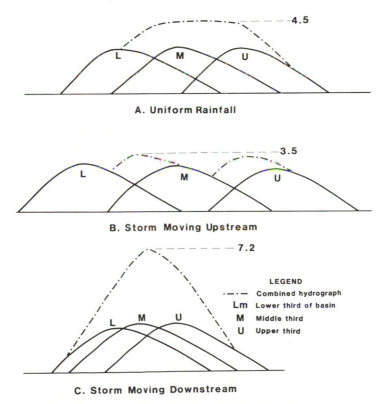

Figure 7-8   Storm Hydrographs on an Elongated Watershed

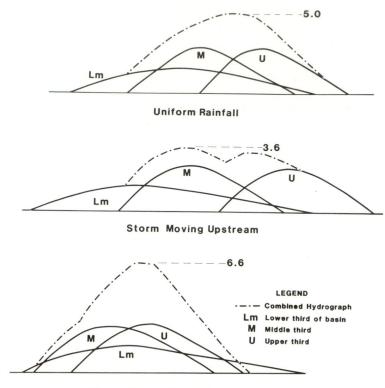

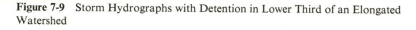

Figure 7-9 Storm Hydrographs with Detention in Lower Third of an Elongated Watershed

upstream the increase is less, from 3.5 to 3.6. In the case of the storm moving downstream, the detention reduces peak flow from 7.2 to 6.6.

Although the numerical values shown are the result of the particular conditions assumed and are not meant to be generally applicable, it is unquestionably true that, in the case either of a spatially undifferentiated rainfall or of a storm moving upstream, the use of detention provisions only in downstream parts of the basin will result in an increase in peak flows rather than a reduction. On the other hand, for a downstream-moving stream, which is the most dangerous type, the detention in the lower basin can contribute to reduction of the flood crest.

Considering the above analysis, the conclusion may be drawn that detention storage is somewhat less valuable in the lower portions of drainage basins, particularly elongated ones, provided no damage center lies downstream of the basin. However, no practical way has been found to use such a conclusion in devising stormwater management ordinances. As far as is known, no planning agency systematically uses such grounds to exempt parts of a basin from programs of stormwater management. Other ecomonic factors influencing development are of preponderant importance; and stormwater management considerations are usually not weighty enough to influence the order of land development. Of course, where detailed planning is to be carried out to develop an optimum stormwater management system, particularly one including structures larger than those built by individual developers, the locational aspects should be taken into consideration. Such cases include planning by the Soil Conservation Service under P.L 566, and planning of master basins by local governmental agencies.

REDUCTION OF PARTICULATE POLLUTION
BY DUAL PURPOSE DETENTION BASINS

General

The idea of using detention basins (or retention basins) to remove pollutants from runoff, although inherent in the older programs of the Soil Conservation Service, was first given viability in urbanizing areas by the studies of nonpoint source pollution started in 1975, under Section 208, P.L. 92-500. It had become apparent by that time that nonpoint and dispersed sources of pollution constituted a major part of the nation's water pollution problem. Several of the early 208 planning studies, in New Jersey, Virginia, and other states, investigated and reported favorably upon possibilities of controlling particulate pollution by detention basins. In these developing areas, detention basins would be desirable in any case, in the interest of flood control.

In order to provide for removal of particulate pollutants at moderate cost, the water quality and flood control objectives must be achieved in the same structure. The concept was outlined in a rcent paper.[10] Briefly, whereas flood damages occur mainly from rare floods, which approximate the size of the 100-year flood, the average pollutant load is contained mainly in the smaller discharges, which occur a number of times each year. The small floods have disproportionately higher concentrations of pollutants, in addition to being hundreds of times more numerous. Therefore, the retention of small floods is important from a water quality viewpoint. From a flood control viewpoint, prolonged retention of large floods would be hazardous, because of the chance of a second storm following the first. Therefore, a sound dual purpose detention basin design criterion must envisage holding the runoff from small storms for a prolonged period of time, but operating the structure for flood control primarily, when runoff from larger storms occurs. This can best be done by a small outlet at the bottom of the detention basin (or just above the permanent pool in a wet basin) sized for slow release of the specified small storm. This may be called the *retention outlet*. See Fig. 7-10. Above the level needed for prolonged retention of the small storm are the main outlets, designed for flood control.

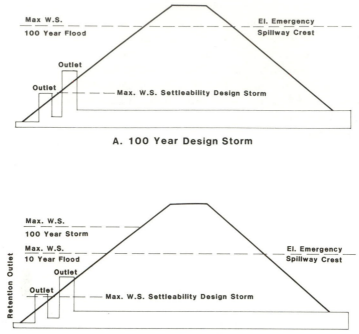

Figure 7-10   Detention Basin with Triple Outlets

Design Concepts

It remains to be decided what size design storm should be used for the purpose of retaining particulates and what length of prolonged release time should be specified. For convenience, the designated storm used to size the small outlet may be designated the *settleability design storm*. The Delaware and Raritan Canal Commission uses as a settleability design storm the runoff from a $1\frac{1}{4}$ inch storm occurring in 2 hours; while the South Florida Flood Management District uses either 1 inch of runoff or the runoff from a 3-year frequency storm, whichever is greater.[11]

An approach to the design of holding basins for water quality protection has been recently described by Griffin et al.[12] This method relies on the accumulation of data by monitoring. It was developed for small (< 100 acres) nonagricultural catchments. The approach is site specific and relies on very few assumptions. Therefore, it should have a high degree of reliability. Optimally, the volume determined by this method could be held by the dual purpose basin being used for flood control, and water quality protection would be provided. However, the construction of additional, separate basins for water quality retention may be desirable in particularly sensitive areas.

Trap Efficiency

The Delaware and Raritan Canal Commission requires the runoff produced by the settleability design storm to be evacuated 90% in 36 hours, or in 18 hours for residential areas. Data on settleability of urban runoff pollutants, summarized in Chap. 4, indicate that retaining runoff over a 36-hour period (with mean retention time over 18 hours) should be sufficient to settle out perhaps 60% of total suspended solids, lead, and hydrocarbons. BOD, copper, and phosphates should settle out in lesser amounts, perhaps 45% of the total. Recent field tests of trap efficiency for a detention basin with an outlet constricted in this manner gave trap efficiencies of suspended sediment of 59% and 81% repectively.[13]

Prediction of Trap Efficiency

A variety of methods can be used to predict trap efficiency of detention basins for various particulate pollutants. Of the older methods, that of Camp is based upon considerable experience and is relatively simple to use.[14] This method depends on the geometry and hydraulics of the basin, and also upon the settling velocity of the suspended matter.

The Camp method of determining trap efficiency requires first the evaluation of two expressions.

$$ WA/Q_0 \quad \text{and} \quad \frac{Wy^{\frac{1}{6}}}{Vn\sqrt{g}} $$

where $A =$ surface area of basin, ft^2;

$Q_0 =$ discharge from basin during settling, cfs;

$W =$ settling velocity;

$y =$ depth of basin, ft;

$V =$ mean velocity of water in basin, ft/sec;

$n =$ Manning coefficient; and

$g = 32.2$.

The trap efficiency of the basin under given conditions is read directly from the curves in Fig. 7-11.

Based upon settling velocities computed from laboratory settleability data,[15] the computed trap efficiency by the Camp method in the case cited above was 69% as compared to the 59% and 81% observed. Other recently derived modeling approaches, which indicate very much higher trap efficiencies,[16] were unverified. More reliable modeling of trap efficiency will no doubt develop, as soon as more data become available.

In principle, some sacrifice in flood control effectiveness of a given amount of storage will occur by requiring prolonged retention for settlement of particulates. This sacrifice is caused by the reduced capacity of flood control outlets

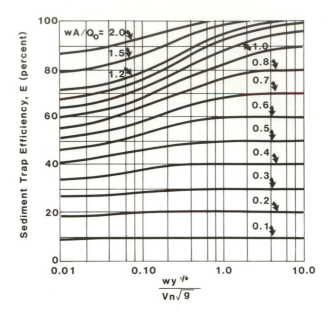

Figure 7-11 Camp's Trap Efficiency Curves

at the lower levels of the detention basin, where only the retention outlet is effective. The relative loss in effectiveness for settleability design storms has been estimated by routing through alternative designs of detention basins. For comparative analysis to determine optimum size of the settleability design storm, a common design criterion was adopted of reducing post-development discharge from a 10-year design storm to 50% of its pre-development level; and this criterion was tested by designing basins for settleability design storms of 0.75, 1.0, 1.25, and 1.5 inches respectively. Results are as shown in the following table.

In these cases, the amount of storage required to control 10-year floods with these alternatives does not change very greatly with the size of settleability design storm specified.

When these results are compared with designs previously discussed, which were designed in the interest of flood control only, an unexpected result appears. The settleability Design 3C, with its requirement of 137,700 cubic feet of storage, controls all three sizes of floods with less storage than Design 2E, which was designed to accomplish this objective without retention of particulates. This result is not really anomalous; it means that the design of two equal sized, dual outlets specified for 2E is not very efficient when floods of a wide range of sizes must be controlled. On the other hand, the requirement of a small retention outlet fits well with this condition.

This is confirmed by Design 3F, which couples the requirement for particulate retention of a 1.25-inch settleability storm to the requirement that for

**TABLE 7-1   Detention Basins Designed for Alternative Sizes
of Settleability Design Storm**

Design 3A—*0.75-in. rainfall inflow*—0.20-ft small outlet and two 16-in. pipes

	Outflow	*Storage*
2-year	8.05	49,900 ft^3
10-year	17.40	94,630
100-year (with spillway)	49.72	121,400

Design 3B—*1.00-in. rainfall inflow*—0.25-ft small outlet and two 18-in. pipes

2-year	8.30	52,050
10-year	17.26	98,030
100-year (with spillway)	41.57	137,800

Design 3C—*1.25-in. rainfall inflow*—0.30-ft small outlet and two 18-in. pipes

2-year	8.38	51.210
10-year	17.20	97,110
100-year (with spillway)	41.23	137,300

Design 3D—*1.50-in. rainfall inflow*—0.30-ft small outlet and two 20-in. pipes

2-year	6.99	58.010
10-year	14.92	102,300
100-year (with spillway)	43.69	138,700

each of the 100-year, 10-year, and 2-year storms, the post-development controlled flow shall not exceed the pre-development maximum. In this case, the following results are obtained;

Storm Tested	Outlets	Target	Outflow	Storage (ft^3)
100-year	small 3.6 in. dual 28 in.	57.3	51.3	105,400
10-year	"	32.3	27.6	69,600
2-year	"	14.1	14.4	42,600

This result shows that the amount of additional storage needed to meet the requirement for retention of particulate pollution is relatively so small that it is overshadowed by variations caused by changes in the design flood requirements and variations in effectiveness of alternative outlet designs.

Flood Control Effects Downstream

As noted in the above sections, design criteria selected for detention basins are always expressed in terms of effects at site, and such detention is relatively ineffective in reducing flood peaks on large rivers. However, there is a great difference in the effects of various criteria on downstream flood flows.

In order to evaluate these differences quantitatively, several of the designs referred to in previous sections were applied to a hypothetical 8000-acre drainage area, of which the runoff from each 20 acres is assumed to be controlled by an identical detention basin. Modeling was accomplished by the SCS TR-20 model. Since this model will not accommodate this number of basins, 25 sub-basins were assumed, in each of which there were 16 identical sub-sub-basins of 20 acres. One 320-acre sub-basin was modeled first, and then the sub-basin outputs were used as inputs for a second modeling of the basin as a whole. The 100-year peak flows before and after development, without detention structures, were 61 and 83 cfs respectively, for the 20-acre site, and 13,200 and 7,900 cfs respectively, for the entire 8000 acres. The effectiveness of three different detention basin designs in reducing peak flows in 2, 10, and 100-year storms is shown in Table 7-2.

TABLE 7-2   Comparison of Effectiveness Downstream of Various Designs

Design and Criterion	Storage, Per Basin	Reduction in Peak Flow for 8000-Acre Watershed Flood		
		2-yr	10-yr	100-yr
1A. Single outlet, control 100-yr flood to pre-D peak	38,000 ft^3	0%	0%	2%
1B. Single outlet, control 10 and 100-yr floods to pre-D peak	89,000 ft^3	1%	7%	30%
3F. Triple outlet, particulate retention, and control 2, 10, and 100-yr storms to pre-D peak	113,000 ft^3	44%	24%	20%

It will be seen that Design 1A, which requires only control of a 100-year design flood at site, has virtually no effect on floods at a point downstream where the stream drains 8000 acres. Design 1B, which controls both 10-year and 100-year storm at site, is somewhat better downstream, but only for large storms. The peaks of floods below the frequency of 10 years, which very largely determine channel erosion tendencies, are very little affected. Design 3F, however, which requires control of 2, 10, and 100-year floods at site, and also retention of particulates, is quite effective in reducing all types of floods in an

8000-acre basin. The reduced peak flows are not greatly in excess of the pre-development peaks. This is largely due to the prolonged retention of part of the runoff for removal of particulates, but also to the requirement to control the peak flow of 2-year floods, as well as those of the larger floods.

The computations for the 8000-acre drainage basin were performed with somewhat different assumptions than those for the 20-acre drainage basins discussed earlier in the chapter. Therefore, the results for a 20-acre basin are not identical.

Detention Basins and Channel Erosion

The idea that reducing peaks of stormwater runoff might be desirable in order to reduce stream erosion as well as to decrease flood heights was expressed in a joint study by three professional societies in 1975.[17] Only recently have studies been made which serve to quantify this relationship.[18, 19]

In analyzing the effect of detention basins upon channel erosion, only a full modeling can give a precise answer, but general indications can be obtained from a simple algorithm, as discussed in more detail in Chap. 6. This algorithm, referred to as the Schoklitsch formula, indicates that the quantities of bed load carried by a channel are directly proportionate to the quantity of flow above a given critical discharge (below which bed load does not move).

If all flood flows were confined within the banks of the stream, it could be concluded directly that, once this minimum level was reached, the given quantity of storm flow would always have the same aggregate erosional effect, regardless of the shape of the hydrograph. However, the existence of overbank flow at higher stages modifies this relationship. The "conventional wisdom" is that a river has greater erosion potential at bankfull stages than at higher flood stages. This conclusion, while not entirely accurate, is suggestive of the correct relationship. The overbank flow ordinarily does not carry bed load, therefore a given quantity of stormwater passing at very high stages may carry less bed load than similar quantities of water passing at bankfall stages, because of the proportion of overbank flow. For example, if the critical discharge is 0.33 of bankfull discharge, and the total discharge is twice bankfull, with the overbank discharge equal to 0.7 bankfull discharge, the relative bed load capacity of the stream in the two situations will be as follows:

Stage	Bed Load per Minute
Bankfull	1.0–0.3 = 0.7
Overbank	2.0–0.7–0.3 = 1.0

Since the bankfull stage would take twice as long to pass a given quantity of water, it would actually pass 40% more bed load in this case. Although the actual amounts vary depending upon the particular circumstances, it follows from this relationship that detention of floodwaters sufficiently to reduce overbank stages may increase the channel erosion capability of a stream.

On the other hand, prolonged retention of part of storm runoff should have a beneficial effect in reducing bed load capability and channel erosion. The retained water will be discharged over an 18 or 36-hour period, whereas the majority of the flood hydrographs on small streams rise rather suddenly and last only a few hours. Therefore, the water retained for a prolonged period will almost certainly be released at stages below the critical velocity for bed load.

It is demonstrable that processes of urbanization characteristically increase the bed load carrying capacity of streams, often by tripling the original capability.[20] As indicated above, some further increase may occur as the result of detention basins, if designed in the interest of flood control only at site, on the basis of a single design storm. However, adding provisions to retain particulate pollutants will at least partially counter this heightening of erosive capability by development.

Detention Basins in Floodplains

In general, stormwater management and floodplain management are separate and different programs, each with its own rationale; but there are some unavoidable interfaces. One of these occurs when it is proposed to develop land, some part of which lies within the floodplain. Of course, it is desirable that all stormwater detention be provided by structures located entirely above the floodplain; but this is not always possible. Much otherwise valuable land is located within the flood hazard area; and unless it lies within the floodway, it would be inequitable to preclude its development entirely. Therefore, the conditions must be examined under which floodplain and stormwater management objectives may be reconciled, as must the extent to which both may be achieved.

Within the flood fringe area, as defined by floodplain management, land development is usually allowed, provided the lower floor of buildings is located slightly above the predicted level of the 100-year flood. The delineation between the flood fringe area and the floodway is drawn so that, in principle, any filling of the flood fringe area will not raise the level of design flows in the floodway by more than a given amount. In other words, developments in the flood fringe area are compatible with allowing some increase in flood heights. On the other hand, the criteria of stormwater management usually aim at preventing any increase in flood heights by development. Therefore, it is clear that the usual laws and ordinances establishing floodplain management cannot be relied on to achieve the objectives of stormwater management.

When land is developed in the floodplain, or only a slight elevation above it, it is almost impossible to avoid locating the detention basin itself in the floodplain. In such a case, at the time the detention basin is needed to store stormwater runoff from the site, there is a chance that the floodplain will already be flooded, and that the detention basin will already be filled by floodwater from the main valley. To the extent that the flood at site coincides with the flood in the main valley, detention storage provided in the floodplain will be ineffective.

Obviously, the size of the drainage area of the main channel is very relevant. If the main channel drains several hundred square miles or more, the chance of interference is rather slight, since the local flooding is more apt to come from short storms than from the prolonged or extensive general rains required to bring the main stem to flood stage. On the other hand, if the floodplain is that of some minor stream, the same storms will probably affect the development site the and floodplain.

The component of detention storage provided on the floodplain at less than two feet below the level of the 100-year flood is less apt to cause interference with local detention storage than the component of storage more than two feet lower, or more than four feet lower.

In the case of the floodplain of a minor stream, a computation showing the probable effect of given detention provisions can be made on the assumption that the design storm, or storms, will occur simultaneously on the site and on the balance of the watershed. Where a design storm of 100-year frequency is used, such a computation will presumably show detention storage within the floodplain to be virtually useless for controlling that storm. Where the design storm is of lesser frequency, such as 10 years, storage provided at elevations less than those defining the flood hazard area may be effective.

For larger drainage basins, the assumption of simultaneity in occurrence of rainfall at site and throughout the watershed may be unduly severe. Many of the storms at the site will occur when the main stream is not in flood. For such cases, a set of numerical coefficients can be drawn up, representing roughly the probability of detention basin storage being effective when the local storm occurs, for basins of given size ranges

The following coefficients have been adopted for use in New Jersey by the Delaware and Raritan Canal Commission.

TABLE 7-3   Relative Effectiveness of Floodplain Detention Storage

	Size of Main Stream		
Elevation	Less than 5 sq. miles	Between 5 and 200 sq. miles	Over 200 sq. miles
Less than two feet below 100-year flood elevation	40	65	90
Between two and four feet below 100-year flood	25	50	75
Over four feet below 100-year flood	10	25	50

As an additional factor, it is clear that the effectiveness of detention basin storage provided as indicated above is affected by net amounts of fill and/or excavation carried out incidental to the development. Therefore, effective detention storage, computed as indicated above, is decreased by any net fill added within the flood hazard area, and increased by roof top storage and by any net excavation between the elevation of ground water and the elevation of the design flood.

The above method of estimation is only accurate to the extent that providing a greater amount of detention storage compensates for a lesser probability of the storage being available when needed. It is clear that this relationship does not hold for large variations, as the increased storage will generally not be as useful as the basic amount, and a great increase would not be useful.

The above approach poses additional problems to planners and engineers when sites are developed in floodplains, as conventional detention basins may not provide a complete solution in such cases. Occasionally, the plan of development may need to be modified so as to place buildings in flood fringe areas on piers or columns rather than on fill, to provide roof top storage, and to rely on gravel or modular pavement roadways and parking areas rather than impervious bitumen. This is a problem area which is just beginning to be explored in depth. Such solutions will add materially to the cost of providing detention, but only sufficiently to meet the same stormwater management criteria which are required elsewhere. They will not absolutely preclude development in any floodplain area, but will restrict the kind of development that will be allowed. Exceptions to the above criteria are made for highways within the flood hazard area, since the requirement for pervious-surfaced paving would introduce other disadvantages which outweigh the advantage gained by a contribution to flood retardation.

Master or Regional Detention Basins

In developing areas where stormwater management ordinances are being enforced, many planners and administrators are becoming concerned regarding the costs of building so many small detention basins, and the cost and difficulty of insuring their proper maintenance. The problem of insect vectors alone (usually mosquitoes) is a major concern. Although the relative economy of larger basins is to some degree countered by extra spillway costs to ensure dam safety, most analysts agree that master or regional detention basins, serving larger areas jointly, are considerably more economical to maintain satisfactorily than are the multiplicity of small basins which they replace. However, the small basins have some favorable aspects. From a public viewpoint, the advantage of the smaller individual detention basins is threefold:

1. They are built when needed, that is, when the individual development is taking place.

2. A single entity, namely the developer, can be held responsible for building them, and for making arrangements for maintenance.

3. They require no public planning or construction funds.

Some ordinances and regulations allow the submission of plans for master basins, but without special provision for encouraging them. Under such ordinances, few of them are apt to be built, because the construction of a detention basin to serve a large area would be required at a time when needed only for the first development. Moreover, master basins can only be located and designed after a thorough and detailed planning process, which is too expensive for most individual developers to undertake. It is seldom feasible to raise money for these purposes from other landowners, who have no immediate prospects of development. This difficulty may be partially overcome if the building of each such basin is required only when the area draining into it has developed to a considerable extent.

In principle, the municipality could encourage master basins by doing the planning itself and requiring developers to make cash contributions. The cash contributions of the early developers could be held in escrow until needed, except that the site for the master basin would be procured at the time of the first major development. This arrangement would provide encouragement to joint facilities; but it would leave two problems. First, the municipality or other entity responsible would have to raise the money for the planning and to finance the entire construction when only part of the contributions had been paid in. Secondly, the regulating agency might have to accept, for a number of years, some flooding resulting from areas partly developed prior to construction of the master basins.

The governing body might require collection of escrow contributions and acquiring of sites as indicated in the first alternative; but it might consider a number of regional detention facilities as a single proposition for purposes of scheduling construction. In such a scheme, if 10 regional facilities were planned, the body would require the site to be purchased for each facility at the time of the first major development in that watershed, but would require the construction of the first basin at the time that the total development in all basins exceeded a given percent of the total. The total contributions in escrow would be pooled for this purpose. The detention basin would be built first which had the greatest proportion of development in its drainge area. Maintenance would be charged to the developers or landwners concerned, but carried out by the county/municipality.

A complication would arise in that the area planned to be served by master detention basins would usually be partly developed by individual homes or minor projects. In this case, the municipality/county would have the option of charging the owners a proportionate fee for the purpose, or of assuming that part of the cost as a public service.

If such a scheme were well administered, the planning and construction costs would, in principle, be defrayed by the escrow funds; and the individual developers would not each have to plan, design, build, and maintain one or more detention basins. It appears that a scheme along these lines would be required to make master detention basins practicable without any material sacrifice in effectiveness, or any large public expenditure for construction. However, there remains the prerequisite of obtaining funds for preparation of a flood control or drainage plan, through which the master basins could be selected. Without some way to obtain public funds for advance planning, programs of master detention basins are apt to be successful only where there is single ownership of a large tract of land, or where the municipality itself is willing to underwrite construction.

MANAGEMENT

Maintenance

From time to time maintenance will be required to protect the integrity of the drainage and detention facilities. Earth embankments are very stable, but they may be worn down by children playing on them or digging, and by holes dug by woodchucks or other rodents. Concrete eventually cracks or crumbles; but usually only after many years. Metal pipes and trash racks may rust, and plastic drainage pipes may collapse. Trees may grow on the embankment and impair the structure when they blow down or rot. However, all these effects occur only very slowly. Once a year the detention basin should be inspected to detect any major structural problems.

Much more frequent problems arise from (a) erosion, (b) sedimentation, and (c) accumulation of leaves and trash.

Erosion

Erosion usually occurs through design defects, downstream of detention basin outlets (where no stilling basin was provided) or below detention basin inlets. Such erosion should be controlled by filling in with rock of suitable size to limit gulleying and prevent formation of pools which might breed mosquitoes, and by paving low flow channels and inflow channels within the basin. Sheet erosion also occurs by heavy rainfall or moving water on other parts of the basin, and should be avoided by keeping the area in grass and mowing several times a year. Bank erosion occurs around the edge of wet basins due to wave action, even where a protective grass covering extends down to the water's edge. Where sufficient granular material is present, a shingle beach may be created, or riprap may be placed.

Sedimentation

Sedimentation occurs in any detention basin, because the retardation of storm runoff even for a few hours allows the heavier sediments to settle out. Runoff from heavily developed areas usually has about 100 ppm of sedimant, or 0.1% by weight of the water inflow. The sediment which settles out may have as high as 0.3% by weight of lead and 5% of hydrocarbons from shopping centers (much less from residential areas.) The hydrocarbons are broken down by bacterial action over a period of time, but the heavy metals accumulate with the sediment. Sediment containing 0.3% of lead in insoluble form can be disposed of in landfills in a normal manner. Of course, runoff from industrial areas handling chemicals and metals may have much larger proportions of lead, cadmium, copper, or other toxics of many different kinds, so that, in special cases, analysis may be required to determine if such sediments require special treatments as toxic and hazardous materials. Oridinarily, however, the accumulated sediment can be removed every year or two and disposed of as fill. The most important erosion and sedimentation period is during construction; and the detention basin usually serves to provide the special retardation required during that period by soil conservation laws.

There is no reason why trees should not be kept in a detention basin. However, they should not be allowed to grow or to spread large roots in embankments or near concrete or masonry structures, which may be shifted and cracked by them.

Accumulation of Leaves and Trash

Leaves blow into most streams, channels, and detention basins every fall. Abandoned paper and containers of every sort are frequent in urban areas. Many persons dispose of grass cuttings, garden refuse, tree branches, and miscellaneous rubbish by leaving it where it can be washed into a stream. With rare exceptions, detention basins may be expected to accumulate a certain amount of such litter from time to time.

If proper trash racks are installed, the material entering will be held on the rack, except for materials fine enough not to block the outlet. The area of the rack should be large enough to hold up quite a large mass of material without impeding the flow of water. After every storm, particularly in the fall, any accumulated leaves and rubbish should be removed, especially from around the trash rack.

Other Considerations

In some areas, it may be desirable to fence detention basins, but this precaution is useless unless the gates are kept locked. Fencing may be required to keep children out of a wet basin, or, in cases where structures are large, to keep children away from steep slopes or walls where falls would be dangerous. Fencing adds to the difficulties of cutting grass, and encourages disposition of trash and debris inside the enclosure. Dense hedges can be used to keep out very small children.

From the viewpoint of operations, there is no reason why detention basins cannot be used for recreation. Of course, if it rains hard, they will fill, but they are no more dangerous from this viewpoint than an open ditch.

Mosquito habitats are the special concern of the mosquito control agencies, and normal detention basin maintenance should take mosquitoes into account. The prescribed floodwater retention period is far less than the minimum time for breeding of mosquitoes. However, mosquitoes can readily breed in pools left by erosion around inlets or outlets, or water backed up by trash accumulated around the edge of trash racks.

In dry basins, all such problems can be avoided by a visit after each storm to fill any eroded holes and remove trash. In wet basins, in order to control mosquitoes, it is necessary to maintain appropriate kinds of fish[21] in the pools, and to avoid excessive vegetation and marsh formation around the borders.

Legal Aspects

Unless maintenance responsibility is assumed by a government agency, the approved plan should lay the responsibility for maintenance upon the landowner, and in event of change of ownership, the liability should be passed to the new owner. Such provisions must be reviewed carefully. The plan should provide that in the event of subdivision a homeowners' association, or equivalent agency, will be formed, which be held permanently liable for maintenance. The individual landowners should be legally obligated to contribute towards payment for maintenance, and the liability should be passed by deed in the event of any change of ownership. In this way, for each basin there will always be a responsible legal entity to turn to, and either a liability on the part of property owners to pay for it, or a government agency which takes responsibility.

CONCLUSIONS

Common practices in building detention basins vary widely, but most are designed to prevent storms after development from causing more flooding than the same storms would have caused prior to the development. The basins designed to cope with a single large design storm require relatively little storage; but they are very ineffective in reducing lesser floods, and have little effect in reducing flood stages further downstream. Basins designed to control only smaller floods may incidentally reduce discharges of larger floods, on account of the action of the spillway and surcharge storage. However, a more conservative design requires a specified degree of control of a number of different size floods, none of which is allowed to create more flooding than it would have prior to the development. For economic design, multiple level outlets are required under such criteria.

In order to make provisions for removing particulate pollution in runoff by dual purpose use of detention basins, it is necessary that a small lower outlet be added, thus insuring slow evacuation of the lower part of the basin. To make such provision requires only a slight amount of additional detention basin capacity, compared to the storage required for basins designed to control design storms of several magnitudes.

Detention basins built in floodplains have reduced effectiveness, particularly if the floodplain is one created by a small stream. Stormwater management requires special provisions for such cases.

Master or regional detention basins, each of which may replace a number of detention basins on individual developments, have considerable advantages in first cost and very great advantages in maintenance costs. However, the difficulties in financing their planning and construction are considerable.

The management of numbers of detention basins presents various problems, particularly as regards maintenance. Special legal provisions are required to insure satisfactory maintenance of detention basins and drainage facilities of large developments, after lots comprising the development are sold to individual owners.

Stormwater management programs are carried out mainly by municipalities and counties; however, by preventing further increases in flood discharges consequent on urbanization, they stabilize otherwise progressively worse flood situations on the larger streams. Such programs are particularly essential to the long-term success of flood plain and channel management programs, as explained in the following chapter.

NOTES—CHAPTER 7

1. "Urban Hydrology for Small Watersheds," Technical Release No. 55, U.S. Soil Conservation Service, Jan. 1975.

2. Clean Water Act; P. L. 92–500 and amendments.

3. "Southeast Water Resources Urban Stormwater Management," Water Resources Research Institute, Univ. of North Carolina, Fall 1979.

4. "Residential Stormwater Management," American Society of Civil Engineers, National Association of Home Builders, and the Urban Land Institute, 1975, pp. 16, 23.

5. G. E. Kamedulski and R. H. McCuen, "Evaluation of Alternative Stormwater Detention Policies," *Journal Water Resources Planning and Management Div.*, *ASCE*, 14806, Sept. 1979.

6. Under OWRT research projects A-058-NJ, "Settleability of Urban Runoff Pollution" and B-084-NJ, "Flood Control Effectiveness of Dual Purpose Deten-

tion Basins." Results are described in an interim report "Modeling of Alternative Criteria for Dual Purpose Detention Basin Design" by William Whipple, Jr. and Samuel D. Faust, Water Resources Research Institute, Rutgers Univ., New Brunswick, N.J., May 1981.

7. William Whipple, Jr. and Joseph V. Hunter, "Settleability of Urban Runoff Pollution," Water Resources Research Institute, Rutgers Univ., New Brunswick, N.J., April 1980.

8. "Storage and Flood Routing," Manual of Hydrology, Pt. 3, Flood Flow Techniques, U.S. Geological Survey, Water Supply Paper 1543-B, 1960, p. 102.

9. D. F. Kibler and G. Aron, "Urban Runoff Management Strategies," *Journal Technical Councils, ASCE,* 15600, TC1, Aug. 1980, p. 1.

10. William Whipple, Jr., "Dual Purpose Detention Basins," *Journal Water Resources Planning and Management Div., ASCE* 14860, Sept. 1979 p. 403

11. Water Resources Institute, 1979.

12. D. M. Griffin, Jr., Clifford W. Randall, and T. J. Grizzard, "Efficient Design of Stormwater Holding Basins Used for Water Quality Protection," *Water Research,* 14, No. 10, Elmsford, N.Y.: Pergamon Press, Oct. 1980, pp. 1549–54.

13. Recent research results, unpublished, from Amwell Road site, Water Resources Research Institute, Rutgers Univ.

14. C. N. Chen, "Design of Sediment Retention Basins," Paper given at symposium on "Evaluation and Control of Soil Erosion in Urbanizing Watersheds," Univ. of Kentucky, Lexington, Ky., 1975.

15. Whipple and Hunter, 1980.

16. C. B. Amandes and P. B. Bedient, "Stormwater Detention in Developing Watersheds," *Journal Environmental Engineering Div., ASCE,* 15335, EE2, April 1980, p. 403.

17. American Society of Civil Engineers, 1975.

18. William Whipple, Jr., James M. DiLouie, and Theodore S. Pytlar, Jr., "Erosional Aspects of Managing Urban Streams," Water Resources Research Institute, Rutgers Univ., New Brunswick, N.J., Jan. 1980.

19. William Whipple, Jr., James M. DiLouie, and Theodore S. Pytlar, Jr., "Erosional Potential of Streams in Urbanizing Areas," *Water Resources Bulletin, AWRA,* 17, No. 1, Feb. 1981, p. 36.

20. Whipple, DiLouie, and Pytlar, 1980.

21. The common goldfish is one of the frequently recommended species to control mosquitoes.

8

Floodplain and Channel Management

L. SCOTT TUCKER

WILLIAM WHIPPLE

GENERAL

The management of floodplains and the improvement of the channels which flow through floodplains are closely related in a physical sense. The programs that deal with floodplains, however, are in many situations different from programs that deal with channels; in other cases such programs are closely related. While the federal definition of floodplain includes areas adjoining coastal water,[1] this chapter deals with management of lands exposed to flooding from river systems, and more specifically from smaller urban streams and creeks.

In a natural setting there is a well-defined channel within the floodplain that carries low flows, typically in the range of the annual flood or the 2-year flood. When a flood is large enough, it overflows the channel banks and extends more widely across the floodplain in overbank flow. As shown in Chap. 7, the effects of urbanization characteristically increase the rate of runoff and total quantity of runoff from a given rainfall.

For the larger flood events, the floodplain provides both a passageway and a temporary storage area for excess waters. Overbank flow is usually shallower and of much less velocity than channel flow. During flood situations, channels may erode in some places and deposit sediment in others; so that over a period of years, there is a tendency for channels to change their configuration, unless confined by erosion resistant rock. As indicated in Chap. 6, many streams in their natural condition were in a state of dynamic balance; meaning that, over a long period of time, the stream received from processes of erosion in its watershed as much bed load as it was capable of carrying, with allowance for reduction of size of particles by stream and weather action along the way. One result of urbanization is to upset this balance by greatly increasing the erosional tendency of a stream. This is the basic reason why so many urban streams must be managed so as to control destructive erosion tendencies, as well as to cope with more frequent high flood stages than occurred in their original undeveloped state.

The main purpose of floodplain and channel management is to investigate problems which have arisen in developed areas, and also additional problems which can be forecast to come with future developments. Floodplain and channel management must incorporate both preventive and remedial considerations.

Elements of the Floodplain

A cross section of a floodplain showing critical elements is seen in Fig. 8-1. Although by geographic definition the term floodplain can include areas flooded even by extremely rare events, floodplain management generally addresses areas flooded at least once in 100 years. Such a condition defines what is called the flood hazard area, or, sometimes, the 100-year floodplain. A narrower area called the floodway includes the channel of the stream and the

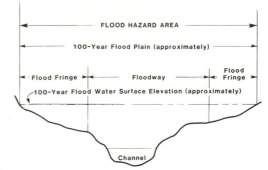

Figure 8-1 Cross Section of a Flood-plain Showing the Various Elements

adjacent land areas that must be reserved in order to discharge the design flood without cumulatively increasing the water surface elevation by more than a given amount. The maximum rise allowed by the National Flood Insurance Program (NFIP) is one foot; but in many situations a lesser amount is more appropriate. The flood hazard area beyond the floodway is called the flood fringe.

Basic Concepts of Floodplain and Channel Management

Three basic approaches to floodplain management have been defined[2] as:

1. Actions to reduce susceptibility to floods,
2. Actions that modify the flood, and
3. Actions that assist individuals and communities in responding to floods.

Actions to reduce susceptibility of a floodplain to flood damage include floodplain regulation of development, governmental development and redevelopment policies, floodproofing, disaster preparedness and response plans, and flood forecasting and warning systems. These approaches are discussed in the paragraphs that follow.

Actions that modify the flood include the various direct control measures such as dams and reservoirs, levees, floodwalls, and other channel improvements. Indirect measures such as land treatment and stormwater detention in urbanizing areas can also modify the nature of floods. In this chapter, channel related improvements are the only structural means covered.

Actions to assist in the response to flood problems include information dissemination and education, methods to spread a flood loss over time, and methods to spread the costs of floods to a wider community.

A great deal of channel management relates mainly to control of the accentuated erosion tendency of the stream. Control can be accomplished in at least four ways, as follows:

1. Lining the channel and banks.
2. Providing for longer detention of stormwater runoff, so that flows are released at velocities below that which moves appreciable quantities of bedload.
3. Creating additional channel roughness. This might be done by adding large numbers of rocks, of sufficient size as not to move at flood stages.
4. Reducing the effective slope of the stream at high stages. This can be done by providing suitably restricted culverts at road-crossings or by adding low dams or drop structures to the stream.

FLOODPLAIN MANAGEMENT

Floodplain Regulation

The cornerstone of a floodplain and channel management program is regulation of the floodplain. The objective of the regulation is to reduce future flood damages by controlling future development in such a manner as to minimize risk. Normally, floodplain regulation is exercised by local governments but is subject to policies of or supervision by the state. This is in accordance with the traditional and constitutional limitation of the powers of the federal government. However, by means of the National Flood Insurance Program, basic policies are specified and a great deal of detailed control is actually exercised by the federal government, local and state governments finding it generally in their interests to comply. The National Flood Insurance Program (NFIP) is described later in this chapter. Also, the Corps of Engineers may require a specified degree of regulation of the floodplain to be carried on as a condition of federal financing of a flood control project.

Floodplain regulation is particularly effective in undeveloped floodplains, where the opportunity to control future development is greatest. In urbanized floodplains the problem of flood damage already exists; but regulation can have a positive effect on damage reduction where older buildings are being rehabilitated or the area is being redeveloped.

The key to successful floodplain regulation is adequate delineation of the flood hazard area and of the floodway. The basis for defining the floodplain is the 100-year flood, which has been accepted by the NFIP for defining the flood hazard area. Mapping at a scale of 1 in. = 200 ft or less, with 2-ft contours, is recommended. Such mapping should include the entire 100-year floodplain and extend slightly beyond. For most situations where stream lengths in excess of one mile are involved, aerial mapping is the most economical mapping method. Tight specifications for mapping can be developed which provide a sound basis for competitive bidding among qualified mapping firms. Prescreening or prequalification is important, however, to insure that all firms submitting bids are qualified to do the work and have good records of performance.

While the mapping is under way, the hydrology can be developed. This involves determining the flow rates for the various flood frequencies of concern. Once the mapping and hydrology are completed, the flows can be routed through the floodplain, using cross-sectional information obtained from the mapping.

An example of a flood hazard area delineation plan and profile is shown in Fig. 8-2. The 100-year and 10-year water surface profiles are shown, so that the water surface elevations can be determined at any point along the channel. In this case, the floodway is not delineated on the plan and profile drawing, but is given instead in tabular form, as shown in Table 8-1. For example at Section 1592, Station 167+90, the floodway is 100 feet wide; and the floodway boundary is 85 feet to the right of the center line and 15 feet to the left of the center line (looking downstream).

The floodplain regulation for a local government can take many different forms. Suggested references in this regard are "Regulation of Flood Hazard Areas to Reduce Flood Losses"[3] and "A Perspective on Flood Plain Regulations for Flood Plain Management."[4] One basic approach involves a rezoning of the flood hazard area. An alternative choice is the overlay approach, which does not change the underlying zoning, but adds restrictions pertaining to the flood hazard. There are one-district ordinances, two-district ordinances, three-district ordinances, and emergency or interim regulations. In addition, there are several ways in which a floodway can be defined depending on the criteria selected. Therefore, each ordinance or regulation must be written specifically to fit the local situation and legal framework of the community and state. The National Flood Insurance Program has published a model regulation based on the minimum criteria of the NFIP;[5] and many states have published model regulations based on the same or different criteria. Because of the complexity and variability of state requirements and authorizing legislation, local needs, information available, and NFIP requirements, each local government should develop its own ordinance to meet its own needs.

In the one-district approach, the entire flood hazard area is regulated as a unit. The two-district approach preserves a passageway for the design flood by prohibiting encroachments into the floodway unless technical evaluation demonstrates that the encroachments will not result in any increase in flood levels. Encroachments are permitted in the flood fringe if they are elevated above or floodproofed to the 100-year flood elevation. The NFIP allows up to a one-foot rise in flood levels created by flood fringe encroachments; but this much of an increase is usually undesirable.

No additional residential construction of any kind should be allowed within the floodway under any circumstances, because it is the most hazardous area of the floodplain.

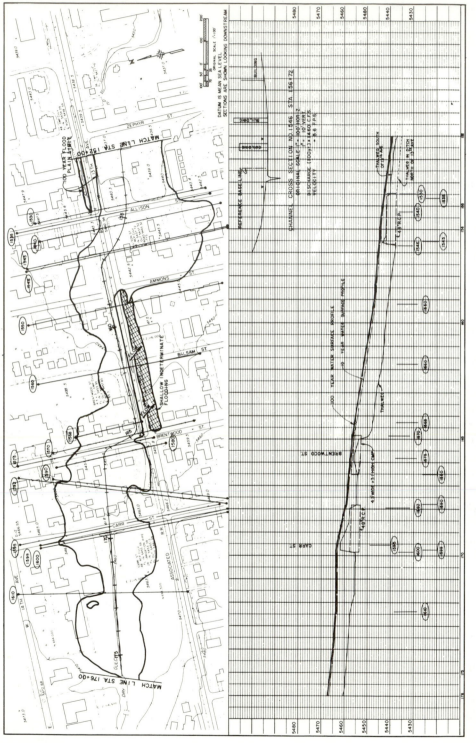

Figure 8-2 Plan and Profile of a Flood Hazard Area Delineation Map

TABLE 8-1 Tabular Floodplain and Floodway Data

Location			Natural Channel				Floodway Data			
Section	Station[a]	Description	100-Year Flow (cfs)	Thalweg[b] Elev.	W.S. Elev.	Top Width (ft)	W.S. Elev.	Top Width (ft)	Dist Rt.[c]	Dist Lt.[d]
1546	156+72		1460	5437.7	5444.9	543	5445.4	360	248	112
1550	159+20		1460	5441.3	5447.4	157[d]	5447.9	100	69	31
1560	161+80		1460	5443.9	5452.0	133[d]	5451.9	36	19	17
1568	164+28		1460	5442.0	5455.3	285[d]	5456.0	30	20	10
1570	164+87		1460	5449.3	5456.2	270[d]	5456.8	125	40	85
1575	165+80	Brentwood Street	1460	5455.5	5457.3	265	5457.3	70	50	20
1580	166+50		1460	5454.4	5458.0	346	5458.1	163	183	−20
1590	167+80		1460	5454.6	5459.2	260[d]	5459.8	105	97	8
1592	167+90		1330	5457.5	5459.9	300	5460.6	100	85	15
1595	169+55	Carr Street	1330	5461.8	5463.2	324	5463.2	150	47	103
1599	169+75		1330	5460.1	5463.6	400	5464.0	150	45	105
1600	169+83		1312	5455.3	5463.6	400	5464.0	150	43	107
1610	172+40		1312	5457.6	5463.6	124	5464.0	43	24	19

[a] Distance above mouth.
[b] Valley bottom or low point in cross section.
[c] Distance right and left (looking downstream) from the reference baseline to the edges of the floodway.
[d] Width of main channel flow only.

Development and Redevelopment Policies

Development and redevelopment policies are not specified by ordinance; but they may be important in the reduction of flood hazards. Such policies are manifested through planning board zoning actions, through the direction and design of governmental facilities, such as sewage treatment plants, through development planning, and through open-space acquisition and the permanent evacuation of floodplain occupants.

Subdivision Ordinances and Building Codes

Subdivision ordinances guide the division of larger parcels of land into smaller lots for the purpose of developments. Subdivision ordinances insure that land development results in the provision of basic facilities in a consistent and sufficient manner. They control improvements such as roads, sewers, water, drainage facilities, and recreational facilities. In terms of floodplain management, subdivision regulations may require the developer to (1) install adequate drainage facilities, (2) show the location of flood hazard areas on the plat, (3) avoid encroachment into the flood hazard areas, (4) determine the most appropriate means of elevating a building above the regulatory flood height, and (5) construct streets and public utilities in such a way that they will not be seriously damaged during a 100-year flood.

Building codes control building design and use of construction materials but do not regulate the type or location of development. Building codes can reduce flood damages to structures by setting forth specifications regarding suitable anchorage to prevent floatation of buildings during floods, minimum protection elevations for the first floor of structures, requirements for electrical outlets and mechanical equipment locations in flood prone structures, restrictions on the use of materials that deteriorate when wetted, and requirements for adequate structural design that can safely withstand the effects of water pressure and flood velocities. Building codes can require a degree of floodproofing, which is discussed further in the following section.

Floodproofing

Building codes as discussed above provide a degree of floodproofing, but other floodproofing measures can be taken that may not be included in local building codes. For local governments involved in the NFIP, it is required that any proposed building, residential or nonresidential, that is to be constructed in defined flood hazard areas should floodproof utility and sanitary facilities and elevate the lowest floor, including basement, to a height at or above the 100-year flood level. Floodproofing can also include walls and levees, temporary and permanent closures, and rearranging or protecting damageable property.

The advantages of floodproofing are that damages to structures and contents are reduced or prevented, and the occupancy of a floodplain site and surrounding infrastructure is allowed under controlled conditions. The limitations of floodproofing are that larger floods can occur that rise above the floodproofed elevations, flooding of surrounding areas still occurs with possible damages to other facilities and services, and during a flooding event the presence of floodproofed buildings may complicate evacuation and assistance efforts.

For details regarding floodproofing techniques, a number of excellent references may be cited.[6-12]

Disaster Warning, Preparedness, and Assistance

The urgency of assistance during flood disasters is suggested by Figs. 8-3 and 8-4. Susceptibility to flood damage can be reduced:

1. If warning is given in ample time before a flood,
2. If a plan exists to communicate the warning to floodplain occupants in time to take preventive measures and/or evacuate,
3. If a plan exists for flood fighting, and
4. If a plan exists that can guide recovery and rehabilitation after a flood.

Figure 8-3   Air Force Helicopter Picking Up Flood Victims

Figure 8-4 Flood Victims Being Rescued by Boat (By Russ Reed, The *Oakland Tribune/Eastbay TODAY.*)

Flood forecasting and warning is related closely to the response of a river system to rainfall. For large rivers, forecasts can be provided several days, and in some cases weeks in advance. Floods on small headwater tributaries peak quickly, and warning times may be a matter of hours; for some cases involving streams with steep gradients, maximum warning time can be one or two hours even with well-developed detection systems.

The National Weather Service (NWS) river forecasting centers (RFC), of which there are 13 in the United States, are responsible for river and flood-stage forecasting. In many headwater areas, there is insufficient time for the RFC to make forecasts. In these areas Weather Service Forecasting Offices (WSFO) or Weather Service Offices (WSO) issue flash flood watches where heavy rain is forecast, or flash flood warnings when precipitation has been observed that is expected to lead to rapid flooding. For headwater streams subject to rapid flash flooding, affected local governments should consider supplementing the WSFO and WSO forecasts with their own flood detection systems. This may be necessary because the WSFO and WSO forecasts tend to be areawide in nature; and for special problem areas, site specific detection may be required.

A complete warning plan consists of detection of the threat, dissemination of warning, and organized evacuation. Improved forecasting and warning systems are of little value unless local communities are prepared to respond. Response to flood forecasts is the responsibility of state and local agencies.

The NWS is involved in detection only and is not staffed to maintain local government level observation networks or response systems. Clearly, if detection/warning/evacuation plans are to be successful, local government must be prepared. The NWS can provide assistance with detection of a flooding threat; and the Federal Emergency Management Agency (FEMA) can help coordinate preparedness efforts among local, state, and federal agencies through the Office of Disaster Response and Recovery; but a successful detection/warning/evacuation plan will simply not succeed unless there is active local government involvement.

For those areas where flash flooding is a real threat, local government should take the initiative to develop a flash flood warning plan. Such a plan should describe in detail the required elements of the warning plan which are:

1. Detection and evaluation of the flood threat,
2. Dissemination of information to the public, and
3. Response to the warning.

The plan should include the input of all potentially responsible agencies and organizations such as sheriff's office, police, fire department, National Weather Service, private meteorological consulting services if they have been retained, public works department, rainfall and/or runoff observers, media, state agencies, and other public and/or private entities with large developments in the floodplain, such as school districts or factories. The plan should contain a step by step procedure of what will happen during a flood emergency including a description of what each party (agency, department, or individual) will be required to do.

A suggested technique is to develop the plan in a loose leaf format. An annual review can be made of the plan and revisions distributed to plan holders. If the warning plan is to be truly effective, it is essential that it be practiced at least annually, with critiques following the practices.

For details regarding flood disaster warning preparedness and assistance references 13 through 27 are suggested.

Flood emergency measures such as flood fighting plans, temporary earthen dikes, and emergency floodproofing should be planned in anticipation of flooding. Such measures must be carefully coordinated with evacuation plans as previously discussed. The Corps of Engineers can usually give technical assistance, and may be able to help with supplies. Frequently, flood fighting plans are improvised at the last minute, and are consequently ineffective. A determined but apparently unsuccessful flood fighting effort is shown in Fig. 8-5. Specific flood fighting plans and tactics depend on the flood characteristics, the physical nature of the flooded area, and resource requirements such as labor, fiscal, supplies, and equipment.

Advance consideration should also be given to recovery measures to be taken after a flood disaster. Rebuilding and redevelopment activities should

Figure 8-5 A Determined But Unsuccessful Flood Fighting Effort (Ottumwa, Iowa, 1947)

be oriented so as to reduce future flood hazards. State and federal agencies usually become actively involved in recovery activities; and a local government should make advance contact with the state and federal agencies that may have a potential involvement in flood disaster recovery. Appropriate state agencies vary from state to state and will have to be determined on an individual basis. The primary federal agency in this regard is FEMA, which will assist states and local governments in developing and improving plans, programs, and capabilities for disaster preparedness, response, and hazard mitigation. FEMA has the responsibility at the federal level to coordinate the federal response during presidentially declared emergencies and disasters and to provide from the President's disaster fund assistance to individuals, the public sector, and certain nonprofit agencies.

Postflood recovery is difficult to plan because of the unpredictable characteristics of major floods, and because psychologically it is difficult to accept the reality of what may seem to be a remote contingency. Nevertheless, consideration should be given to postflood recovery to the extent practicable. Postflood recovery measures are difficult to rehearse, which is one of the reasons that planning is difficult. An important aspect of postflood recovery is to prevent redevelopment from occurring in such a way that the same flood hazard is allowed to be rebuilt in the floodplain. After a disaster interested federal and state agencies may have a tendency to finance the rebuilding of structures that would better be relocated. In some cases, grants or loans can be counterproductive if they encourage rehabilitation of structures located in high hazard areas. If no thought is given to this aspect of postflood recovery, rebuilding in the floodplain will be difficult to control.

After a major flood disaster, aid from public and quasipublic agencies is often in the form of donations of food, clothing, grants, and loans. Relief may also be in the form of tax adjustments.

Under provisions of P.L. 92-234, Flood Disaster Protection Act, and P.L. 93-288, Disaster Relief Act of 1974, owners of flood damaged property may be required to purchase flood insurance as a condition for obtaining federal financial aid.

Information and Education

Modern techniques of education and information dissemination are very important in a floodplain management program, because of the necessity for widespread public support if a sound program is to be implemented, and also because the public must have an understanding of the flood situation if it is to act rationally during a crisis.

Education and information are always means to an end; and as such each part of the effort should be oriented towards the specific end desired. For example, it is desirable that citizens living or working in flood hazard areas be advised of the potential dangers. This can be done in several ways. One way is to post high water marks throughout a floodplain, using several signs or posts showing the water surface elevation of a historic flood, or of the 100-year flood. Unfortunately, such posted marks usually disappear in a year or two, sabotaged by persons whose interests are that such disagreeable facts not be recalled. Another approach is to publish in local newspapers the flood hazard area delineation map. Such a publication can advise of the hazard, of what action may be taken by the individual, and of where to call for additional information. Local television newscasts can be used to reinforce the warning.

In Denver, brochures have been mailed to the occupants of all building addresses located within identified 100-year floodplains. Such brochures are more likely to be retained for future reference than a newspaper article. This brochure includes a floodplain map and gives notice that the building in question is subject to occasional flooding. The brochure advises occupants to obtain flood insurance or floodproofing, to observe the level of water in the stream and stay tuned to the radio or television for possible flood warnings, to plan escape routes to higher ground, and to evacuate the area in times of impending flood, or when official advice is given. The brochure also identifies the responsible agencies to be contacted for further information. Such brochures are mailed annually before the spring season when floods are most likely.

It is very desirable for all those involved with real estate transactions to be fully aware of flood hazards. If local ordinances regulate floodplains, and planning boards are alert and well informed, official action can prevent major encroachments upon flood hazard areas by vulnerable developments. However, it is also very desirable that all those intending to buy or to improve facilities in the floodplain be aware of the situation. All real estate agents should be given full information as to flood hazards, so that prospective buyers can be advised. The banking industry also needs the information in order to evaluate prospective mortgages and the need for flood risk insurance, and to protect the interests of all concerned. Educational programs can be effective with both the real estate and the banking industries. Similar information can also be useful to prospective developers, in order to help their adjustment to floodplain regulation. Such programs reduce friction and political resistance from the building industry by giving them an understanding of the reason for regulating floodplain construction.

Seminars can be sponsored by public agencies or professional groups periodically to provide and disseminate information on floodplain management issues. For example, design criteria, flood insurance program, or flood warning systems can be presented to appropriate interest groups.

Flood Insurance

In principle, flood insurance is a means of spreading flood losses over time and to a large number of other people who share a similar risk. For all practical purposes flood insurance was not available until 1968, when the National Flood Insurance Act was passed. The 1968 Act was amended by the Disaster Protection Act of 1973, and again in 1976 and 1977.

As with other types of insurance, such as fire insurance, flood insurance provides compensation to those who suffer losses from flooding. However, unlike other common forms of insurance, flood insurance has been heavily subsidized by the federal government; so that premiums collected from persons covered have generally reimbursed only a part of the cost of paying for losses.

As originally conceived by Gilbert White and others, the main purpose of the federal flood insurance program was to restrict future development and prevent future flood damages in designated hazard areas. However, the high degree of subsidy in the emergency program means that not only is the impact of flood damages distributed between participants covered, but also the federal taxpayer has paid a large share of the costs of the program. The financial benefit which this arrangement represents to local interests within the floodplain not only provides a "carrot" to induce local communities to adopt federally desired floodplain regulations, but also provides an inducement to continue the program.

There is no doubt that to states with a high proportion of occupied floodplains, the federal subsidy is a major objective in itself. Although, in principle, actuarially estimated flood insurance premiums are supposed ultimately to be imposed, it is hard to see how the federal subsidy could be generally eliminated. Under present arrangements, the conversion to the regular program does not eliminate the subsidized "first layer" insurance for existing structures.

Flood insurance is an important element of a floodplain management program. It provides a rapid and efficient way for individuals who have suffered flood damages to obtain funds to help them recover. Without flood insurance an individual has to depend on more cumbersome federal or state disaster aid programs that could be in the form of low interest loans, could be long delayed, or might not be available to all those suffering losses.

Flood insurance is made available on the basis that the community in which the property is located will adopt and administer floodplain land use control and building code measures that meet or exceed Federal Insurance Administration (FIA) requirements. It is sometimes called a "carrot and stick" approach, with the carrot being the availability of insurance; but there is really no federal stick, only the deprival of the carrot, if the local government does not adopt minimum land use regulation measures.

The NFIP has two levels of involvement by a community. A community is eligible for the "emergency program" as soon as FIA has notified the community that the community has flood hazard areas. The FIA will prepare a flood hazard boundary map for the flood risk areas. If the community chooses not to enter the program, citizens within the community cannot obtain flood insurance, and theoretically at least may be ineligible for federal or federally related flood disaster assistance.

If the community chooses to enter the emergency program, limited amounts of flood insurance coverage are available for existing structures and their contents at subsidized rates without regard to the degree of risk involved. This coverage is called "first layer." The total amount of insurance available under the emergency program is given in Table 8-2, and varies depending on use of the structure and where located.

After a community has entered the emergency program, the FIA will prepare a more detailed map called a flood insurance rate map (FIRM). When the FIRM is completed, the community is then supposed to enter the "regular program" and a "second layer" of additional coverage is made available at nonsubsidized (actuarial) rates for all existing structures. Under the regular program, actuarial rates of insurance are also charged for all structures for which construction was started after the effective date of the FIRM. The limits of coverage under the regular program also are shown in Table 8-2. The subsidized rates or premiums that are paid for the purchase of flood insurance under the emergency program are as follows:

Type of Structure	Rate per Year per $100 Coverage on Structure*	Rate per Year per $100 Coverage on Contents*
1. Residential	$0.40	$0.50
2. All other	0.50	1.00

*Plus $20.00 annual fee for all policies to defray operating expenses.

TABLE 8-2   Limits of Coverage Available Under the Emergency and Regular Programs

	Emergency Program (First Layer)	Regular Program	
		Second Layer	Total Amount Available
Single family residential:			
Except in Hawaii, Alaska, Guam, and U.S. Virgin Islands	$35,000	$150,000	$185,000
In Hawaii, Alaska, Guam, and Virgin Islands	50,000	150,000[a]	185,000
Other residential:			
Except in Hawaii, Alaska, Guam, and U.S. Virgin Islands	100,000	150,000	250,000
In Hawaii, Alaska, Guam, and Virgin Islands	150,000	150,000[b]	250,000
Small business	100,000	150,000	250,000
Churches and other properties	100,000	100,000	200,000
Contents (per unit):			
Residential	10,000	50,000	60,000
Small Business	100,000	200,000	300,000
Churches, Other Properties	100,000	100,000	200,000

[a]Add to $35,000.
[b]Add to $100,000.
Source: Federal Emergency Management Agency.

These rates are subject to change by the Federal Insurance Administrator. Full actuarial rates vary with the degree of risk, but average much higher than the subsidized rates.

Both the flood hazard boundary map and the FIRMs are prepared at the expense of the federal government, under the direction of the FIA. As of late 1979 over 16,000 communities had been identified by the FIA as having flood hazards. However, as of the same date, only about 10% of those communities were in the regular program.[28]

A community must agree to adopt and enforce minimum regulatory standards for both the emergency and regular programs. Under the emergency program the community must agree to do the following as a minimum for the entire community:

1. Require permits for all construction within the community so that it may determine whether the proposed construction is within the flood prone areas.
2. Review proposed development to assure that all applicable government permits have been obtained.
3. Review all permit applications to determine if proposed building sites are reasonably free from flooding.

If a proposed development is in a flood prone area then the community must also require the following:

1. Adequate design and anchorage to prevent floatation.
2. Use of construction materials and utility equipment resistant to flood damage.
3. Sanitary sewer systems and water systems to be designed to minimize infiltration.
4. Adequate drainage to be provided.
5. Utilities to be located and constructed to minimize flood damage.

Once a community is in the regular program, it must adopt floodplain regulations requiring all new construction and substantial improvements to have the lowest floor, including basement, elevated to or above the 100-year flood level. In this connection, substantial improvements are defined as those costing more than 50% of the market value of the building. If the FIA has defined a floodway, the community must regulate it so as to prevent encroachment upon it such as fill or new construction. In some states, such as New Jersey, all floodplains in the state are required to meet these requirements, whether or not they have entered the regular program of the FIA.

CHANNEL MANAGEMENT

General

This section covers the general case of channel management in urbanizing areas, where the characteristic problems include flood peaks and channel erosion intensified by development, and also the necessity for consideration of environmental values. Channels may be designed or redesigned as part of a comprehensive planning approach; and the interprogram relationships of channel improvement with flood control and stormwater management are covered in Chap. 9.

On navigable rivers and in some urban areas on smaller streams, design and construction of channels and bank protection may be undertaken by the Corps of Engineers or the Soil Conservation Service, in accordance with their respective planning and design criteria. Problems and approaches outlined below pertain mainly to nonfederal intrastate urban channel management on the smaller streams. In such programs channel management may be explicitly recognized as the objective of a definite program, or more frequently, the major drainageways are viewed as public facilities necessary for orderly urban development, as are streets and water supply mains.

Urban streams are commonly subjected to abuse by deposition of trash and debris; and they may experience erosion damage, which requires public action to correct. Therefore, whether or not a community explicitly adopts a channel maintenance and improvement program, it is apt to have some work of this nature.

General Design Criteria

In the past, streams have often been modified to counter increasing flood peaks by straightening and lining natural channels so as to increase their hydraulic capacity. In many cases this has increased velocities sufficiently to increase stream erosion tendencies, has destroyed environmental values of natural streams, and has resulted in hastening floodwaters downstream, to the detriment of downstream flood prone areas. These conditions have led to widespread criticism of the federal agencies concerned, and to a general reassessment of the proper way to design channels.

The straightening and lining of channels should only be undertaken when the downstream effects of such actions have been identified and addressed. Channel straightening and lining should not be permitted if it will result in detrimental effects downstream. Consideration of the effect of such actions on fish life, flood storage, erosion, and other environmental factors should also be a part of the evaluation process.

Drop Structures and Culverts

Increasingly, it is becoming necessary to modify channel characteristics in order to deal with increased erosion tendencies, as explained in Chap. 6. Measures may be desirable to reduce the effective slope of the stream at high stages by means of energy dissipation devices, either drop structures or restricted-size culverts, or even by adding to the stream rock of sufficient size to increase channel roughness and not to be carried away at high stages.

Drop structures consist of a small dam or weir, followed by a stilling basin of sufficient capacity to dissipate hydraulic energy at high stages. An energy dissipating drop structure with stilling basin is shown schematically in Fig. 8-6. Design criteria for stilling basins may be found in standard civil engineering textbooks.

A. L O W   F L O W

B. H I G H   F L O W

Figure 8-6   Typical Stilling Basin

The drop structure, including adjacent banks, must be built of masonry or heavy rock so as to resist erosion. At low stages a deep pool will form, which will be advantageous for fish. However, in residential areas, such a pool may represent a hazard to small children. In such cases, a special design may be used, which will act as an energy dissipator at flood stages, but will allow normal low flows to pass through the drop structure. See Fig. 8-7. An alternate form of energy dissipator allows the flows to cascade down heavy rock. The rock must be of size large enough to dissipate the necessary energy of flood flows. This method can also be applied to a V-shaped channel rather than the flat channel illustrated. See Fig. 8-8. Any of these drop structures can be effective in limiting the progress of channel erosion by reducing the general water surface slope at flood stages.

As indicated in Chap. 6, road culverts and bridges through which small streams pass frequently become inadequate to pass the increased flood flows resulting from urbanization, and consequently form obstructions to passage of flood flows. This results in the creation of what is in effect a very small impound-

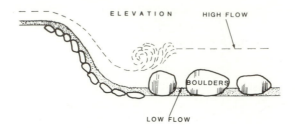

ELEVATION   HIGH FLOW

BOULDERS

LOW FLOW

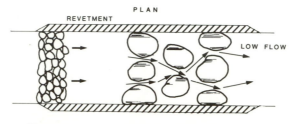

PLAN

REVETMENT

LOW FLOW

Figure 8-7 Special Design Dissipator (No Pool)

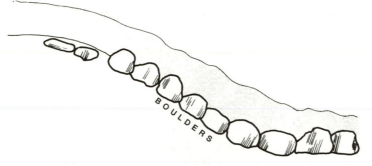

BOULDERS

Figure 8-8 Special Design—B Energy Dissipator

ment, with a deep pool downstream caused by erosion; an energy-dissipating drop structure has been unintentionally created. The usual civil engineering design criterion is that such "inadequate" structures should automatically be replaced by larger structures capable of passing a large flood with only a few inches freeboard. Such an approach can be misguided unless the effects are analyzed. In basins where a large number of existing restricted-sized culverts back up water during floods, the replacement with larger culverts may be seriously damaging, from both flood control and stream erosion viewpoints. Culvert design criteria should favor the use wherever practicable of small-sized culverts, which will back up water during time of flood, and allow part of it to flow over the road. These small culverts can be considered on land other than flat floodplains, except where overflow over heavily traveled roads or other unacceptable damage would result. The flood pool created behind such crossings should not cause damage or problems to upstream property owners. Further, the downstream slope of the crossing should be reinforced to prevent failure when overtopped. Figure 8-9 shows the effect of a restricted-size culvert in reducing flood velocities and limiting the progress of channel erosion.

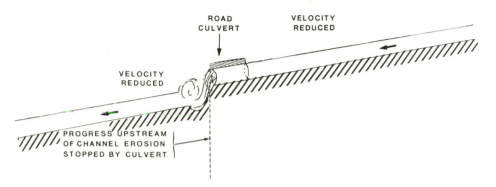

Figure 8-9   Local Effect of Culvert During Flood

Bank Protection

It is now generally considered that structural provisions for bank protection along streams should be held to a minimum, both because of cost and for environmental and aesthetic reasons. Publicly financed bank protection works are usually undertaken where necessary to protect public property, although private property also may be protected, in cases considered by municipal engineers to be of high priority.

More frequently, the protection of private property from eroding banks is considered to be the responsibility of riparian landowners. At times, over-aggressive landowners push heavy fill well out into the stream, forcing the current across to the opposite side and sometimes adversely affecting the flood carrying capacity of the stream, or causing erosion of the opposite bank. Good and bad practices of bank protection are well understood by river engineers; see Figs. 8-10, 8-11, and 8-12. If the erosion power of a stream has been allowed to increase seriously above its stability range, a considerable amount of bank protection will probably be unavoidable. However, it should be held to the minimum essential for protection of valuable property, generally along unstable concave banks. Only where flood damage is extensive, and as part of a carefully engineered flood control plan, should a stream be generally straightened and lined. The preservation of the natural character of a stream is preferable from an environmental viewpoint.

Where it is desired to make riparian landowners responsible for protecting

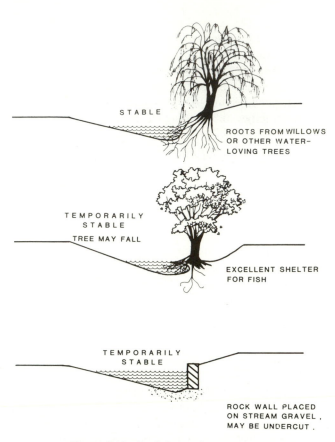

STABLE

ROOTS FROM WILLOWS
OR OTHER WATER-
LOVING TREES

TEMPORARILY
STABLE

TREE MAY FALL

EXCELLENT SHELTER
FOR FISH

TEMPORARILY
STABLE

ROCK WALL PLACED
ON STREAM GRAVEL,
MAY BE UNDERCUT.

Figure 8-10   Bank Protection Measures

their own property, it is desirable to have some form of municipal review and
approval of plans. Such control is necessary in order to avoid some of the
unsatisfactory practices discussed above. This can be accomplished by a properly enforced stream encroachment ordinance.

Channel Design

Several different types of channel can be used depending on the situation.
Grasslined and open, natural channels offer the best opportunities for using
the available space for greenways and pedestrian trails. Critical design criteria
for grasslined channels include a velocity limitation to minimize erosion, a
limitation on side slopes to allow development and maintenance of an adequate
grass cover, provision of a low flow or trickle channel to make maintenance
easier and less costly, and provision of a maintenance access trail. Limiting
velocities are usually in the range of 5 to 7 feet per second depending on the
soil. For highly erodible soils even lower maximum velocities may be necessary.

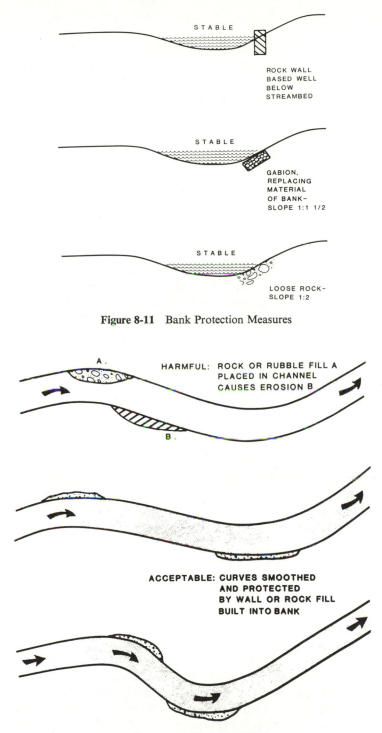

STABLE

ROCK WALL
BASED WELL
BELOW
STREAMBED

STABLE

GABION,
REPLACING
MATERIAL
OF BANK-
SLOPE 1:1 1/2

STABLE

LOOSE ROCK-
SLOPE 1:2

Figure 8-11 Bank Protection Measures

A.

HARMFUL: ROCK OR RUBBLE FILL A
PLACED IN CHANNEL
CAUSES EROSION B

B.

ACCEPTABLE: CURVES SMOOTHED
AND PROTECTED
BY WALL OR ROCK FILL
BUILT INTO BANK

Figure 8-12 Bank Protection Measures

Channel sideslopes should be no steeper than a 1:4 ratio of vertical distance to horizontal distance; grass is difficult to establish on steeper slopes and mowing machines cannot be used on steeper slopes. Maintenance is difficult and expensive if mowing has to be done by hand.

Low Flow Channels

In humid climates generally and in other areas where there is a well-maintained base flow between storms, streams usually maintain natural low flow channels, which are free or almost free of vegetation. Except where slopes are very flat, such channels usually have beds composed of rock, gravel, or other resistant materials. Such channels have practically no tendency for erosion at low or medium flows, except where erodible materials are exposed in the banks.

In semi-arid or arid climates, base flows are smaller, and the banks of a stream are less likely to be protected by vegetation. Under these circumstances, artificial low flow or trickle channels should be used, in order to confine normal base flows and runoff from minor rainfall events to a small protected area. A low flow channel will:

1. Keep the remainder of the channel bottom dry and accessible for routine maintenance, such as mowing and trash removal;
2. Control erosion and meandering caused by small flows; and
3. Minimize sediment deposition.

Several types of trickle channels are:

1. Natural material,
2. Rocklined,
3. Concrete, and
4. Underground pipe.

A general guideline for a semi-arid climate is to design a low flow or trickle channel with a capacity of 0.5 to 1.0% of the design flow for the entire channel. The tradeoff is to keep the size and cost low but to minimize frequency of overtopping.

A low flow channel of natural material is the least expensive type to construct; but it is the most prone to problems and the most difficult to maintain. This type of low flow channel may be desirable in park areas, where a natural look is important for aesthetic reasons. Rocklined low flow channels can be aesthetically pleasing and effective if properly designed. However, they tend to encourage sediment deposition and vegetative growth, which decrease the design capacity and increase maintenance problems. They are also subject to vandalism, either by adults who take the rock for lawns and gardens, or by children who like throwing the rocks into the water. This problem can be discouraged by using rock sized to a minimum of 12 inches.

Concrete low flow channels prevent erosion in the area they cover, prevent vegetative growth, and provide sufficient velocity to minimize deposition. They also allow mowing right up to the edge of the concrete. Concrete low flow channels can be V-shaped, trapezoidal, or rectangular. Design configurations for rectangular and trapezoidal concrete low flow channels are shown in Figs. 8-13 and 8-14. Shallow V-shaped channels have a tendency to suffer erosion at the interface of the concrete and the grasslined channel bottom.

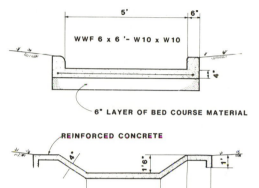

Figure 8-13 Rectangular Concrete Low Flow Channel

Figure 8-14 Design Configuration of Trapezoidal Concrete Low Flow Channel

Combination low flow channels can be installed with a concrete bottom, with rock imbedded in the concrete to form the channel sides. This combination can offer aesthetic advantages, and will also help slow the water near the interface with the grass channel, thus reducing erosion in the area. A design configuration for a rock and concrete combination low flow channel is shown on Fig. 8-15.

Underground low flow pipes can be used when it is desired to keep the entire channel bottom dry under normal weather conditions; but experience

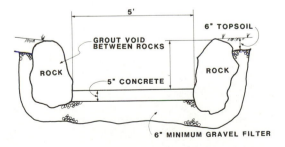

Figure 8-15 Design Configuration of Combination Concrete and Rock Low Flow Channel

with underground pipes has been mixed. One problem is to insure that all low flows get into the pipe. Otherwise marshy, swampy conditions will develop. Another problem is clogging. This can be particularly severe when upstream areas are developing and low flows are heavily laden with sediment. If low flow pipes are used they should meet the following criteria:

1. Minimum diameter—24 in.
2. Minimum velocity—3 fps at a depth of $\frac{1}{2}$ diameter
3. Design capacity—at least 0.5% of 100-year design discharge
4. Access—provide manholes at 300-ft to 500-ft intervals

A common problem with grasslined channels is the delivery of tributary flows to the trickle channel. Too often, tributary flows are released at the top of the major channel and allowed to run down the side of the channel to the bottom. See Fig. 8-16. This causes erosion to the major channel and can also damage the trickle channel or collect water outside the trickle channel. Tributary flows should be delivered to the trickle channel by pipes extending to the trickle channel, or concrete rundowns similar to that shown in Fig. 8-17.

In fine sandy soils, low flow or trickle channels are of questionable value. Experience has indicated that low flow channels in such soils tend to fill with sediment or to wash out during high flows. The dilemma is that a channel designed to carry the 100-year discharge without excessive damage must have a slope limited to keep velocities within acceptable range such as 5 fps or less. For smaller runoff events, velocities may be so low that the low flow will deposit

Figure 8-16 Erosion Caused by Inadequate Rundown

Figure 8-17   Concrete Rundowns Extending to Low Flow Channel

sediment. If the slope is designed to keep the low flow channels self-cleaning, excessively high velocities very likely may occur during flooding events, resulting in significant erosion damage. In fine-grained sandy soils, it is probably best to do without a low flow or trickle channel.

URBAN FLOODPLAIN AND CHANNEL PLANNING

The purpose of this section is to outline some aspects of procedures for planning, through which the objectives and technology discussed in previous sections are to be applied to specific drainage basins. Also, examples are given of planning efforts by the Urban Drainage and Flood Control District of metropolitan Denver. Three stages of planning are covered, as follows:

1. Policy planning stage—drainage criteria manual
2. Framework planning stage—areawide planning
3. Implementation planning stage—master planning

The planning examples are limited to the area of urban floodplains and channels and to local or intrastate regional jurisdictions. They are specific in nature and are not intended to imply that all plans must be developed similarly. On the contrary, agencies involved in planning must define their own needs and tailor their efforts to meet those specific needs.

193

Design and operational criteria are needed for effective planning, implementation, and operation. Criteria provide the basis for consistent planning and design. Without such criteria, designs will vary from project to project depending on the engineer. For example, it is essential to provide maintenance access to all major drainageway improvements. This should be stated in a formal manner, so that an engineer working for a local government or a developer will be aware of the requirement and incorporate it into the design.

Established criteria that are thoughtfully developed and consistent with the goals and objectives of the local government will help insure that plans and designs are workable, that legal constraints are consistently considered, that procedures for estimating rainfall and runoff are consistent from plan to plan, that maintenance access is consistently provided, that standard hydraulic design criteria are consistently met, and so forth. Criteria may be developed for the entire spectrum of urban stormwater management, although criteria documents cited below are limited to floodplains and channels.

The Urban Storm Drainage Criteria Manual[29] was developed by the Denver Regional Council of Governments in 1969 for use in the Denver metropolitan region. It has been adopted and used by all local governments in the region since it was completed in 1969. It has been updated and maintained since 1970 by the Urban Drainage and Flood Control District. The criteria manual contains the following major chapter topics:

Volume I	*Volume II*
Drainage Policy	Major Drainage
Colorado Drainage Law	Hydraulic Structures
Planning	Inlets and Culverts
Rainfall	Storage
Runoff	Irrigation Ditches
Storm Sewers	Floodproofing
Streets	Auxiliary Uses
Stormwater Inlets	

The criteria manual is in the form of two loose leaf volumes. This provides the capability of making changes by exchanging the revised pages. Many criteria manuals have since been developed and adopted throughout the United States, and there are many examples and precedents from which to choose.

For a local government interested in developing and adopting a stormwater management criteria manual, the usual way to proceed is to retain a consulting engineer with demonstrated experience in the urban flood management field. If sufficient staff capability in terms of time and experience is available, a criteria manual could be developed in-house, but generally it will be necessary to hire a consultant. In any event, the staff of the agency for which the criteria manual is being developed must be closely involved in that development.

In some cases, an active program is initiated without time to prepare a formal criteria manual; in this event, criteria from elsewhere should be quickly adapted for the purpose.

Areawide Planning—Framework Planning

Definition of the problems in floodplain areas of a city, county, or region should be accomplished if possible. Such an effort can provide the basic reference material needed to develop priorities, categorize problems, determine and define hydrologic characteristics, and define basin boundaries.

In the case of the Urban Drainage and Flood Control District, the total area was divided into drainage basins having a tributary area of 1000 to 3000 acres and limited by natural watershed boundaries, or by physical features such as roads or railroads that restrict runoff during major storms. The size of the area included in a basin took building density into account, allowing larger basins to be used in rural areas.

Standard U.S. Geological Survey $7\frac{1}{2}$-minute quandrangle maps were used to portray the information because of their availability, convenient scale, and detail of existing physical features. The entire region of evaluation, about 1200 square miles, was shown on a total of 27 maps. The maps were reproduced at both the original scale and a reduced scale.

To facilitate collection and correlation of drainage basin information, and to provide for an orderly system of identifying, indexing, and retrieving data, a numbering scheme for major drainage channels, tributary basins, and sub-basins was developed for the region in the example. Narrative descriptions were prepared for each of 398 drainage basins identified in the study. The information developed was presented as shown on Table 8-3.

The maps have been used as part of a regional flood hazard information system, used to locate flooding problems, and used by local governments and the public in defining and illustrating problems. The basic information has also been of use to public agencies, developers, and consultants as input to hydrologic studies. A good information base is a necessary part of a sound floodplain and channel management program.

Master Planning—Implementation Planning

Master planning for floodplains and channels is valuable for a coordinated approach to flood hazard mitigation. It provides a systematic procedure to develop the hydrology, to define the nature and extent of flooding problems, to identify solutions to the flooding problems, to analyze benefits and costs of the various available solutions, and to formalize the adoption and presentation of a selected plan. A good master plan will provide a blueprint for solving existing problems and for preventing future problems. Thus planning for major drainageways is a mix of remedial and preventive considerations. This level of

TABLE 8-3   Summary of Sub-basin Information

5400—Little Dry Creek	1-05-5400-01
Major Basin	*Sub-basin Number*
June 1971	Little Dry Creek
Date Prepared, Revisions	*Tributary Basin*
27—Highlands Ranch, 21—Englewood	
Mapping Number/Name	
Cherry Hills Village, Greenwood Village, Englewood, Arapahoe Co.	
City/County	

A	4.96	sq. miles	CT	0.34	Slope	0.006
L	6.47	miles	CP	0.46	Population Density	0.03–11.15
LCA	4.02	miles	PERV	65 %		

Land Use Index   2.20–4.42

Basin/Floodplain Development Status	Classification	B
Development Residential, commercial		
Boundaries Natural contours		
Features Downtown Englewood, Cinderella City		
Problems High value commercial development in low areas		

Channel Status	Classification	B
Definition Poorly defined		
Capability Poor		
Structures Bridges at University Blvd. and Quincy Ave. inadequate		
Inadequate culverts		

Drainage and Flood Control Information
Master Plan

Other Reports/Studies   Sellards & Grigg, Inc. Storm Drainage Plan for Englewood, Jan. 1971 and FPI—Vol. IV, Oct. 1968

Improvements   Channel improved on downstream end

Floodplain Status   Developed heavily near mouth

Flood History   3 major floods since 1903

Remarks: Corps of Engineers Report Vol. I, Oct. 1963 of the S. Platte River covers the mouth of this basin. Englewood Dam helps control flooding in this basin but status is uncertain. S. Platte River channel improvement under consideration from Chatfield Dam to Denver City limits. Denver priority #18.

planning is oriented toward a specific problem area, a major drainageway and tributaries, and emphasizes specific solutions and recommendations.

Master planning for floodplains and channels must be performed in a systematic manner. All governmental entities with jurisdictional control along the drainageway must be involved, and the entire drainageway should be included. In many areas, the problems are multijurisdictional. For these cases multijurisdictional understandings and/or agreements must be reached regarding the objectives of a master planning effort, the coordination of the study, how the study will be conducted, and the method of financing the study. In some areas there may be a regional agency that can coordinate multijurisdictional master planning efforts. Where several incorporated areas are involved but include only one county, the effort could be coordinated by the county. In other areas it may be necessary for the individual local governments to develop a special means of coordinating the master planning effort.

A systematic procedure for conducting a master planning effort is important because it will provide the basis for defining the scope of work. The local governments should know what they want done before going to a consulting engineer for proposals to do the work. If the effort is to be conducted with in-house staff, a well-defined process is still needed to give the study direction.

A master planning process is shown schematically in Fig. 8-18. The primary areas of effort and the basic sequence of the process are to acquire and develop facts, to determine present and future runoff and basin problems, to identify major drainage concepts, to select a plan, and to prepare a master plan or preliminary design. Each one of these primary areas of effort consists of several sequential activities shown in Fig. 8-18. The steps shown are illustrative, and are not meant to imply that this exact procedure must be followed. The steps appropriate for any given area should be designed to fit the local situation.

For the planning process set forth in Fig. 8-18, the outputs include: an interim report summarizing problems, outlining feasible solutions or approaches, evaluating the costs and benefits of the feasible approaches, and a recommended structural plan; a flood hazard area delineation report; a report consisting of a preliminary design of the master plan and written documentation supporting the plan; and a report containing all backup calculations including hydrologic and hydraulic calculations and benefit and cost analyses. The flood hazard area delineation report was discussed previously in this chapter.

The third major area of effort, called "Identify Major Drainage Concepts" in Fig. 8-18 consists of identification of solutions to the problem, evaluation of those solutions, development of a recommended approach, and preparation of an interim report that includes a recommended plan. Approaches that should be given consideration, in addition to floodplain regulation, may include some or all of the following:

1. Maintaining the existing configuration.
2. A natural type waterway (where feasible) following the general historic channel determined from old aerial photographs, old mapping, and from local records.
3. The installation of major underground conduits along the general course of the historic stream channel, using local right-of-way whenever possible.

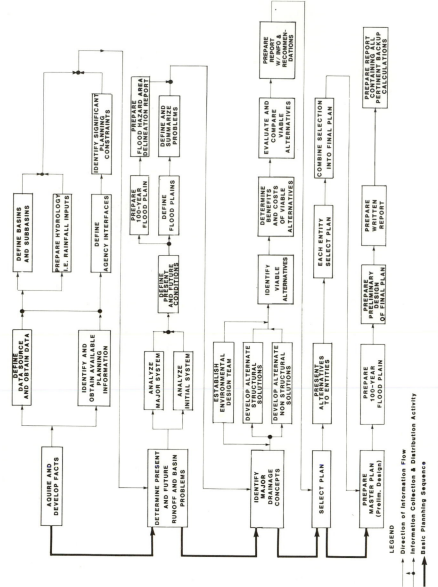

Figure 8-18   Steps in Master Planning for Urban Floodplains and Channels

4. The use of lined flood channels in order to reduce right-of-way requirements.

5. Selected or limited structure improvements or additions (culverts, bridges, irrigation crossings, etc.) and channel improvements (realignment, erosion control, low flow protection, maintenance access, velocity control, etc.).

6. Acquisition of flood prone properties and relocation of occupants.

7. Nonstructural methods such as flash flood warning, flood insurance, evacuation plans, etc.

8. Relocating channel to other than historic routes.

9. Other.

The operation and maintenance aspects of each of the best alternate plans should consider the following:

1. Erosion control,

2. Removal of debris,

3. Repair of structures,

4. Shoaling of channel,

5. Reseeding and planting of grassed areas,

6. Bank stabilization,

7. Rip rap, and

8. Access to entire length of drainageway.

The plan selected will usually consist of a mix of structural and nonstructural solutions.

Following completion of the interim report, the local governments involved must arrive at a selected plan by whatever process is consistent with local policy, the fourth major area of activity. This may consist of public hearings, neighborhood meetings, or review sessions with the local governing body. The final plan will very likely vary from the plan recommended in the interim report. The fifth major area of activity consists of preparing the preliminary design and final report for the selected plan.

Following formal adoption of a plan, steps must be taken to determine phases of the program and annual budgets, and to initiate final planning and design of individual projects.

Use of Consultants

When master plan studies or criteria studies are to be conducted by engineering consultants under contract to local government, a difficult task for the local government is the preparation of a scope of work. A thorough and complete scope of work is necessary, because it is the basis for defining the work to be done by the engineer. If it is well defined, then it is easier to reach a fair price for the work to be performed, and both the local government and consultant will have a common understanding of what is to be done and what is to be accomplished. The scope of work should be prepared by the local government even before the procedure is initiated to select an engineer. This can be an onerous task, but the local government must first understand what it wants done before it starts to find an engineer to do the work. Sometimes, a preliminary contract is let to prepare the scope of work.

Program Interfaces

Urban floodplain and channel planning may have important interrelationships with existing or proposed flood control developments, and with the nature of stormwater management required of land developers upstream from potential drainage centers. These program interfaces are covered in the next chapter.

NOTES—CHAPTER 8

1. "A Unified Program for Floodplain Management," U.S. Water Resources Council, Washington, D.C., Sept. 1979, p. III–3.

2. Water Resources Council 1979, p. IV–1.

3. "Regulation of Flood Hazard Areas to Reduce Flood Losses," Vol. 1 Pts. I–IV and Vol. 2 Pts. V–VI, U.S. Water Resources Council, 2120 L. St., N.W., Washington, D.C. 20037.

4. "A Perspective on Flood Plain Regulations for Flood Plain Management," U.S. Army Corps of Engineers, Office of the Chief, Washington, D.C. 20314, June 1976.

5. "Guide for Ordinance Development," Community Assistance Series No. 1(d) National Flood Insurance Program, Federal Emergency Management Agency, 451 7th St., S.W., Washington, D.C. 20410, June 1978.

6. John R. Sheaffer, "Introduction to Flood Proofing," Center for Urban Studies, University of Chicago, Chicago, Ill., April 1967.

7. William K. Johnson, "Physical and Economic Feasibility of Nonstructural Flood Plain Management Measures," the Hydrologic Engineering Center, U.S. Army Corps of Engineers, March 1978.

8. Charles M. Anderson et al., "Manual for the Construction of Residential Basements in Non-Coastal Flood Environs.," National Association of Homebuilders Research Foundation, Inc., July 1975.

9. "Elevated Residential Structures," Federal Insurance Administration, U.S. Department of Housing and Urban Development, 1977.

10. John G. Carling et al., "Handbook of Flood-Resistant Construction Specifications," Pennsylvania Department of Community Affairs, Dec. 1976.

11. "Flood Proofing: Example of Raising a Private Residence," Technical Services Report, South Atlantic Division, U.S. Army Corps of Engineers, March 1977.

12. Richard D. Black, "Flood Proofing Rural Residences," Department of Agricultural Engineering, Cornell University, May 1975.

13. "State Comprehensive Emergency Management; National Governor's Association," U.S. Government Printing Office, Washington, D.C., 1978.

14. "Flood Forecast and Warning System Evaluation," National Weather Service, Susquehanna River Basin, New York, Pennsylvania, and Maryland, 1979.

15. "Second Conference on Flash Floods," American Meteorological Society, 45 Beacon St., Boston, Mass. 02108, March 1980.

16. William G. Gay and William W. Chenault, "Improving Your Community's Emergency Response—An Introduction to Disaster Planning," Defense Civil Preparedness Agency, Human Sciences Research, Inc., McLean, Va., Nov. 1973.

17. "Disaster Preparedness Checklist," U.S. Department of Commerce, Federal Disaster Assistance Administration, Dec. 1974.

18. "Disaster Operations, A Handbook for Local Governments," U.S. Department of Defense, Defense Civil Preparedness Agency, June 1972.

19. "Standards for Civil Preparedness—Summary for Public Officials," U.S. Department of Defense, Defense Civil Preparedness Agency, Dec. 1972.

20. George P. Wessman, "Flash Flood Warnings—Federal Plus Local Action," Natural Hazards Observer, 1978.

21. James H. Owen, "Guide for Flood and Flash Flood Preparedness Planning," National Oceanic and Atmospheric Administration, National Weather Service, April 1976.

22. "Planning Guide, Self-Help Flood Forecast and Warning System," Swatara Creek Watershed Pa., Susquehanna River Basin Commission, Mechanicsburg, Pa., Nov. 1976.

23. "Neighborhood Flash Flood Warning Program Manual," Susquehanna River Basin Commission, Mechanicsburg, Pa., Oct. 14, 1976.

24. "A Description of a Conceptual Model of a Total Readiness System for Disaster," Commonwealth of Massachusetts, System Element II (The Warning System), Civil Defense Agency and Office of Emergency Preparedness.

25. "Handbook of State and Federal Officials," Federal Disaster Assistance Administration, Dec. 1973.

26. H. M. Mogil and H. G. Groper, "NWS's Severe Local Storm Warning and Disaster Preparedness Programs," *Bull. Amer. Meteor. Soc.*, 58, 1977.

27. "Flash Flood Handbook," State Council of Civil Defense, Commonwealth of Pennsylvania, 1978.

28. Rutherford H. Platt and George M. McMullen, "Post-Flood Recovery and Hazard Mitigation: Lessons from the Massachusetts, February 1978," Water Resources Research Center, University of Massachusetts, Amherst, Mass., May 1980.

29. "Urban Storm Drainage Criteria Manual," Vols. I and II, prepared by Wright-McLaughlin Engineers, Urban Drainage and Flood Control District, Denver, Colo., 1969.

9

General Planning and Management Aspects

WILLIAM WHIPPLE

L. SCOTT TUCKER

GENERAL

Stormwater and floodplain management are not separate fields, they have interfaces with each other, with long-established federal activities, and with municipal activities in land use control, environmental improvement, and public health. These interfaces are real and important; but they are poorly reflected in existing institutional arrangements, either for planning or for financing. As outlined in Chap. 2, each federal program is administered by an executive agency, under budgets and authorization controlled by the designated congressional committees. However, there has been very little federal influence over local or state channel and stormwater management programs. Even the Soil Conservation Service, with its widespread and effective network of conservation districts, can only work within the functional limits prescribed by its authorizing legislation and appropriations; and it acts only very cautiously to influence the programs of states and substate bodies.

Naturally, intelligent and conscientious individuals in various agencies, both federal and state, make sporadic efforts to reconcile and adjust governmental actions perceived to be deficient or conflicting; but the interface problems between different agencies and levels of government in stormwater management remain extremely serious. Some of these important problems are discussed in this chapter.

FEDERAL COMPREHENSIVE APPROACHES

General Planning

A Water Resources Council report[1] categorized planning programs in terms of the areas addressed. *Multi-sectorial planning* is defined as coordinated planning for all sectors of public endeavor, such as land use, housing, transportation, and water resources. *Sectorial planning* is integrated planning within one sector, such as water resources. In this sector, planning may be integrated for such programs as flood control, water supply, and hydroelectric power. This is what has traditionally been known as comprehensive river basin planning. *Functional planning* is directed to meet needs within one function, such as urban floodplain management within the water resources sector.

The stages of planning are also distinguished by levels. Policy planning, for example, involves the definition of overall goals and program objectives, policy development, overall budget and priority analysis, dissemination of program guidelines, and evaluation of results. *Framework planning* involves the identification of general problems and needs, outlining a range of possible alternate futures, inventory of available resources and general opportunities, assessment of overall adequacy of resources, and determination of need for further specific investigations. The next level of planning in terms of specificity is *general appraisal planning*, which attempts to evaluate alternative measures for meeting proposed goals and objectives. It should include recommendations for action plans and programs for specific units of governments. For example, Level B planning under the Water Resources Council is general appraisal planning. Finally, *implementation planning* includes investigations of specific structural or nonstructural measures or systems of measures, in sufficient detail to determine their feasibility, including determination whether it would be physically and politically possible to implement the plan and potentially possible to finance the plan. The most common example is project planning.

River Basin Planning

Comprehensive planning of river basins is an approach through which, about a generation ago, it was felt that all water problems could be resolved; but current expectations are much more modest. In principle, it has been possible to study all of the alternatives in flood hazard mitigation by means of a Level B comprehensive plan, under Water Resources Council guidelines or by the planning of a single federal agency. At times, some of the issues have been treated in this way. However, the political weakness of the Water Resources Council and the hybrid nature of our institutional arrangements—federal, state, and local—has greatly limited such an approach. The federal agencies which, in practice, have conducted such studies have no responsibility for stormwater management and for channel improvement on the smaller streams, which are controlled locally; and the criteria for floodplains is established nationwide by federal regulation, and cannot be modified by processes of regional or river basin planning as they have existed. For these reasons, comprehensive river basin planning has not been effective in solving problems within the different flood management programs.

Section 208 Planning and Best Management Practices

In the areawide water quality planning under Section 208 P. L. 92-500 (now known as the Clean Water Act), starting in 1975, a nationwide effort was launched to develop broad-based plans for water quality and related matters, prepared at the local level. Initially, heavy funding and technical support was given by the U.S. Environmental Protection Agency. Some of the first-year plans suggested innovative approaches to modeling flood control and water quality objectives into a combined stormwater management program. However, in later phases the support was greatly reduced and the scope narrowed.

The mechanism for implementing such a program was intended to be the designation of "best management practice" (BMP), which would be adopted areawide for general application. This type of approach implicitly assumes that the BMP in question is properly suited for general areawide application, rather than being subject to determination on a local or site specific basis. It also makes the implicit assumption, which is often very questionable, that the planning body making the designation has the authority (and sufficient funding resources) to insure that the BMP will actually be utilized.

It does not now appear likely that this type of planning will be the vehicle for major progress in stormwater management in most areas. However, the problems and possible solutions discussed below will be the same whether or not approached through Section 208 planning, and whether or not the term BMP is adopted for preferred or mandated design criteria.

PROGRAM INTERFACES

Floodplain Management

The physical objective of the federal floodplain management program is quite clear; it is to minimize the impact of future flood damages within the defined flood hazard area, which corresponds to the area flooded by a design flood statistically predicted to be equalled or exceeded once in 100 years. The prediction of a design flood is based upon the historic record of past floods in the area in question, with an implicit assumption that a flood cycle similar to that of the past will be repeated in the future. In fully urbanized areas, this assumption is quite a reasonable one. However, in areas that are largely undeveloped, it is not reasonable at all. As shown in Chap. 3, peak flood discharges are usually greatly increased by processes of urbanization; so that a flood hazard area outlined by the usual criteria may turn out later to be seriously inadequate in extent. Existing federal guidelines allow intensive urban development just outside the designated flood hazard line, and also within that line, elevated just above the level of a predicted 100-year frequency flood. If, due to urbanization, higher floods occur, all of this carefully located development may be innundated.

In principle, the choice of a 100-year design flood for floodplain management purposes is probably better than any other arbitrary standard available. This was one of the conclusions of the National Science Foundation Flood Hazard Mitigation Study.[2] However, for best results, the designation of a flood hazard area should take into account:

1. Future changes in hydrology and increases in flood heights due to urbanization.
2. Extent and character of present and future stormwater management programs.
3. Any changes in sizes and characteristics of floods to be brought about by structural flood control, or by soil and water conservation programs.

Stormwater Management

If a watershed is to be subject to future urbanization, the increased flooding tendencies can be countered to some extent by stormwater management, as brought out in Chap. 7, rather than by total reliance upon remedial flood control measures. An example is the program of the Albuquerque Metropolitan Arroyo Flood Control Authority, which has the sole purpose of protecting the valley floors from flooding.[3]

The effectiveness of different stormwater management criteria in controlling flood discharges varies greatly, some criteria being effective only locally on very small watersheds, while others are more effective when applied to the watersheds of larger streams. In any case, stormwater management does not materially reduce the total volume of the flood wave; so that, for rivers, the initial assumption should be that flood peaks will be increased by any future development. If sound stormwater management practices are not adopted, the future flood peaks will be even higher. Even though criteria designed from a purely local viewpoint might require detention of stormwaters for only a few hours, interests of communities downstream are served by requiring longer periods of detention for at least part of the runoff. Therefore, county and state interests favor retaining some influence over local stormwater management criteria.

The long term effectiveness of stormwater management practices must also be considered. Onsite detention facilities that are not maintained or monitored by public agencies are likely to become ineffective over a period of time. If safety in downstream floodplains depends on such facilities being fully effective, then long-term inspection and maintenance programs must be developed by the responsible public agency, which is, practically without exception, a unit of local government.

Reservoir Flood Control

Reservoir flood control has long suffered from a major inherent defect; the general reduction in peak flood stages which it brings about has usually resulted in a further invasion of the floodplain by new developments, thus creating at a lower elevation a new set of damage prone properties, similar to the original damage prone properties which the reservoir was designed to protect. In such a case, there is a negative component of flood control effects, called project-induced damages, meaning flood damages to property which would not have been located in the flood hazard area except for the illusory impression of protection created by the project. It is for this reason that many analysts have concluded that no more federal flood control reservoirs should be built without a concurrent requirement for floodplain regulation downstream.

This is a matter of federal policy, which is implemented in some cases by the Corps of Engineers; but for general application it would require a basic decision to be mandated by Congress.

Substate Flood Control and Channel Programs

As regards the planning of substate level flood control programs, some exceptionally complex issues arise, particularly those concerning the basis for design and the economics of a hybrid federal/state/local flood hazard mitigation system. In the first place, it is practically a fixed rule for nonfederal managers to avoid spending nonfederal money for any purpose for which federal funds are obtainable. Therefore, one must assume that any substate level flood control program, whether regional, county, or municipal, will exclude projects that are likely to be funded by the Corps of Engineers, the Soil Conservation Service, or other federal construction agencies.

The most common type of improvement in such substate programs is erosion control of channels and banks. This type of work is often included in federal programs, particularly on large rivers; but if not specifically authorized as part of a federal program, there are no major federal programs either to compensate property owners for the losses, or to contribute financially to the costs of the remedial work. For this reason, the planning agency can apply a traditional balance of benefits against costs, from its own accounting stance (using Water Resources Council terminology). This approach is conceptually simple, even though estimates of benefits may be difficult to make.

One alternative approach to erosion control, that of leaving it to each property owner to protect his own property, is often adopted, usually by default. However, as shown in Chap. 8, unless some public agency reviews and approves the plans, the result may be a hodgepodge of poorly designed and impermanent bank protection structures, which may cause erosion to neighbors downstream, worse than what the structure was designed to protect against.

For engineering reasons, bank and channel erosion control are often undertaken as part of a general channel improvement program, which includes increasing the capacity of the channel to accommodate larger flood discharges without damaging overflows. The Los Angeles County Flood Control District has perhaps the largest channel improvement program of any metropolitan area; but it also needs structures to reduce flood flows. Such channel programs raise some difficult policy problems. The question as to the design criteria to be adopted for general channel improvement is particularly complex.

Assuming that the environmental issue has been faced, as described in Chap. 8, and that it has been decided that channel flood capacity is to be increased, the question is "How much?" Unlike levees, channel improvements help to reduce the damaging overbank flow of floods of all sizes, including those larger than that for which the works were designed. Therefore, if a channel which originally carried a 2-year flood at bankfull stage is improved so as to pass (say) a 20-year frequency flood at bankfull stage, it will also greatly reduce the overbank flow of a 100-year flood.

An attempt might be made to optimize the choice of design criteria for a channel improvement by considering the incremental benefits to be obtained by a further degree of improvement. However, a difficult policy question must be faced. Increasingly, properties in flood hazard areas are covered by subsidized federal flood insurance, and even those losses not covered are often reimbursed by federal flood relief. If property is so covered, the federal government compensates for flood losses suffered, within the limits of coverage. Therefore, a locally financed improvement which has the effect of reducing such losses would not create a corresponding financial benefit to the community locally. From an economic viewpoint, the decision in such cases should be made in the national interest (from a national accounting stance, to use the definition of the Water Resource Council). However, although most local governments are not yet sufficiently familiar with the flood insurance program to reduce local support on this account, no one should be surprised if sooner or later the availability of heavily subsidized flood insurance comes to act as a disincentive to local attempts to reduce the damages.

In all cases, it must be borne in mind that channel improvements, which hasten the flood discharges on their way, always tend to increase flood discharges downstream. This may or may not create unacceptable flood damages, depending upon the circumstances. The state should exercise sufficient control over channel improvement by substate entities to make sure that downstream interests are adequately protected.

Practical constraints often control the design of channel improvements. For example, for crossings of major highways, policy generally favors providing channel capacity equal to 100-year discharge. The special inconvenience and hazards due to any interruption of vehicle traffic on major highways are in this case controlling factors.

In most cases, channel improvements of less than 100-year flood capacity must be considered; and a variety of different aspects may influence the design criteria. For example, if channels are designed of much lesser capacity than the 100-year peak flood discharge, encroachment might be encouraged within the floodplain, based upon the illusory public perception that protection had been provided. On the other hand, channel improvements of lesser capacity may be more satisfactory from an environmental viewpoint, and more justifiable economically. Some of these problems will be simplified if the floodplain management program and the channel improvement are approached in an integrated planning effort.

In summary, there can be no simple generally preferable standard of channel improvement capacity, nor is there a definitely established methodology for determining optimum channel capacity on a site specific basis. This appears to be one of the fields of engineering where empirical methods of decision making are unavoidable.

INTRASTATE PLANNING

State Legislation

Broad planning approaches, going beyond the limits of a single program, are recognized by some states to be so important that state law requires master plans to be completed by local government. Pennsylvania passed a Stormwater Management Act in 1978 which requires each county to "prepare and adopt a watershed stormwater management plan for each watershed located in the county as designated by the department."[4] Each plan is to include at the minimum the following:

1. Survey of existing runoff characteristics,
2. Survey of existing obstructions,
3. Assessment of projected and alternative land development patterns and the potential impact on runoff quantity and quality,
4. Analysis of present and projected development in flood hazard areas and its sensitivity to damages from future flooding,
5. Survey of existing damage problems and proposed solutions,
6. Review of existing and proposed stormwater collection systems and their impacts,
7. Assessment of alternative runoff control techniques,
8. Identification of existing and proposed flood control projects,
9. Designation of areas to be served by storm water facilities within 10 years, and who will construct and operate the facilities,
10. Identification of the floodplains within the watershed,
11. Development of criteria and standards,
12. Establishment of priorities for implementation of action within each plan, and
13. Setting forth provisions for periodically reviewing and updating the plan.

Another state that requires the preparation of master plans is Maryland. A Maryland law provides that the state, in cooperation with local governments, "shall conduct studies of the watersheds, which studies shall define as a minimum (1) the existing magnitude and frequency of flood events, (2) the magnitude and frequency of flood events based on planned development, and (3) alternative management techniques according to their effectiveness in controlling floods and minimizing flood damage."[5] Local governments are required by Maryland law to "prepare a flood management plan based on an evaluation of the alternative management techniques and other findings" including the watershed studies conducted by the state. The statutes list management techniques that may be included in the local government planning process which are:

1. Flood control laws,
2. Levees and dikes,
3. Stormwater detention or retention structures,
4. Flood warning systems,
5. Public acquisition,
6. Floodproofing,
7. Storm drain and stream maintenance,
8. Tax adjustment policies,
9. Subdivisions, zoning, and related ordinances, and
10. Other practical methods.

Planning of this broad scope can be very valuable for solving the interface problems outlined earlier in this chapter. However, as was the case with Section 208 planning, conceptually sound planning approaches may fail to achieve their potential if continued funding and available expertise are not sufficient. Information on institutional aspects of stormwater management in various parts of the United States is contained in a recent report.[6]

Planning and Public Participation

There is a tendency for public bodies, at all levels of government, to short-circuit the planning process in order to "get on with the work." Within recent years, some long and, at times, inordinate delays have resulted from the necessity of considering a multiplicity of views from various persons, particularly as regards environmental aspects. However, it is better to face these problems squarely and openly in order to be sure that all legitimate interests have been properly considered. Consideration of national agency goals and of technical aspects is essential; but it is not enough. If a reasonable amount of public participation is provided for, public support for the program will be easier to maintain. A single federal agency, operating within its budget and the terms of its authorizing acts, cannot possibly forsee how its decisions will affect the plans of local governments and the desires of many interested groups of individuals. Selection of criteria for application areawide, whether or not designated as BMP, should be sufficiently flexible to allow for legitimate site specific and other local differences. The Soil Conservation Service provides an excellent example of how this can be done, acting through locally based conservation districts, with technical support from the federal agency. Some of the public participation activities of other federal agencies have been very superficial by comparison.

Implementation of flood management programs requires financing. As indicated above, some programs, including major flood control works, are federally funded; and federal financing is beyond the scope of this book. Also, as indicated in Chaps. 7 and 8, many stormwater management and floodplain management programs are paid for mainly by developers. However, even for these programs, there may be considerable nonfederal costs; including such items as planning, subdivision regulations, enforcement of building codes, information and education efforts, and sometimes maintenance of facilities constructed at the cost of federal agencies, private interests, or local agencies. Other aspects of flood management must be paid for mainly or entirely by state or local entities. It is to the field of such nonfederal financing that this section is addressed.

Financing needs can be categorized into two basic areas: (1) existing development, or problems needing remedial treatment, and (2) new development, or situations offering the opportunity to prevent problems. Some practices for financing flood management projects are listed in Table 9-1. These

TABLE 9-1 Methods of Financing Floodplain
and Channel Management Projects

Development Status	Source of Funds
Existing developments	General tax fund
	Special assessments
	Service charges or fees
	Federal or state assistance
	Bonds
	Private funds
New developments	Developer fees
	Developer provided facilities
	Dedications
	Floodplain regulation

financing methods are discussed in this section from the point of view of local government.

General Tax Revenues

All local governments have basic tax revenues to support their operations including property taxes, sales taxes, fees, licenses, etc. There is always considerable competition for these funds; and it is difficult to obtain large amounts of monies for capital projects from general fund revenues. When flooding problems exist on major drainageways in developed areas, structural improvements are expensive, and right-of-way is costly, as are engineering and construction. Consequently, general tax revenues are not good sources of funding for flood management projects requiring large capital outlays. There are exceptions, however. For example, a portion of a sales tax can be committed to capital projects including floodplain and channel management projects. Also, general tax revenues are generally the only source of funds available for planning, plan review, inspection, mapping, and similar activities. Maintenance of facilities is also usually a general tax revenue funded activity.

Special Assessments

A special assessment is a compulsory charge on selected properties for an identified improvement which benefits the owners of the selected properties and which is undertaken in the interest of the public.[7] Special assessment projects may be undertaken by general purpose local governments or special purpose districts. The authority for local governments to levy special assessments is derived from the state. Consequently, special assessment statutory requirements vary from state to state, and even from city to city depending on city charters.

Special assessments can in general be initiated in one of three ways. The first is by local government legislative body (council, commissioners, aldermen, etc.) action with consent of the property owners, usually expressed in the form of a petition. This is the most common means of initiating a special assessment. A second way is by local government legislative body action which may be stopped only by opposing petition or remonstrance. A third way is by local government legislative action without the consent of the subject property owners and not subject to remonstrance. Usually a public hearing is required before an assessment is confirmed; and a preliminary hearing is held before a project is approved.

The basis for assessment is usually spelled out mathematically to indicate benefit, such as front footage, lot area, etc. The benefit provides the foundation for levying a special assessment on owners of property in the assessed district. The amounts assessed must be proportional to the benefits received and must not exceed the cost of the project, and the total amount assessed must not exceed the total benefit resulting from the project. Determining an assessment that is related to benefit poses two problems. One is determining specifically who benefits, and the second is determining the amount of special benefit to be received by each property owner.

Because of rather general statements of principles in enabling legislation, much has been left to the interpretation of courts. In Colorado, for example, the State Supreme Court has defined the basis for an assessment as follows:

1. Irrespective of the method of apportionment, all special assessments are fundamentally and basically founded upon special benefits without which they cannot stand; and

2. The amount of assessment cannot exceed the value of the special benefit.

The court, however, did not define special benefit, and for drainage and flood control this has posed problems. In the absence of legislative definition, the final decision rests with courts if the assessment is challenged. Because of the limiting definition of benefits accepted by the courts, the state legislature in Colorado adopted the following definition of benefits:[8]

"Determination of special benefits—factors considered. (1) The term 'benefit,' for the purposes of assessing a particular property within a drainage system improvement district, includes, but is not limited to, the following:

(a) Any increase in the market value of the property;

(b) The provision for accepting the burden from specific dominant property for discharging surface water onto servient property in a manner or quantity greater than would naturally flow because the dominant owner made some of his property impermeable;

(c) Any adaptability of property to a superior or more profitable use;

(d) Any alleviation of health and sanitation hazards accruing to particular property or accruing to public property in the improvement district, if the provision of health and sanitation is paid for wholly or partially out of funds derived from taxation of property owners of the improvement district;

(e) Any reduction in the maintenance costs of particular property or of public property in the improvement district, if the maintenance of the public property is paid for wholly or partially out of funds derived from taxation of property owners of the improvement district;

(f) Any increase in convenience or reduction in inconvenience accruing to particular property owners, including the facilitation of access to and travel over streets, roads, and highways;

(g) Recreational improvements accruing to particular property owners as a direct result of drainage improvement."

Even with this rather inclusive list, there is still the difficulty of determining and assigning numerical values to the benefits to each property.

The approach of the City of Bellevue, Washington, for the financing of stormwater runoff management is interesting. Traditionally, the management of stormwater has been a "free" service of local governments, with the costs being borne by the taxpayers as a whole. However, the City of Bellevue decided to approach the management and disposal of stormwater as a "utility service" to the owners of the land from which the stormwaters flow. For this service, a utility fee commensurate with the value of the service provided is demanded and received. The municipal government is very careful to define the stormwater charges as a utility service fee and not a tax. This makes it possible to demand payment from all landowners, public and private, from whose property stormwaters flow. This includes traditionally nontaxable institutions such as churches and colleges, and even includes the State Highway Department for their roads and the City of Bellevue itself. This type of funding was made possible by a state enabling law.

Service Charges or Fees

Service charges or fees should be distinguished from general fund taxes and special assessments because of the different legal requirements placed on each. Service charges or fees are generally used to defray the costs incurred for particular services rendered. It is important in a service charge to provide some tangible service or commodity. Also, there should be a relation between the charges imposed and value of the services received, and a commitment to use the fees collected for the provision and/or maintenance of a particular service. Common examples of service charges are fees paid for water and sewer services, parking, use of toll roads, and use of parks.

Service charges or fees are not widely used to finance flood management programs, but they are becoming more common because of increased competition for limited general fund tax dollars. The fee should be related to the flood management service provided, the most common basis being area of impervious surface. There are exceptions; Aurora, Colorado, for example, has a drainage fee that is related to the size of the water service line. While this method of determining the fee does not appear to be related to the service, it has worked in Aurora for a number of years.

In New Jersey, substantial fees are beginning to be imposed for the review by the municipality of the developer's plans for stormwater management and drainage. In one case, an initial deposit of $1,500 is required for each development, which may be partially refunded if the actual costs of the review are less than this amount. However, it is more common for fees to be nominal, the costs of a detailed engineering review being borne by the general revenues.

Service charges have been adopted by both large and small cities. Denver, with a population of about 500,000, has a drainage fee that involves billing each individual property in the city. Boulder, Colorado, with a population of about 80,000, also has a drainage fee. In the case of Boulder the drainage fee supports a drainage utility. Drainage fees can also be used to finance revenue bonds. Some disadvantages of service charges include the need to obtain large amounts of detailed data about the location and size of properties and their impervious areas, the need for a system to bill each individual property, and the resistance of many property owners, particularly those who live uphill and do not have drainage and flood control problems. Uphill property owners may not have flood problems; but they do send additional runoff waters downhill, exacerbating downstream flood problems.

Bonds

Bonds are not an additional source of revenue, because they create an equivalent liability which must be met from future revenues. Bonds do permit an entity to borrow against future revenues in order to develop sufficient capital to finance a public works improvement. General criteria to justify a bonding approach are to:

1. Provide the capital requirements of a self-supporting enterprise such as water and sewer.
2. Provide capital for projects costly in terms of entity's fiscal resources.
3. Provide capital for projects with long utility.
4. Provide capital for projects that reoccur infrequently.

Flood management projects meet the criteria well, except for the first one, as they are not revenue producers. Bonding is a popular method of developing capital for flood management projects.

There are two basic types of bonds, the general obligation (GO) bond and the revenue bond. General obligation bonds are guaranteed by the full faith and credit of the issuing entity. They may actually be repaid from a fee type revenue source; but if there were ever to be insufficient revenues the entity would have to use general tax revenues to pay the interest and principal. The revenue bond is paid solely from earnings of the project for which the funding was provided, and is not guaranteed by the full faith and credit of the issuing agency. The advantage of GO bonds is that the interest rate is lower. A GO bond generally has to be approved by a vote, whereas revenue bonds frequently do not. The necessity for voting is a disadvantage for drainage and flood control projects, because typically a relatively small portion of the population is subject to flooding, even though the entire population may be contributing to the problem. Also, there is usually a limit on the GO bonding capacity of an entity.

Private Funds

A private property owner may fund improvements to solve an existing drainage or flood control problem on his property. Except for minor improvements this is unusual, because such problems generally involve more than one property owner and tend to be too expensive for a single property owner to bear the full cost.

Development Fees and Developer Provided Facilities

Developers have typically been required to provide drainage facilities such as curb and gutter, inlets, and storm sewers. Many communities are now requiring developers to provide detention facilities. Developer provided floodplain and channel improvements have not been so common. Many communities are now requiring developers either to avoid the floodplain or to provide facilities in conformance with floodplain regulations.

A method for financing flood management projects impacting an entire basin is to spread the cost of required facilities over the entire basin. The rationale or justification is that development should finance those improvements that are necessitated by the development. The method of accomplishing this is with a drainage development fee.

The basic approach is to charge a unit drainage development fee, based upon acreage involved for all developments in a given drainage basin. Such a development fee would be calculated at a level to provide for the estimated cost of required facilities in the basin. The unit drainage development fee would vary from basin to basin depending on the facilities required. A drainage development fee should not be used to finance improvements required to solve existing problems, except to the extent that new development aggravates an existing problem. Costs of improvements used to determine the unit drainage development fee should include preliminary planning, preliminary design, final design, right-of-way acquisition, and construction and construction-related services. The drainage development fee could be used to finance master detention basins, discussed in Chap. 7.

One of the difficulties with drainage development fees is that an improvement may be needed before enough monies have accumulated in the basin fund to finance the project. This may require the local government to "frontend" or loan the basin fund enough monies to finance the necessary improvements.

A drainage development fee can be adopted by ordinance by a local government. Such an ordinance should include sections on facilities that can be provided by a developer, criteria for the design of facilities, engineering studies of drainage basins, delineation of drainage basins, the unit drainage fee, payment of fees, right-of-way required, option to local government to require developer to construct needed facilities, drainage basin funds, cooperation of surrounding entities, local government cooperation with and assistance of developers, and administration of the drainage development fee.

Dedications

When new developments infringe on a floodplain, the developer must consider the expense of meeting floodplain regulation requirements, as explained in Chap. 8. An option to such physical infringement on the floodplain is to avoid the floodplain. This is more viable when the floodplain does not constitute a large portion of the total parcel being developed. In such case, the developer may compare the cost and potential revenues of developing in the floodplain versus not developing in the floodplain. If the cost of developing in the floodplain in conformance with floodplain regulations is more than or about the same as not developing in the floodplain, the developer may choose to leave the floodplain alone and dedicate that area to the local government, park district, forest preserve, or other public land use entity.

CONCLUSION

The planning, financing, and administration of stormwater management and related programs on small streams are generally neglected, and to the extent that they are done, are done by highly varied methods. This complexity is due not only to the differences in state laws and institutions and the general delegation of certain powers to municipalities but also to the fact that several federal agencies impact upon and control important aspects; without being able to manage the field as a whole. Consequently, research has been feeble, policy has been cautious and segmented, and planning has been generally weak. The ambitious and potentially valuable approaches of early 208 planning were abortive. Waiting for a further growth of federal bureaucracy and a further extension of federal funding to do the job is not the way. It is time for states to realize that there is a policy vacuum; and that they should set policy and define the institutional context for planning and management. Whether by watershed or by county, programs should be established on the basis that the smaller streams belong to the communities and should be managed by them for their own benefit, with just enough state and federal control to ensure that broader interests are protected. It is because of the general lack of adequate technology and of planning guidance that this book has been written.

NOTES—CHAPTER 9

1. Harvey O. Banks, "Water Resources Planning," National Water Commission, U.S. Water Resources Council, Washington, D.C., May 1972.
2. "A Report on Flood Hazard Mitigation," National Science Foundation, Washington, D.C., Sept. 1980, p. 5.
3. H.G. Poertner, "Stormwater Management in the United States," Report to Office of Water Research and Technology, Department of the Interior, Sept. 1980.
4. "Storm Water Management Act," Commonwealth of Pennsylvania, P.L. 864, No. 167, SB 744, 1978.
5. Annotated Code of Maryland, Article—Natural Resources, Sections 8-9A-01 through 11.
6. Poertner, 1980.
7. A.G. Bueher, *Public Finance*, New York: McGraw Hill, 1948, p. 528.
8. Colorado Revised Statutes, S 37-23-101.5, 1973.

Glossary

Accounting stance Viewpoint from which a calculation of financial or economic advantage should be made. For example, a state accounting stance takes account only of costs and of benefits within that state. (This term stems from usage of the U.S. Water Resources Council.)

Aggradation Tendency of a stream to deposit in a channel more sediment than it removes, and hence to build the bed higher.

Algorithm Mathematical statement of a basic relationship used in analysis.

Atmospheric fallout The polluting substances falling out of the air onto land and water surfaces.

Automatic sampling Samples taken by an automatic, unattended device.

Bank protection Structures placed along the banks of a stream to resist erosion by the current.

Bed load Sediment which moves along or near the bottom of streams.

Best management practices Management or design criteria adopted for areawide application (BMP.) This term is used mainly in EPA planning.

BMP Best management practices.

Buffer Strip of natural vegetation adjacent to a stream (in a developed area).

Bureau of Reclamation Irrigation and Power Agency of the Department of the Interior.

Calibration The exercise of changing model coefficients until the model simulates measured results with satisfactory accuracy.

"Carrot" Positive economic inducement to comply with government policies or regulations (slang).

Channel erosion *See* stream erosion.

Channel roughness Irregularities in channel configuration which tend to retard the flow of water and to dissipate its energy.

Composite samples The taking of a number of samples over a given period of time, which samples are then combined for analysis.

Cost-effective A proposal or practice which provides the desired result at a lesser economic cost than any alternative (differentiated from approaches which maximize net economic benefit or environmental quality).

csm/in. Cubic feet per second per square mile for each inch of rainfall.

Culvert Large pipe or other conduit through which a small stream passes under a road or street.

Dedication Legally donating land or rights of way to government.

Degradation *See* stream erosion.

Design storm, flood The storm or flood which is used as the basis for design, i.e., against which the structure is designed to provide a stated degree of protection or other specified result.

Detention (1) The holding of stormwaters for shorter periods of time than would ordinarily be classed as flood control storage. (2) Sometimes used to apply to both detention and retention, jointly used.

Dissipator or energy dissipator *See* drop structures.

Drop structures Sections of channel designed to reduce the elevation of flowing water without increasing its velocity.

Dual purpose detention basins Those which combine holding of water for detention purposes, with more prolonged holding for other purposes, particularly the settling of particulates.

Empirical methods Methods which are based mainly on observation of actual events.

Erosional disequilibrium Tendency of erosion to continue indefinitely rather than to stabilize at a low rate.

EPA U.S. Environmental Protection Agency.

220

First flush   Commonly observed phenomenon in which the concentration of pollutants is higher in the earlier stages of a storm event.

FEMA   Federal Emergency Management Agency.

FIA   Federal Insurance Agency.

Flood control   (1) Structural projects other than floodproofing, designed for reducing flood damages on large streams, including programs such as those of the SCS (P. L. 566) and Corps of Engineers. (2) Aspects of other programs which have the effect of physically controlling floods, as distinguished from aspects of those programs which may favor other goals.

Flood fringe   Part of the flood hazard area outside of the floodway.

Flood hazard area   Area subject to flooding by 100-year frequency floods.

Flood management or flood hazard mitigation   Any program or activity designed to reduce damages from flooding, including stream erosion.

Floodplain   Geographically the entire area subject to flooding. In usual practice, it is the area subject to flooding by 100-year frequency floods.

Floodplain and channel management program   Includes floodplain management and channel management. Does not include stormwater management or major programs of flood control.

Floodplain management   Programs carried out within the floodplain, designed to reduce impact of floods. All except floodproofing are nonstructural.

Floodway   The channel of a stream and adjacent areas reserved to facilitate passage of a 100-year frequency flood.

Flow-weighted composite sampling   Composite samples weighted by taking for an analysis a quantity of each sample proportionate to the flow of the stream at the time the sample was taken.

fps   Feet per second, a measure of velocity.

Frequency (of storms, floods)   Average recurrence interval of events, over long periods of time.

Grab samples   Samples obtained by removing a quantity of water from the source at a given time.

Histogram   Plotting of rainfall over a period of time.

Home owners association   Organization created to administer property of joint interest, such as open space and detention basins, on behalf of owners of individual homes or lots.

100-year storm   Size of storm equalled or exceeded on the average once in 100 years (with given duration.)

100-year flood   Size of flood which might be expected to be equalled or exceeded once in 100 years on the average, over a long period of time (with given conditions).

Hydrograph   A graph of runoff time history.

Hyetograph   A graph of rainfall time history.

Insect vector   See vector.

Institutional aspects   Aspects relating to governmental organization and procedures.

Isohyetal lines   Lines connecting points of equal rainfall.

Level B planning   Federal water resources general appraisal planning conducted under guidelines of the Water Resources Council.

Manning coefficient   The coefficient of roughness in the most commonly used formula for flow in open channels.

Master detention basins   A single detention basin, built to fulfill the stormwater management function of a number of smaller detention basins, one or more on each site. Sometimes called regional basins.

Meandering streams   Those flowing with flat slopes and long looping curves.

Model, modeling Mathematical systems analysis by computer, applied to evaluate relationships of rainfall–runoff; runoff–pollution; runoff–bed load, or other aspects of planning.

Modular pavement Prefabricated pavement used to allow infiltration of water.

NOAA National Oceanic and Atmospheric Administration.

Nonpoint source pollution Pollution from sources other than waste treatment plants and direct wastewater discharges. *See* point source pollution.

NFIP National Flood Insurance Program.

NWS National Weather Service.

Particulate pollution Pollution which occurs as particulate matter in water, as distinguished from dissolved matter.

PMP Probable maximum precipitation.

Point source pollution That arising from direct wastewater discharges or from treatment plant effluents. (Legally, the Clean Water Act also includes stormwater runoff entering a stream through a pipe, ditch, or channel.)

Pollutant loadings Total quantity of pollutant (as distinguished from concentrations).

Pollutant loading function or loading curve Graph of flow of pollutant loading in a storm event with time. Sometimes called pollutograph (slang).

Pollution, particulate *See* particulate pollution.

Post-development The condition of the given site and drainage area after the anticipated development has taken place.

Pre-development The condition of the given site and drainage area prior to development.

Project-induced damages Flood damage caused by reason of false confidence in a project which induces undue development within the floodplain.

Rainfall duration The length of time over which a discrete rainfall event lasts.

Rainfall frequency The average recurrence interval of rainfall events, averaged over long periods of time.

Rainfall intensity The rate of accumulation of rainfall, usually in inches or millimeters per hour.

Rational method A traditional, very simple method of estimating runoff from rainfall, described in Chap. 3.

Real terms or real value Value expressed in terms of constant dollars, i.e., corrected for currency depreciation.

Regional detention basins *See* master detention basin.

Retention In stormwater management programs, the holding of water for periods of time long enough to allow settling of particulates, or infiltration.

Retention outlet Small outlet at the bottom of a detention basin sized for slow release of water, and settling out of particulates.

Revetment (riprap) Forms of bank protection, usually using rock. Riprap is a term applied to stone which is dumped rather than placed more carefully.

RFC River forecasting centers of NWS.

Riprap *See* revetment.

Runoff curve number Index number used by the Soil Conservation Service as a measure of the tendency of rainfall to run off into streams rather than evaporate or infiltrate.

Runoff pollution Polluting substances contained in stormwater runoff. Also called (loosely) nonpoint source pollution.

SCS U.S. Soil Conservation Service.

Section 208 P. L. 92-500 That provision of law which called for a nationwide system of areawide water quality planning, supposed to encompass both point sources and nonpoint sources of pollution.

Section 208 planning Areawide planning conducted under Section 208 of P. L. 92-500 under EPA sponsorship.

Settleability Removal of suspended particulate pollution through sedimentation. Measured as percent removal of a specified pollutant during a given period of time, or with a given design criterion.

Settleability design storm Specified rainfall event used to determine the amount of runoff to be retained for particulate removal.

State of the art The current state of knowledge of a given subject.

"Stick" Negative inducement to dissuade local agencies or interests from actions not desired by higher governmental levels (slang).

Stilling basin Pool of water conventionally used, as part of a drop structure or other structure, to dissipate energy.

Stochastic events Irregularly variable, but not completely uncertain, as the weather.

Storm drainage (1) Programs onsite or in small watersheds which deal with moving stormwaters downstream efficiently rather than detaining or storing them. Includes features of roof top drains, driveway gutters, storm drains, and eventually outfall channels. (2) Term often used loosely to include programs of stormwater detention. (This is not a good usage for clarity.)

Storm event sampling Sampling intended to represent accurately the total water quality characteristics of an entire storm event.

Storm hydrology The branch of hydrology that concentrates on the calculation of runoff from storm rainfall.

Stormwater management The control of storm runoff onsite or on small streams, by means of land use control, detention storage, erosion control, and/or drainage.

Stormwater model Mathematical method of solving stormwater problems by computer technology.

Stream erosion Also called channel erosion or degradation. The tendency of a stream to dig its channel deeper by erosion.

Suspended load Sediment which is carried with and remains suspended in the water of a stream.

Trap efficiency The effectiveness of a detention basin in removing specified pollutants under given operating conditions.

Trash rack Racks, gratings, or mesh designed so as to prevent leaves and rubbish from plugging the outlets from a dam or detention basin.

TDS Total dissolved solids in water.

10, 15-year storm, flood *See* 100-year storm, flood.

Unit hydrograph The temporal sequence of flows corresponding to one inch of rainfall, or comprising a total of one inch of runoff.

USGS U.S. Geological Survey.

USLE Universal Soil Loss Equation.

Vector Water-related organism that carries pathogens (to humans). Example: the mosquito.

Verification Checking a calibrated model against a data set not used in the calibration process.

Index

A

Agricultural Regional Services, 74
Air borne pollution, Washington, D.C. and New Jersey, 65
Air borne pollution and washout, 60, 64, 69
Albuquerque Metropolitan Arroyo Flood Control District, 207
American Public Works Association, 28
American Society of Civil Engineers, 28
Analysis of runoff pollution data, 82
Annual average pollution loadings, estimation of, 83
Atlanta, 34, 35
Atmospheric fallout, 65
Aurora, Colo., 215
Automatic sampling, 73
Automatic sampling equipment, 77
Automobiles as sources of runoff pollution, 61

B

Bacterial contamination in runoff, 59, 86, 88
Bank protection, 187-89
Bellevue, Washington, 214
Best management practices, 11, 137, 205
Biochemical oxygen demand, 59
Bond financing, 216
Boulder, Colo., 215
Buffer, 127
Buffer strip, 127
Bureau of Land Management, 21
Bureau of Reclamation, 21, 74

C

Calibration and verification of models, 113
California (see Los Angeles County Flood Control District, San Francisco)
Camp method, 153